German

lonely planet

phrasebooks
and
Gunter Muehl

German phrasebook
4th edition – February 2011

Published by Lonely Planet Publications Pty Ltd
ABN 36 005 607 983

Lonely Planet Offices
Australia Locked Bag 1, Footscray, Victoria 3011
USA 150 Linden St, Oakland CA 94607
UK 2nd fl, 186 City Rd, London, EC1V 2NT

Contact
talk2us@lonelyplanet.com.au
lonelyplanet.com/contact

Cover illustration Andy Lewis

ISBN 978 1 74179 333 8

10 9 8 7 6 5 4 3 2 1

Printed in China

MIX
Paper from
responsible sources
FSC™ C021741
FSC
www.fsc.org

acknowledgments

This 4th edition of Lonely Planet's *German* phrasebook is based on the previous three editions by the Lonely Planet Language Products team, translator Gunter Muehl for the German translations and pronunciation guides, and Birgit Jordan who also provided German language expertise as well as content. For this edition, new content was provided by German translator Mario Kaiser with contributions by Robyn Loughnane. *Vielen Dank Mario, Robyn, Gunter und Birgit!*

Thanks also to the others who contributed to the previous editions on which this one is based:

Jane Atkin, Karina Coates, Francesca Coles, Adrienne Costanzo, Quentin Frayne, Ben Handicott, Jim Jenkin, Piers Kelly, Yukiyoshi Kamimura, Emma Koch, Paul Piaia, Fabrice Rocher, Karin Vidstrup Monk, Meg Worby, and last but not least, Daniel New who created the inside illustrations.

Lonely Planet Language Products

Associate Publisher: Tali Budlender
Managing Editor: Annelies Mertens
Editor: Branislava Vladisavljevic
Managing Layout Designer: Celia Wood
Layout Designer: Wibowo Rusli
Cartographer: Wayne Murphy
Production Support: Yvonne Kirk, Glenn van der Knijff

acknowledgments

make the most of this phrasebook ...

Anyone can speak another language! It's all about confidence. Don't worry if you can't remember your school language lessons or if you've never learnt a language before. Even if you learn the very basics (on the inside covers of this book), your travel experience will be the better for it. You have nothing to lose and everything to gain when the locals hear you making an effort.

finding things in this book

For easy navigation, this book is in sections. The Tools chapters are the ones you'll thumb through time and again. The Practical section covers basic travel situations like catching transport and finding accommodation. The Social section gives you conversational phrases, pick-up lines, the ability to express opinions – so you can get to know people. Food has a section all of its own: gourmets and vegetarians are covered and local dishes feature. Safe Travel equips you with health and police phrases, just in case. Remember the colours of each section and you'll find everything easily; or use the comprehensive Index. Otherwise, check the two-way traveller's Dictionary for the word you need.

being understood

Throughout this book you'll see coloured phrases on the right-hand side of each page. They're phonetic guides to help you pronounce the language. You don't even need to look at the language itself, but you'll get used to the way we've represented particular sounds. The pronunciation chapter in Tools will explain more, but you can feel confident that if you read the coloured phrase slowly, you'll be understood.

communication tips

Body language, ways of doing things, sense of humour – all have a role to play in every culture. 'Local talk' boxes show you common ways of saying things, or everyday language to drop into conversation. 'Listen for ...' boxes supply the phrases you may hear. They start with the phonetic guide (because you'll hear it before you know what's being said) and then lead in to the language and the English translation.

german

Denmark
Copenhagen ○

Berlin ●

GERMANY

Brussels ○
Belgium

Luxembourg
Luxembourg ○

Prague ○
Czech Republic

Liechtenstein

Bern ● Vaduz ○
Vienna ○

Switzerland **Austria**

○ Budapest

Hungary

0 ———— 200 km
0 ———— 100 mi

■ official language
■ widely understood

For more details see the **introduction**.

EUROPE

Romantic, flowing, literary ... not usually how German is described, but maybe it's time to reconsider. After all, this is a language that has played a major role in the history of Europe and remains one of the most widely spoken languages on the continent. Outside Europe, it's taught throughout the world and chances are you're already familiar with a number of German words that have entered English – 'kindergarten', 'kitsch' and 'waltz' are all of German origin.

German is spoken by approximately 100 million people, and is the official language of Germany, Austria and Liechtenstein, and one of the official languages of Belgium, Switzerland and Luxembourg. It's also understood in a number of countries in Eastern Europe. German did not spread across the rest of the world with the same force as English, Spanish and French. This is largely due to the fact that Germany only became a unified nation in 1871 and never established itself as a colonial power.

In recent years, however, the reunification of East and West Germany has seen the language become more important in global politics and economics. Its role in science has long been recognised and German literature lays claim to some of the most famous written works ever printed. Just think of the enormous influence of Goethe, Nietzsche, Freud and Einstein.

at a glance ...

language name: German

name in language:
Deutsch doytsh

language family:
West Germanic

key country: Germany

approximate number of speakers: 100 million

close relatives:
Afrikaans, Dutch, English, Frisian, Yiddish

donations to English:
numerous contributions including: aspirin, chromosome, eiderdown, hamburger, hamster, kindergarten, plunder, poodle, spanner

introduction

German is commonly divided into two forms – Low German (*Plattdeutsch*) and High German (*Hochdeutsch*). Low German is an umbrella term used for the dialects spoken in Northern Germany. High German is considered the standard form and is understood throughout German-speaking communities: it's the form of German used in this book.

Both German and English belong to the West Germanic language family, along with a number of other languages including Dutch and Yiddish. What this means is that as well as having recognisable words, the grammar of German will also make sense to an English speaker. Don't be put off by the fact that words can have 'different endings' or that there are many ways of saying 'the'. Even with a slight grasp of German grammar, you'll still manage to get your point across.

From the Swiss Alps to the cosy cafes of Vienna, this book gives you the words you need to get by, as well as all the fun, spontaneous phrases that will enrich your experience. Need more encouragement? Remember, the contact you make through using German will make your travels unique. Local knowledge, new relationships and a sense of satisfaction are on the tip of your tongue, so don't just stand there, say something!

> abbreviations used in this book

f	feminine	**pl**	plural
inf	informal	**pol**	polite
m	masculine	**sg**	singular
n	neuter		

German is not difficult to pronounce because almost all of its sounds are also found in English.

vowel sounds

As in English, vowels can be pronounced short or long with different meanings (compare 'ship' and 'sheep'). Vowels are pronounced crisply and cleanly with your mouth tenser than in English, eg *Tee* (tea) is pronounced tay, not *tay·ee*.

symbol	english equivalent	german example	transliteration
a	run	*hat*	hat
ah	rather	*habe*	hah·be
ai	aisle	*mein*	main
air	hair	*Bär*	bair
aw	saw	*Boot*	bawt
ay	say	*leben*	lay·ben
e	red	*Bett, Männer*	bet, *me*·ner
ee	bee	*fliegen*	flee·gen
er	teacher	*schön*	shern
i	bit	*mit*	mit
o	pot	*Koffer*	ko·fer
oo	moon	*Schuhe*	shoo·e
ow	house	*Haus*	hows
oy	boy	*Leute, Häuser*	loy·te, hoy·zer
u	foot	*unter*	un·ter
ü	ee with rounded lips	*zurück*	tsu·rük

consonant sounds

All German consonant sounds exist in English, except for the kh and r sounds, but all you need is a little practice.

The kh sound is generally like the 'ch' in 'Bach' or the Scottish 'loch', pronounced at the back of the throat. After the vowels e and i it's pronounced more forward in your mouth, almost like a sh sound. A kh sound, however, will always get you by. In this book we've used one symbol for both sounds to simplify things.

The r sound is pronounced at the back of the throat, almost like saying a g sound, but with some friction – a bit like gargling.

symbol	english equivalent	german example	transliteration
b	**big**	*Bett*	bet
ch	**chili**	*Tschüss*	chüs
d	**din**	*dein*	dain
f	**fun**	*vier*	feer
g	**go**	*gehen*	gay·en
h	**hit**	*helfen*	hel·fen
k	**kick**	*kein*	kain
kh	**Bach**	*Sprache*	shprah·khe
l	**loud**	*laut*	lowt
m	**man**	*Mann*	man
n	**no**	*nein*	nain
ng	**sing**	*singen*	zing·en
p	**pig**	*Preis*	prais
r	**run**	*Reise*	rai·ze
s	**so**	*heiß*	hais
sh	**show**	*schön*	shern
t	**tin**	*Tag*	tahk
ts	**hits**	*Zeit*	tsait
v	**van**	*wohnen*	vaw·nen
y	**yes**	*ja*	ya
z	**zoo**	*sitzen*	zi·tsen
zh	**pleasure**	*Garage*	ga·rah·zhe

word stress

Stress in German is straightforward – almost all native German words are pronounced with stress on the first syllable. There are just a couple of things to watch out for.

Some prefixes aren't stressed, like *ver-* in the verb *verstehen* fer·*shtay*·en (understand). Also, words borrowed from other languages keep their original stress, like *Organisation* or·ga·ni·sa·*tsyawn* (organisation) and *Student* shtu·*dent* (student) and therefore may have the stress on a different syllable than in English.

While these are handy rules of thumb, you can always rely on our coloured pronunciation guides which show the stressed syllable in italics.

intonation

German intonation is quite similar to that of English. If you're asking a question, your voice goes up at the end, just like in English: *Bist du fertig?* bist du *fer*·tikh (Are you ready?) or *Tee?* tay (Tea?). If you start with a question word, however, your voice falls, also like in English: *Woher kommst du?* vo·*hair* komst du (Where are you from?).

Note that, like in English, a rise in intonation can indicate that the speaker hasn't finished. For example, if someone asks you where you're from, you can say *Melbourne ... eine Stadt ... in Australien* mel·*bawn* ... *ai*·ne shtat ... in ow·*stra*·li·en (Melbourne ... a city ... in Australia), rising on the first two parts, and everyone will wait with bated breath!

reading & writing

The relationship between German sounds and the characters that represent them in writing is consistent, so once you become familiar with them, you should be able to pronounce a new word without a hitch. The examples in the tables on the previous pages show the correspondence between the sounds (in the first column) and how they're typically spelt (in the third column). However, there are a few points worth noting:

- The letter ß stands for *ss* (but the rules for when you can use ß or *ss* are confusing to Germans themselves, so you can ignore these!).
- The letters *sp* and *st* at the start of a word are pronounced like shp and sht, eg *Sport* (sport) is pronounced shport.
- Final *d*, *g*, and *b* are 'unvoiced', ie pronounced more like t, k and p, eg *Geld* (money) is pronounced gelt.

Don't be intimidated by the length of some German words. Unlike English, which often uses a number of separate words to express a single notion, German tends to join words together. After a while you'll start to recognise parts of words and find it easy to understand longer words. For example, *Haupt-* howpt· means 'main', so *Hauptpost* howpt·post means 'main post office', and *Hauptstadt* howpt·shtat is 'main city', ie 'capital'.

german alphabet								
A a	ah		B b	bay		C c	tsay
D d	day		E e	ay		F f	ef
G g	gay		H h	hah		I i	ee
J j	yot		K k	kah		L l	el
M m	em		N n	en		O o	aw
P p	pay		Q q	koo		R r	er
S s	es		T t	tay		U u	oo
V v	fow		W w	vay		X x	iks
Y y	üp·si·lon		Z z	tset			

This chapter is designed to explain the main grammatical structures you need in order to make your own sentences. Look under each heading – listed in alphabetical order – for information on functions which these grammatical categories express in a sentence. For example, demonstratives are used for giving instructions, so you'll need them to tell the taxi driver where your hotel is, etc. A glossary of grammatical terms is included at the end of the chapter to help you.

adjectives & adverbs

describing people/things • doing things

Adjectives don't change their form if they come after 'be' in a sentence. However, if they come before a noun, adjectives have either 'strong' endings (if used without an article) or 'weak' endings (if used with an article). Strong endings change to match the gender, number and case of the noun, but weak endings don't indicate this. See also **articles**, **case**, **gender** and **plurals**.

My meal is cold.	*Mein Essen ist kalt.*	main *e·sen* ist kalt
	(lit: my-nom-n-sg meal is cold)	
cold meal	*kaltes Essen*	*kal·tes e·sen*
	(lit: cold-nom-n-sg meal)	
the cold meal	*das kalte Essen*	das *kal·te e·sen*
	(lit: the-nom-n-sg cold meal)	

| | weak endings | | | | strong endings | | | |
	m sg	f sg	n sg	pl	m sg	f sg	n sg	pl
nom	-e	-e	-e	-en	-er	-e	-es	-e
acc	-en	-e	-e	-en	-en	-e	-es	-e
dat	-en	-en	-en	-en	-em	-er	-em	-en
gen	-en	-en	-en	-en	-en	-er	-en	-er

grammar

13

Most adjectives in German can also be used as adverbs in their basic form (with no endings), and they usually come towards the end of the sentence.

a quiet restaurant	*ein ruhiges Restaurant*	ain *roo*·ikh·es res·to·*rang*
	(lit: a-nom-n-sg quiet-nom-n-sg restaurant)	
Keep quiet!	*Sei ruhig!*	zai *roo*·ikh
	(lit: be quiet)	

articles

German has various forms of both the definite article (ie 'the' in English) and the indefinite article (ie 'a' or 'an' in English), depending on the gender, number and case of the noun (see **case**, **gender** and **plurals**). If you just use the nominative (dictionary form), you'll still be understood.

definite article ('the')				
	m sg	f sg	n sg	pl
nom	*der* dair	*die* dee	*das* das	*die* dee
acc	*den* dayn	*die* dee	*das* das	*die* dee
dat	*dem* daym	*der* dair	*dem* daym	*den* dayn
gen	*des* des	*der* dair	*des* des	*der* dair

indefinite article ('a/an')				
	m sg	f sg	n sg	pl
nom	*ein* ain	*eine* ai·ne	*ein* ain	*keine* * kai·ne
acc	*einen* ai·nen	*eine* ai·ne	*ein* ain	*keine* kai·ne
dat	*einem* ai·nem	*einer* ai·ner	*einem* ai·nem	*keinen* kai·nen
gen	*eines* ai·nes	*einer* ai·ner	*eines* ai·nes	*keiner* kai·ner

*kein is the negative indefinite article meaning 'no'

be

describing people/things • making statements

Just like in English, the verb *sein* zain (be) has different forms depending on the subject of the sentence. For information on negative forms, see **negatives**.

SEIN (be) – present tense					
I	am	*ich*	*bin*	ikh	bin
you sg inf	are	*du*	*bist*	doo	bist
you sg pol	are	*Sie*	*sind*	zee	zind
he/she/it	is	*er/sie/es*	*ist*	air/zee/es	ist
we	are	*wir*	*sind*	veer	zind
you pl inf	are	*ihr*	*seid*	eer	zait
you pl pol	are	*Sie*	*sind*	zee	zind
they	are	*sie*	*sind*	zee	zind

case

doing things • giving instructions • indicating location • naming people/things • possessing

German has a system of four cases (shown through word endings) which are used to indicate the 'role' of certain words in a sentence and their relationship to other words (ie whether it's the subject, direct or indirect object). Pronouns, adjectives and articles all take different endings for case, while nouns take case endings only in a few instances – a noun's case is generally indicated by the article or adjective accompanying it (see **adjectives & adverbs** and **articles**).

The word lists, **culinary reader** and **dictionaries** in this book provide words in the nominative case – you can just use this case, even if another case would be grammatically correct in a sentence, and you'll still be understood. The main functions of the four cases in German are explained in the table on the following page. See also **prepositions**.

nominative nom – shows the subject of a sentence

The tour guide is handsome.
  Der Reiseführer ist schön. dair rai·ze·fü·rer ist shern
  (lit: the-nom tour-guide-nom is handsome)

accusative acc – shows the direct object of a sentence

I love the tour guide.
  Ich liebe den Reiseführer. ikh lee·be dayn rai·ze·fü·rer
  (lit: I love the-acc tour-guide-acc)

dative dat – shows the indirect object of a sentence

I gave my ticket to the tour guide.
  Ich habe dem Reiseführer ikh hah·be daym rai·ze·fü·rer
  meine Fahrkarte gegeben. mai·ne fahr·kar·te ge·gay·ben
  (lit: I have the-dat tour-guide-dat my-acc ticket-acc given)

genitive gen – shows possession

What's the tour guide's name?
  Wie ist der Name vee ist dair nah·me
  des Reiseführers? des rai·ze·fü·rers
  (lit: how is the-nom name-nom the-gen tour-guide-gen)

demonstratives

giving instructions • indicating location • pointing things out

The easiest way to point something out in German is to use *das ist* das ist (this/that is) and *das sind* das zint (these/those are).

That's my bag; those are her suitcases.
  Das ist meine Tasche; das ist mai·ne ta·she
  das sind ihre Koffer. das zint ee·re ko·fer
  (lit: that is my-nom-f-sg bag those are her-nom-m-pl suitcases)

The demonstrative *dieser* dee·zer (this) changes to match the noun's gender, number and case (see **case**, **gender** and **plurals**). The table opposite shows all the forms – as you can see, they follow the same pattern as the definite article (see **articles**).

demonstratives

	m sg	f sg	n sg	pl
nom	*dieser* dee·zer	*diese* dee·ze	*dieses* dee·zes	*diese* dee·ze
acc	*diesen* dee·zen	*diese* dee·ze	*dieses* dee·zes	*diese* dee·ze
dat	*diesem* dee·zem	*dieser* dee·zer	*diesem* dee·zem	*diesen* dee·zen
gen	*dieses* dee·zes	*dieser* dee·zer	*dieses* dee·zes	*dieser* dee·zer

gender

naming people/things

In German, all nouns (words which denote a thing, person or idea) have masculine, feminine or neuter gender. You can recognise the noun's gender by the article, demonstrative, possessive or any other adjective accompanying the noun, as they change form to agree with the noun's gender (see **adjectives & adverbs**, **articles**, **demonstratives**, **possessives**). The gender of words is also indicated in the dictionary, but here are some general rules:

- nouns ending in *-er, -ig* or *-ing* are generally masculine
- nouns ending in *-in, -heit* or *-keit* are generally feminine
- nouns which refer to young people and animals are neuter

The gender of words is indicated with m (masculine), f (feminine) and n (neuter) throughout this phrasebook where relevant. See also the box **m before f**, page 115.

have

possessing

Possession can be indicated in various ways in German (see also **possessives**). One way is with the verb *haben* hah·ben (have), shown on the next page. For negative forms, see **negatives**.

HABEN (have) – present tense					
I	have	*ich*	*habe*	ikh	*hah*·be
you sg inf	have	*du*	*hast*	doo	hast
you sg pol	have	*Sie*	*haben*	zee	*hah*·ben
he/she/it	has	*er/sie/es*	*hat*	air/zee/es	hat
we	have	*wir*	*haben*	veer	*hah*·ben
you pl inf	have	*ihr*	*habt*	eer	hapt
you pl pol	have	*Sie*	*haben*	zee	*hah*·ben
they	have	*sie*	*haben*	zee	*hah*·ben

negatives

negating

To make a negative statement in German, just add the word *nicht* nikht (not) after the verb, or after the object if included.

I don't smoke.	*Ich rauche nicht.*	ikh *row*·khe nikht
	(lit: I smoke not)	
I don't love you.	*Ich liebe dich nicht.*	ikh *lee*·be dikh nikht
	(lit: I love you-acc-sg-inf not)	

In sentences with the indefinite article *ein* ain (a/an) or no article, the negative article *kein* kain is used instead of *nicht*.

I see a taxi.	*Ich sehe ein Taxi.*	ikh *zay*·e ain *tak*·si
	(lit: I see a-acc-n-sg taxi)	
I don't see a taxi.	*Ich sehe kein Taxi.*	ikh *zay*·e kain *tak*·si
	(lit: I see no-acc-n-sg taxi)	

personal pronouns

making statements • naming people/things

Personal pronouns ('I', 'you' etc) change their form in German for person, number and case (see **case**). It's similar in English, which has eg 'I' and 'me' as the subject and object pronouns.

There are two forms of the second-person singular pronoun (ie 'you') in German. Use the polite form *Sie* zee when talking to anyone you don't know well, and the informal forms *du* du (singular) and *ihr* eer (plural) only with people you know well or who are younger than you. Phrases in this book use the form of 'you' that is appropriate to the situation. Where both forms are used, they are indicated by pol and inf.

personal pronouns

	nom		acc		dat		gen	
I	*ich*	ikh	*mich*	mikh	*mir*	meer	*meiner*	mei·ner
you sg inf	*du*	du	*dich*	dikh	*dir*	deer	*deiner*	dai·ner
you sg pol	*Sie*	zee	*Sie*	zee	*Ihnen*	ee·nen	*Ihrer*	ee·rer
he	*er*	air	*ihn*	een	*ihm*	eem	*seiner*	zai·ner
she	*sie*	zee	*sie*	zee	*ihr*	eer	*ihrer*	ee·rer
it	*es*	es	*es*	es	*ihm*	eem	*seiner*	zai·ner
we	*wir*	veer	*uns*	uns	*uns*	uns	*unser*	un·zer
you pl inf	*ihr*	eer	*euch*	oykh	*euch*	oykh	*euer*	o·yer
you pl pol	*Sie*	zee	*Sie*	zee	*Ihnen*	ee·nen	*Ihrer*	ee·rer
they	*sie*	zee	*sie*	zee	*ihnen*	ee·nen	*ihrer*	ee·rer

plurals

naming people/things

The most common ways of forming plurals in German are:

- no plural endings and often an umlaut added over the vowel, mostly for masculine nouns ending in a consonant: *Spiegel* shpee·gel (mirror), *Spiegel* shpee·gel (mirrors); *Boden* baw·den (soil), *Böden* ber·den (soils)
- adding -e and often an umlaut over the vowel for nouns ending in a consonant, mostly single-syllable masculine

nouns: *Tag* tahk (day), *Tage* tah·ge (days); *Zug* tsook (train), *Züge* tsoo·ge (trains)
- adding -*er* and often an umlaut over the vowel, mostly for single-syllable neuter nouns: *Bild* bilt (picture), *Bilder* bil·der (pictures); *Blatt* blat (leaf), *Blätter* ble·ter (leaves)
- adding -*s* to all nouns ending in a vowel, except those ending in -*e,* and to most English loanwords: *Auto* ow·to (car), *Autos* ow·tos (cars); *Park* park (park), *Parks* parks (parks)
- adding -*n* to nouns ending in -*e,* and adding -*en* to almost all feminine nouns: *Junge* yung·e (boy), *Jungen* yung·en (boys); *Frau* frow (woman), *Frauen* frow·en (women)

possessives

possessing

A common way of indicating possession is by using possessive adjectives before the noun they refer to. Like other adjectives, they agree with the noun in gender, number and case (see also **case**, **gender** and **plurals**). The table below shows only the nominative case, singular forms; for other cases and for plural see **demonstratives** as they follow the same pattern.

possessive adjectives	m sg		f sg		n sg	
my	*mein*	main	*meine*	mai·ne	*mein*	main
your sg inf	*dein*	dain	*deine*	dai·ne	*dein*	dain
your sg pl	*Ihr*	eer	*Ihre*	ee·re	*Ihr*	eer
his	*sein*	zain	*seine*	zai·ne	*sein*	zain
her	*ihr*	eer	*ihre*	ee·re	*ihr*	eer
its	*sein*	zain	*seine*	zai·ne	*sein*	zain
our	*unser*	un·zer	*unsere*	un·ze·re	*unser*	un·zer
your pl inf	*euer*	o·yer	*eure*	oy·re	*euer*	o·yer
your pl pol	*Ihr*	eer	*Ihre*	ee·re	*Ihr*	eer
their	*ihr*	eer	*ihre*	ee·re	*ihr*	eer

prepositions

giving instructions • indicating location • pointing things out

Like English, German uses prepositions to explain where things are in time or space. All prepositions in German require the noun to be in a certain case (see **case**), most frequently the dative.

prepositions					
after	*nach*	nakh	from	*von*	fon
at (time)	*um*	um	in (place)	*in*	in
before	*vor*	fawr	to	*zu*	tsoo

questions

asking questions • negating

The easiest way of forming 'yes/no' questions is to add *nicht wahr* nikht var (literally 'not true') to the end of a statement, similar to 'isn't it?' in English. You can also turn a statement into a question by putting the verb before the subject of the sentence.

The hotel is nearby, isn't it?
 Das Hotel ist nahe, nicht war?   das ho·tel ist nah·e nikht var
 (lit: the-nom-n-sg hotel is near not true)

Is the hotel nearby?
 Ist das Hotel nahe?   ist das ho·tel nah·e
 (lit: is the-nom-n-sg hotel near)

As in English, there are question words for more specific questions. They go at the start of the sentence, followed by the verb.

question words					
how	*wie*	vee	where	*wo*	vaw
what	*was*	vas	who	*wer*	vair
when	*wann*	van	why	*warum*	va·rum

verbs

Most German verbs are regular, with the infinitive ending in *-(e)n*.
Tenses are formed by adding various endings for each person to
the verb stem (the dictionary form without the *-(e)n*). The endings
are shown in the following tables. See also **be**, **have** and **negatives**.

> present tense

present tense – *SAGEN* (say)				
I	say	*ich*	*sage*	ikh *zah·ge*
you sg inf	say	*du*	*sagst*	doo zahkst
you sg pol	say	*Sie*	*sagen*	zee *zah·gen*
he/she/it	says	*er/sie/es*	*sagt*	air/zee/es zahkt
we	say	*wir*	*sagen*	veer *zah·gen*
you pl inf	say	*ihr*	*sagt*	eer zahkt
you pl pol	say	*Sie*	*sagen*	zee *zah·gen*
they	say	*sie*	*sagen*	zee *zah·gen*

> past tense

past tense – *SAGEN* (say)				
I	said	*ich*	*sagte*	ikh *zahk·te*
you sg inf	said	*du*	*sagtest*	doo *zahk·test*
you sg pol	said	*Sie*	*sagten*	zee *zahk·ten*
he/she/it	said	*er/sie/es*	*sagte*	air/zee/es *zahk·te*
we	said	*wir*	*sagten*	veer *zahk·ten*
you pl inf	said	*ihr*	*sagtet*	eer *zahk·tet*
you pl pol	said	*Sie*	*sagten*	zee *zahk·ten*
they	said	*sie*	*sagten*	zee *zahk·ten*

> future tense

For future tense, use the construction 'werden + infinitive' (like 'going to …' in English). The verb *werden* vair·den (lit: 'become') changes form for each person as shown in the table below.

I'm going to travel to Berlin.
>	*Ich werde nach Berlin fahren.* ikh vair·de nakh ber·*lin* fah·ren
>	(lit: I am-going-to to Berlin travel)

future tense				
I	am going to	*ich*	werde	ikh *vair*·de
you sg inf	are going to	*du*	wirst	doo virst
you sg pol	are going to	*Sie*	werden	zee *vair*·den
he/she/it	is going to	*er/sie/es*	wird	air/zee/es virt
we	are going to	*wir*	werden	veer *vair*·den
you pl inf	are going to	*ihr*	werdet	eer *vair*·det
you pl pol	are going to	*Sie*	werden	zee *vair*·den
they	are going to	*sie*	werden	zee *vair*·den

word order

making statements

In a straightforward German statement, the verb is the second element, usually following the subject of the sentence. So, if the sentence starts with an adverb such as 'tomorrow', the order of the subject and the verb is reversed to keep the verb as the second element. See also **negatives** and **questions**.

I'm going to Berlin.
>	*Ich gehe nach Berlin.*	ikh gay·e nakh ber·*lin*
>	(lit: I go to Berlin)

Tomorrow I'm going to Berlin.
>	*Morgen gehe ich nach Berlin.*	mawr·gen gay·e ikh nakh ber·*lin*
>	(lit: tomorrow go I to Berlin)

grammar glossary

adjective	a word that describes something – '**German** beer is up there with the world's **best**'
adverb	a word that explains how an action is done – 'it **supposedly** doesn't give you a hangover'
article	the words 'a', 'an' and 'the'
case (marking)	word ending which tells us the role of a thing or person in the sentence
demonstrative	a word that means 'this' or 'that'
direct object	the thing or person in the sentence that has the action directed to it – 'most visitors just drink **it**'
gender	classification of *nouns* into classes (like masculine, feminine and neuter), requiring other words (eg *adjectives*) to belong to the same class
indirect object	the person or thing in the sentence that is the recipient of the action – 'others go to **breweries**'
infinitive	dictionary form of a *verb* – 'to **learn** about beer'
noun	a thing, person or idea – 'and its **production**'
number	whether a word is singular or plural – '**breweries** use four **ingredients**: **malt**, **yeast**, **hops**, **water**'
personal pronoun	a word that means 'I', 'you' etc
possessive adjective	a word that means 'my', 'your' etc
possessive pronoun	a word that means 'mine', 'yours' etc
preposition	a word like 'for' or 'before' in English
subject	the thing or person in the sentence that does the action – '**monasteries** still produce beer too'
tense	form of a *verb* that tells you whether the action is in the present, past or future – eg 'drink' (present), 'drank' (past), 'will drink' (future)
verb	a word that tells you what action happened – 'you **can visit** them on brewery tours'
verb stem	part of a *verb* that doesn't change – eg '**tast**e' in '**tast**ing' and '**tast**ed'

There are two forms of the second-person singular pronoun 'you'. Use the polite form *Sie* zee with anyone you don't know well, and only use the informal form *du* doo with people you know very well. All the phrases in this chapter use *Sie* unless indicated otherwise.

Do you speak English?
Sprechen Sie Englisch?	shpre·khen zee eng·lish
Sprichst du Englisch?	shprikhst doo eng·lish

Does anyone speak English?
Spricht hier jemand	shprikht heer yay·mant
Englisch?	eng·lish

I'd like an interpreter who speaks English.
Ich brauche einen	ikh brow·khe ai·nen
Dolmetscher, der	dol·me·tsher dair
Englisch spricht. m	eng·lish shprikht
Ich brauche eine	ikh brow·khe ai·ne
Dolmetscherin, die	dol·me·tshe·rin dee
Englisch spricht. f	eng·lish shprikht

Do you understand (me)?
Verstehen Sie (mich)?	fer·shtay·en zee (mikh)

Yes, I understand (you).
Ja, ich verstehe (Sie).	yah ikh fer·shtay·e (zee)

No, I don't understand (you).
Nein, ich verstehe (Sie) nicht.	nain ikh fer·shtay·e (zee) nikht

I (don't) understand.
Ich verstehe (nicht).	ikh fer·shtay·e (nikht)

I'd like to practice German.
Ich möchte Deutsch üben.	ikh merkh·te (doytsh) ü·ben

I speak a little German.
Ich spreche ein	ikh shpre·khe ain
bisschen Deutsch.	bis·khen doytsh

What does 'Kugel' mean?
Was bedeutet 'Kugel'?	vas be·doy·tet koo·gel

How do you ...?	Wie ...?	vee ...
pronounce this	*spricht man dieses Wort aus*	shprikht man dee·zes vort ows
say 'ticket' in German	*sagt man 'ticket' auf Deutsch*	zagt man ti·ket owf doytsh
write *'Schweiz'*	*schreibt man 'Schweiz'*	shraipt man shvaits
Could you please ...?	*Könnten Sie ...?*	kern·ten zee ...
repeat that	*das bitte wiederholen*	das bi·te vee·der·haw·len
speak more slowly	*bitte langsamer sprechen*	bi·te lang·za·mer shpre·khen
write it down	*das bitte aufschreiben*	das bi·te owf·shrai·ben

false friends

Many German words look like English words but have a completely different meaning, so be careful! Here are a few examples:

blank	blank	**shiny**
not 'blank', which is *leer* leer		
Chef	shef	**boss**
not 'chef', which is *Koch* kokh		
komisch	kaw·mish	**strange**
not 'comical', which is *lustig* lus·tikh		
Konfektion	kon·fekt·tsyawn	**ready-made clothes**
not 'confectionary', which is *Konfekt* kon·fekt		
sensibel	zen·zee·bel	**sensitive**
not 'sensible', which is *vernünftig* fer·nünf·tikh		
Tip	tip	**advance information**
not 'tip', which is *Trinkgeld* trink·gelt		

cardinal numbers

		kardinalzahlen
0	*null*	nul
1	*eins*	ains
2	*zwei*	tsvai
3	*drei*	drai
4	*vier*	feer
5	*fünf*	fünf
6	*sechs*	zeks
7	*sieben*	zee·ben
8	*acht*	akht
9	*neun*	noyn
10	*zehn*	tsayn
11	*elf*	elf
12	*zwölf*	zverlf
13	*dreizehn*	drai·tsayn
14	*vierzehn*	feer·tsayn
15	*fünfzehn*	fünf·tsayn
16	*sechzehn*	zeks·tsayn
17	*siebzehn*	zeep·tsayn
18	*achtzehn*	akht·tsayn
19	*neunzehn*	noyn·tsayn
20	*zwanzig*	tsvan·tsikh
21	*einundzwanzig*	ain·unt·tsvan·tsikh
22	*zweiundzwanzig*	tsvai·unt·tsvan·tsikh
30	*dreißig*	drai·tsikh
40	*vierzig*	feer·tsikh
50	*fünfzig*	fünf·tsikh
60	*sechzig*	zekh·tsikh
70	*siebzig*	zeep·tsikh
80	*achtzig*	akht·tsikh
90	*neunzig*	noyn·tsikh
100	*hundert*	hun·dert
1000	*tausend*	tow·sent
1,000,000	*eine Million*	ai·ne mil·yawn

ordinal numbers

1st	erste	*ers·te*
2nd	zweite	*tsvai·te*
3rd	dritte	*dri·te*
4th	vierte	*feer·te*
5th	fünfte	*fünf·te*

fractions

brüche

a quarter	ein Viertel	ain *fir·tel*
a third	ein Drittel	ain *dri·tel*
a half	eine Hälfte	ai·ne *helf·te*
three-quarters	drei Viertel	drai *fir·tel*
all	alles	*a·les*
none	nichts	nikhts

amounts

mengen

How much?	Wieviel?	vee·*feel*
How many?	Wie viele?	vee *fee·le*
(100) grams	(100) Gramm	(*hun·*dert) gram
half a dozen	ein halbes Dutzend	ain *hal·*bes *du·*tsent
a kilo	ein Kilo	ain *kee·*lo
a packet	eine Packung	ai·ne *pa·*kung
a slice	eine Scheibe	ai·ne *shai·*be
a tin	eine Dose	ai·ne *daw·*ze
less	weniger	*vay·*ni·ger
(just) a little	(nur) ein bisschen	(noor) ain *bis·*khen
much/a lot	viel	feel
many	viele	*fee·*le
more	mehr	mair
some	einige	*ai·*ni·ge

For other useful amounts, see **self-catering**, page 156.

TOOLS

28

telling the time

die uhrzeit

What time is it?	*Wie spät ist es?*	vee shpayt ist es
It's (10) o'clock.	*Es ist (zehn) Uhr.*	es ist (tsayn) oor
Quarter past (one).	*Viertel nach (eins).*	fir·tel nahkh (ains)
Twenty past (one).	*Zwanzig nach (eins).*	tsvan·tsikh nahkh (ains)
Half past one.	*Halb zwei.*	halp tsvai
	(lit: half two)	
Twenty to (one).	*Zwanzig vor (eins).*	tsvan·tsikh fawr (ains)
Quarter to (one).	*Viertel vor (eins).*	fir·tel fawr (ains)
It's 2.12 pm.	*Es ist*	es ist
	14:12.	feer·tsayn oor tsverlf
At what time?	*Um wie viel Uhr?*	um vee feel oor
At …	*Um …*	um …
am	*vormittags*	fawr·mi·tahks
pm	*nachmittags/*	nahkh·mi·tahks/
	abends	ah·bents

the time of your life

To denote the time between noon and midnight, use *nach-
mittags* nahkh·mi·tahks for times between noon and 6pm,
and *abends* ah·bents for times from 6pm to midnight.

days of the week

die wochentage

Monday	*Montag* m	mawn·tahk
Tuesday	*Dienstag* m	deens·tahk
Wednesday	*Mittwoch* m	mit·vokh
Thursday	*Donnerstag* m	do·ners·tahk
Friday	*Freitag* m	frai·tahk
Saturday	*Samstag* m	zams·tahk
Sunday	*Sonntag* m	zon·tahk

the calendar

> months

January	*Januar* m	yan·u·ahr
February	*Februar* m	fay·bru·ahr
March	*März* m	merts
April	*April* m	a·pril
May	*Mai* m	mai
June	*Juni* m	yoo·ni
July	*Juli* m	yoo·li
August	*August* m	ow·gust
September	*September* m	zep·tem·ber
October	*Oktober* m	ok·taw·ber
November	*November* m	no·vem·ber
December	*Dezember* m	de·tsem·ber

> seasons

summer	*Sommer* m	zo·mer
autumn	*Herbst* m	herpst
winter	*Winter* m	vin·ter
spring	*Frühling* m	frü·ling

dates

das datum

What date?
  Welches Datum?   vel·khes dah·tum

What date it is today?
  Der Wievielte ist heute?   dair vee·feel·te ist hoy·te

It's (18 October) today.
  Heute ist (der   hoy·te ist (dair
  18. Oktober).   akh·tsayn·te ok·taw·ber)

present

die gegenwart

now	*jetzt*	yetst
right now	*jetzt gerade*	yetst ge·*rah*·de
this ...		
afternoon	*heute*	*hoy*·te
	Nachmittag	*nahkh*·mi·tahk
month	*diesen Monat*	*dee*·zen *maw*·nat
morning	*heute Morgen*	*hoy*·te *mor*·gen
week	*diese Woche*	*dee*·ze vo·khe
year	*dieses Jahr*	*dee*·zes yahr
today	*heute*	*hoy*·te
tonight	*heute Abend*	*hoy*·te *ah*·bent

past

die vergangenheit

day before yesterday	*vorgestern*	*fawr*·ges·tern
last month	*letzten Monat*	*lets*·ten *maw*·nat
last night	*vergangene Nacht*	fer·*gang*·e·ne nakht
last week	*letzte Woche*	*lets*·te vo·khe
last year	*letztes Jahr*	*lets*·tes yahr
since (May)	*seit (Mai)*	zait (mai)
a while ago	*vor einer Weile*	fawr *ai*·ner *vai*·le
(three) days ago	*vor (drei) Tagen*	fawr (drai) *tah*·gen
(half an) hour ago	*vor (einer halben) Stunde*	fawr (*ai*·ner *hal*·ben) *shtun*·de
(five) years ago	*vor (fünf) Jahren*	fawr (fünf) *yah*·ren
yesterday ...	*gestern ...*	*ges*·tern ...
afternoon	*Nachmittag*	*nahkh*·mi·tahk
evening	*Abend*	*ah*·bent
morning	*Morgen*	*mor*·gen

future

day after tomorrow	*übermorgen*	ü·ber·mor·gen
in (six) days	*in (sechs) Tagen*	in (zeks) tah·gen
in (five) minutes	*in (fünf) Minuten*	in (fünf) mi·noo·ten
next month	*nächsten Monat*	naykhs·ten maw·nat
next week	*nächste Woche*	naykhs·te vo·khe
next year	*nächstes Jahr*	naykhs·tes yahr
tomorrow ...	*morgen ...*	mor·gen ...
afternoon	*Nachmittag*	nahkh·mi·tahk
evening	*Abend*	ah·bent
morning	*früh*	frü
until (June)	*bis (Juni)*	bis (yoo·ni)
within a month	*in einem Monat*	in ai·nem maw·nat
within an hour	*in einer Stunde*	in ai·ner shtun·de

during the day

It's early.	*Es ist früh.*	es ist frü
It's late.	*Es ist spät.*	es ist shpayt
afternoon	*Nachmittag* m	nahkh·mi·tahk
dawn	*Dämmerung* f	de·me·rung
day	*Tag* m	tahk
evening	*Abend* m	ah·bent
midday	*Mittag* m	mi·tahk
midnight	*Mitternacht* f	mi·ter·nakht
morning	*Morgen* m	mor·gen
night	*Nacht* f	nakht
noon	*Mittag* m	mi·tahk
sunrise	*Sonnenaufgang* m	zo·nen·owf·gang
sunset	*Sonnen-*	zo·nen·
	untergang m	un·ter·gang

How much is it?
Wie viel kostet es?   vee feel *kos*·tet es

Can you write down the price?
Können Sie den Preis   *ker*·nen zee dayn prais
aufschreiben?   *owf*·shrai·ben

Do you accept ...?	*Nehmen Sie ...?*	*nay*·men zee ...
credit cards	*Kreditkarten*	kre·*deet*·kar·ten
debit cards	*Debitkarten*	*day*·bit·kar·ten
I'd like to ...	*Ich möchte ...*	ikh *merkh*·te ...
arrange a transfer	*einen Transfer tätigen*	*ai*·nen trans·*fer tay*·ti·gen
cash a cheque	*einen Scheck einlösen*	*ai*·nen shek *ain*·ler·zen
change money	*Geld umtauschen*	gelt *um*·tow·shen
change travellers cheques	*Reiseschecks einlösen*	*rai*·ze·sheks *ain*·ler·zen
get a cash advance	*eine Barauszahlung*	*ai*·ne *bahr*·ows·tsah·lung
get change for this note	*diesen Schein wechseln*	*dee*·zen shain *vek*·seln
withdraw money	*Geld abheben*	gelt *ap*·hay·ben
Where's the nearest ...?	*Wo ist der/die nächste ...?* m/f	vaw ist dair/dee *naykhs*·te ...
automatic teller machine	*Geldautomat* m	*gelt*·ow·to·maht
foreign exchange office	*Geldwechsel-stube* f	*gelt*·vek·sel·shtoo·be

What's the ...?	Wie ...?	vee ...
charge for that	hoch sind die Gebühren dafür	hawkh zint dee ge·bü·ren da·für
commission	hoch ist die Kommission	hawkh ist dee ko·mi·syawn
exchange rate	ist der Wechselkurs	ist dair vek·sel·kurs

I'd like ..., please.	Ich möchte bitte ...	ikh merkh·te bi·te ...
my change	mein Wechselgeld	main vek·sel·gelt
a receipt	eine Quittung	ai·ne kvi·tung
a refund	mein Geld zurückhaben	main gelt tsu·rük·hah·ben

It's free.
Das ist umsonst.   das ist um·zonst

It costs (30) euros.
Das kostet (30) Euro.   das kos·tet (drai·tsikh) oy·ro

There's a mistake in the bill.
Da ist ein Fehler   dah ist ain fay·ler
in der Rechnung.   in dair rekh·nung

Do you want to sign or use your PIN?
Möchten Sie unterschreiben   merkh·ten zee un·ter·shrai·ben
oder Ihre PIN benutzen?   aw·der ee·re pin be·nu·tsen

For more money-related phrases, see **banking**, page 77.

For more money-related phrases, see **banking**, page 77.

money talks

Talking about prices is really easy in German because you don't need to add a plural ending to the currency. Twenty dollars is simply *zwanzig Dollar* tsvan·tsikh do·lahr. Below are a few currencies translated into German to get you started:

cent	Cent m	sent
dollar	Dollar m	do·lahr
euro	Euro m	oy·ro
franc	Franc m	frank
pound	Pfund n	pfunt
rouble	Rubel m	roo·bel
yen	Yen m	yen

getting around

herumreisen

At what time does the ... leave?	*Wann fährt ... ab?*	van fairt ... ap
boat	*das Boot*	das bawt
bus	*der Bus*	dair bus
train	*der Zug*	dair tsook

At what time does the plane leave?
Wann fliegt das Flugzeug ab? van fleekt das *flook*·tsoyk ap

At what time does it arrive?
Wann kommt es an? van komt es an

At what time's the ... bus?	*Wann fährt der ... Bus?*	van fairt dair ... bus
first	*erste*	*ers*·te
last	*letzte*	*lets*·te
next	*nächste*	*naykhs*·te

I'd like a/an ... seat.	*Ich hätte gern einen ...*	ikh *he*·te gern *ai*·nen ...
aisle	*Platz am Gang*	plats am gang
(non-)smoking	*(Nicht)raucher-platz*	(nikht·)row·kher·plats
window	*Fensterplatz*	*fens*·ter·plats

listen for ...

... ist ge·*shtri*·khen *... ist gestrichen.*	The ... is cancelled.
... hat fer·*shpay*·tung *... hat Verspätung.*	The ... is delayed.
dee·zer halt ist *Dieser Halt ist ...*	This stop is ...
dair *nairkh*·ste halt ist *Der nächste Halt ist ...*	The next stop is ...

How long will it be delayed?
Wie viel Verspätung wird es haben? — vee feel fer·*shpay*·tung virt es *hah*·ben

Is this seat free?
Ist dieser Platz frei? — ist *dee*·zer plats frai

That's my seat.
Dieses ist mein Platz. — *dee*·zes ist main plats

Can you tell me when we get to (Kiel)?
Könnten Sie mir bitte sagen, wann wir in (Kiel) ankommen? — *kern*·ten zee meer *bi*·te *zah*·gen van veer in (keel) *an*·ko·men

I want to get off here.
Ich möchte hier aussteigen. — ikh *merkh*·te heer *ows*·shtai·gen

buying tickets

Where can I buy a ticket?
Wo kann ich eine Fahrkarte kaufen? — vaw kan ikh *ai*·ne *fahr*·kar·te *kow*·fen

Do I need to book?
Muss ich einen Platz reservieren lassen? — mus ikh *ai*·nen plats re·zer·*vee*·ren *la*·sen

A ... ticket to (Berlin).	Eine ... nach (Berlin).	*ai*·ne ... nahhk (ber·*leen*)
1st-class	Fahrkarte erster Klasse	*fahr*·kar·te *ers*·ter *kla*·se
2nd-class	Fahrkarte zweiter Klasse	*fahr*·kar·te *tsvai*·ter *kla*·se
child's	Kinderfahrkarte	*kin*·der·fahr·kar·te
one-way	einfache Fahrkarte	*ain*·fa·khe *fahr*·kar·te
return	Rückfahrkarte	*rük*·fahr·kar·te
student's	Studentenfahrkarte	shtu·*den*·ten·fahr·kar·te

Two (return tickets), please.
Zwei (Rückfahrkarten) bitte.   tsvai (*rük*·fahr·kar·ten) *bi*·te

How much is it?
Was kostet das?   vas *kos*·tet das

It's full.
Es ist ausgebucht.   es ist *ows*·ge·bookht

How long does the trip take?
Wie lange dauert die Fahrt?   vee *lang*·e *dow*·ert dee fahrt

Is it a direct route?
Ist es eine direkte   ist es *ai*·ne di·*rek*·te
Verbindung?   fer·*bin*·dung

Can I get a stand-by ticket?
Kann ich ein Standby-Ticket   kan ikh ain stend·*bai*·ti·ket
bekommen?   be·*ko*·men

I'd like to …	*Ich möchte meine*	ikh *merkh*·te *mai*·ne
my ticket, please.	*Fahrkarte bitte …*	*fahr*·kar·te *bi*·te …
cancel	*zurückgeben*	tsu·*rük*·gay·ben
change	*ändern lassen*	*en*·dern *la*·sen
collect	*abholen*	ab·*ho*·len
confirm	*bestätigen*	be·*shtay*·ti·gen
	lassen	*la*·sen

---

getting there

German distinguishes between different types of journeys, depending on the transport used:

| *Fahrt* f | fahrt | **journey by road or rail** |
| *Flug* m | flook | **journey by plane** |

This distinction is reflected in the names of the tickets used for these journeys:

| *Fahrkarte* f | *fahr*·kar·te | **train/bus/underground ticket** |
| *Flugticket* n | *flook*·ti·ket | **plane ticket** |

This chapter mostly uses *Fahrkarte fahr*·kar·te, except in the plane section, so make sure you use the appropriate word when you're buying tickets.

luggage

gepäck

My luggage has been ...	*Mein Gepäck ist ...*	main ge·*pek* ist ...
damaged	*beschädigt*	be·*shay*·dikht
lost	*verloren*	fer·*law*·ren
	gegangen	ge·*gang*·en
stolen	*gestohlen*	ge·*shtaw*·len
	worden	*vor*·den

My luggage hasn't arrived.
Mein Gepäck ist   main ge·*pek* ist
nicht angekommen.   nikht *an*·ge·ko·men

I'd like a luggage locker.
Ich hätte gern ein   ikh *he*·te gern ain
Gepäckschließfach.   ge·*pek*·shlees·fakh

Can I have some coins/tokens?
Können Sie mir   *ker*·nen zee meer
ein paar Münzen/   ain pahr *mün*·tsen/
Wertmarken geben?   *vert*·mar·ken *gay*·ben

plane

flugzeug

When's the next flight to (Frankfurt)?
Wann ist der nächste   van ist dair *naykhs*·te
Flug nach (Frankfurt)?   flook nahkh (*frank*·furt)

What time do I have to check in?
Wann muss ich   van mus ikh
einchecken?   *ain*·che·ken

For phrases about getting through customs, see **border crossing**, page 48.

bus

Which bus goes to ...?	*Welcher Bus fährt ...?*	vel·kher bus fairt ...
Cologne	*nach Köln*	nakh kerln
the station	*zum Bahnhof*	tsum *bahn*·hawf
the youth hostel	*zur Jugend- herberge*	tsur *yoo*·gent· her·ber·ge
the city centre	*zum Stadt- zentrum*	tsum *shtat*· tsen·trum

This/That one.	*Dieser hier./Der da.*	*dee*·zer heer/dair dah
Bus number ...	*Bus Nummer ...*	bus *nu*·mer ...

Where's the bus stop?
Wo ist die Bushaltestelle? vo ist dee *bus*·hal·te·shte·le

What's the next stop?
Welches ist der nächste vel·khes ist dair *naykh*·ste
Halt? halt

I'd like to get off (at Alexanderplatz).
Ich möchte (am Alexander- ikh *merkh*·te (am a·lek·*san*·der·
platz) aussteigen. plats) *ows*·shtai·gen

For bus numbers, see **numbers & amounts**, page 27.

---

where to?

German uses two different words for the English word 'to'.
With place names, use *nach* nakh:

to Germany	*nach Deutschland*	nakh *doytsh*·lant
to Salzburg	*nach Salzburg*	nakh *zalts*·boorg

For all other destinations, use *zum/zur/zum* tsum/tsur/
tsum with masculine/feminine/neuter nouns:

to the station	*zum Bahnhof* m	tsum *bahn*·hawf
to the youth hostel	*zur Jugend- herberge* f	tsur *yoo*·gent· her·ber·ge
to the city centre	*zum Stadt- zentrum* n	tsum *shtat*· tsen·trum

train

What station is this?
Welcher Bahnhof ist das?   vel·kher *bahn*·hawf ist das

What's the next station?
Welches ist der   vel·khes ist dair
nächste Bahnhof?   naykhs·te *bahn*·hawf

Does this train stop at (Freiburg)?
Hält dieser Zug in   helt *dee*·zer tsook in
(Freiburg)?   (*frai*·boorg)

Do I need to change trains?
Muss ich umsteigen?   mus ikh *um*·shtai·gen

Which carriage	*Welcher*	vel·kher
is (for) ...?	*Wagen ...?*	vah·gen ...
1st class	*ist erste Klasse*	ist *ers*·te *kla*·se
dining	*ist der*	ist dair
	Speisewagen	*shpai*·ze·vah·gen
Munich	*geht nach*	gayt nahkh
	München	*mün*·khen

boat

boot

Are there life jackets?
Gibt es Schwimmwesten?   gipt es *shvim*·ves·ten

What's the sea like today?
Wie ist das Meer heute?   vee ist das mair *hoy*·te

I feel seasick.
Ich bin seekrank.   ikh bin zay·krangk

taxi

taxi

I'd like a taxi ...	*Ich hätte gern*	ikh *he*·te gern
	ein Taxi für ...	ain *tak*·si für ...
at (9am)	*(neun Uhr)*	(noyn oor)
now	*sofort*	zo·fort
tomorrow	*morgen*	*mor*·gen

Where's the taxi stand?
Wo ist der Taxenstand?   vaw ist dair *tak*·sen·shtant

Are you free?
Sind Sie frei?   zint zee frai

Please put the meter on.
Schalten Sie bitte den   *shal*·ten zee *bi*·te dayn
Taxameter ein.   tak·sa·*may*·ter ain

How much is it to ...?
Was kostet es bis ...?   vas *kos*·tet es bis ...

How much is the flag fall/hiring charge?
Wie hoch ist die   vee hawkh ist dee
Grundgebühr?   *grunt*·ge·bür

Please take me to (this address).
Bitte bringen Sie mich zu   *bi*·te *bring*·en zee mikh tsoo
(dieser Adresse).   (dee·zer a·*dre*·se)

Please slow down.
Fahren Sie bitte langsamer.   *fah*·ren zee *bi*·te *lang*·za·mer

Please wait here.
Bitte warten Sie hier.   *bi*·te *var*·ten zee heer

| Stop at the corner. | *Halten Sie an der Ecke.* | hal·ten zee an dair e·ke |
| Stop here. | *Halten Sie hier.* | hal·ten zee heer |

For other useful phrases, see **directions**, page 59, and **money**, page 33.

car & motorbike

> car & motorbike hire

I'd like to hire a/an ...	*Ich möchte ein ... mieten.*	ikh *merkh*·te ain ... *mee*·ten
4WD	*Allradfahrzeug*	al·raht·fahr·tsoyk
automatic	*Fahrzeug mit Automatik*	fahr·tsoyk mit ow·to·mah·tik
car	*Auto*	ow·to
manual	*Fahrzeug mit Schaltung*	fahr·tsoyk mit shal·tung
motorbike	*Motorrad*	maw·tor·raht

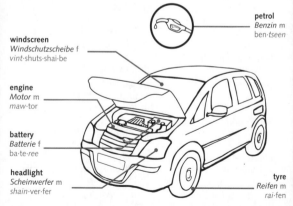

petrol
Benzin m
ben·*tseen*

windscreen
Windschutzscheibe f
vint·shuts·shai·be

engine
Motor m
maw·tor

battery
Batterie f
ba·te·ree

headlight
Scheinwerfer m
shain·ver·fer

tyre
Reifen m
rai·fen

How much	*Wie viel kostet*	vee feel *kos*·tet
is it per ...?	*es pro ...?*	es praw ...
day	*Tag*	tahk
hour	*Stunde*	*shtun*·de
week	*Woche*	*vo*·khe

Does that include insurance/mileage?
Ist eine Versicherung/   ist *ai*·ne fer·*zi*·khe·rung/
Kilometerzahl inbegriffen?   kee·lo·*may*·ter·tsahl *in*·be·gri·fen

> on the road

Does this road go to ...?
Führt diese Straße   fürt *dee*·ze *shtrah*·se
nach ...?   nahkh ...

What's the ...	*Was ist die Höchst-*	vas ist dee *herkhst*·
speed limit?	*geschwindigkeit ...?*	ge·shvin·dikh·kait ...
city	*in der Stadt*	in dair shtat
country	*auf dem Land*	owf daym lant
motorway	*auf der*	owf dair
	Autobahn	*ow*·to·bahn

road signs

Ausfahrt	*ows*·fahrt	**Exit**
Ausfahrt	*ows*·fahrt	**Keep Clear**
Freihalten	*frai*·hal·ten	
Baustelle	*bow*·shte·le	**Roadworks**
Einbahnstraße	*ain*·bahn·shtrah·se	**One-way**
Einfahrt	*ain*·fahrt	**Entrance**
Einfahrt	*ain*·fahrt	**No Entry**
Verboten	fer·*baw*·ten	
Gefahr	ge·*fahr*	**Danger**
Halteverbot	*hal*·te·fer·bawt	**No Stopping**
Mautstelle	*mowt*·shte·le	**Toll**
Parkverbot	*park*·fer·bawt	**No Parking**
Radweg	*raht*·vayk	**Cycle Path**
Sackgasse	*zak*·ga·se	**No Through Road**
Stopp	shtop	**Stop**
Überholverbot	ü·ber·*hawl*·fer·bawt	**No Overtaking**
Umleitung	*um*·lai·tung	**Detour**

(How long) Can I park here?
(Wie lange) Kann ich hier parken?	(vee *lang*·e) kan ikh heer *par*·ken

Where do I pay?
Wo muss ich bezahlen?	vaw mus ikh be·*tsah*·len

Where's a petrol station?
Wo ist eine Tankstelle?	vaw ist *ai*·ne *tangk*·shte·le

diesel	*Diesel* m	*dee*·zel
leaded	*verbleites Benzin* n	fer·*blai*·tes ben·*tseen*
LPG	*Autogas* n	*ow*·to·gahs
petrol (gas)	*Benzin* n	ben·*tseen*
regular	*Normalbenzin* n	nor·*mahl*·ben·tseen
unleaded	*bleifreies Benzin* n	*blai*·frai·es ben·*tseen*

> **problems**

I need a mechanic.
Ich brauche einen Mechaniker.	ikh *brow*·khe *ai*·nen me·*khah*·ni·ker

My car/motorbike has broken down (at ...).
Ich habe (in ...) eine Panne mit meinem Auto/Motorrad.	ikh *hah*·be (in ...) *ai*·ne *pa*·ne mit *mai*·nem *ow*·to/*maw*·tor·raht

I had an accident.
Ich hatte einen Unfall.	ikh *ha*·te *ai*·nen *un*·fal

The car/motorbike won't start.
Das Auto/Motorrad springt nicht an.	das *ow*·to/*maw*·tor·raht shpringkt nikht an

I have a flat tyre.
Ich habe eine Reifenpanne.	ikh *hah*·be *ai*·ne *rai*·fen·pa·ne

I've lost my car keys.
Ich habe meine Autoschlüssel verloren.	ikh *hah*·be *mai*·ne *ow*·to·shlü·sel fer·*law*·ren

---

listen for ...

vel·khes fa·bri·*kaht*/mo·*del* ist es	
Welches Fabrikat/ Modell ist es?	**What make/model is it?**

I've locked my keys inside the car.
Ich habe meine Schlüssel ikh *hah*·be *mai*·ne *shlü*·sel
im Wagen eingeschlossen. im *vah*·gen *ain*·ge·shlo·sen

I've run out of petrol.
Ich habe kein Benzin mehr. ikh *hah*·be kain ben·*tseen* mair

Can you fix it?
Können Sie es reparieren? *ker*·nen zee es re·pa·*ree*·ren

When will it be ready?
Wann ist es fertig? van ist es *fer*·tikh

bicycle

fahrrad

Where can I ...?	*Wo kann ich ...?*	vaw kan ikh ...
buy a second-	*ein gebrauchtes*	ain ge·*browkh*·tes
hand bike	*Fahrrad kaufen*	*fahr*·raht *kow*·fen
hire a bicycle	*ein Fahrrad mieten*	ain *fahr*·raht *mee*·ten

How much	*Wie viel kostet*	vee feel *kos*·tet
is it per ...?	*es für ...?*	es für ...
day	*einen Tag*	*ai*·nen tahk
hour	*eine Stunde*	*ai*·ne *shtun*·de

I have a puncture.
Ich habe einen Platten. ikh *hah*·be *ai*·nen *pla*·ten

I'd like to have my bicycle repaired.
Ich möchte mein Fahrrad ikh *merkh*·te main *fahr*·raht
reparieren lassen. re·pa·*ree*·ren *la*·sen

Can I take my bike on the train?
Kann ich mein Fahrrad kan ikh main *fahr*·raht
im Zug mitnehmen? im tsook *mit*·nay·men

Are there cycling paths?
Gibt es Fahrradwege? geept es *fahr*·raht·vay·ge

Is there bicycle parking?
Gibt es Fahrrad-Parkplätze? geept es *fahr*·raht·park·ple·tse

bicycle path map	*Fahrradkarte* f	*fahr*·raht·kar·te
bicycle pump	*Fahrradpumpe* f	*fahr*·raht·pum·pe

local transport

Where's the nearest metro station?

Wo ist der nächste	vaw ist dair *naykhs*·te
U-Bahnhof?	oo·bahn·hawf

Which line goes to (Potsdamer Platz)?

Welche Linie geht zum	*vel*·khe *lee*·ni·e gayt tsum
(Potsdamer Platz)?	(pots·*dah*·mer plats)

day ticket	*Tageskarte* f	*tah*·ges·kar·te
ticket for	*Mehrfach-*	*mair*·fakh·
multiple trips	*fahrkarte* f	fahr·kar·te
tram	*Straßenbahn* f	*shtrah*·sen·bahn
tram stop	*Straßenbahn-*	*shtrah*·sen·bahn·
	haltestelle f	hal·te·shte·le
underground	*U-Bahn* f	oo·bahn
underground station	*U-Bahnhof* m	oo·bahn·hawf
urban railway	*S-Bahn* f	es·bahn
weekly ticket	*Wochenkarte* f	vo·khen·kar·te

For phrases on disabled access, see **senior & disabled travellers**, page 83.

---

ticket machines

Buying tickets from machines is very common in Germany, Austria and Switzerland. Some common terms are:

Automat Gibt	ow·to·*maht* geept	**Change Given**
Rückgeld	*rük*·gelt	
Bitte Wählen	*bi*·te vay·len	**Please Choose**
Kennzahl Eingeben	*ken*·tsahl *ain*·ge·ben	**Enter Code**
Korrektur	ko·rek·*toor*	**Correction**
Taste Drücken	*tas*·te drü·ken	**Press Button**
Zahlbar mit ...	*tsahl*·bar mit ...	**Pay with ...**

If you can't get the machine to work, you can always try asking someone:

Wie funktioniert das?
  vee fungk·tsyaw·*neert* das   **How does this work?**

passport control

passkontrolle

I'm here ...	Ich bin hier ...	ikh bin heer ...
in transit	auf der Durchreise	owf dair durkh·rai·ze
on business	auf Geschäftsreise	owf ge·shefts·rai·ze
on holiday	im Urlaub	im oor·lowp
to study	zum Studieren	tsum shtu·dee·ren

I'm here for ...	Ich bin hier für ...	ikh bin heer für ...
(four) days	(vier) Tage	(feer) tah·ge
(three) weeks	(drei) Wochen	(drai) vo·khen
(two) months	(zwei) Monate	(tsvai) maw·na·te

I'm going to (Salzburg).
Ich gehe nach (Salzburg).   ikh gay·e nahkh (zalts·burg)

I'm staying at the ...
Ich wohne im ...   ikh vaw·ne im ...

listen for ...

... bi·te	..., bitte.	**Your ..., please.**
ee·ren rai·ze·pas	Ihren Reisepass	passport
eer vee·zum	Ihr Visum	visa
rai·zen zee ...	Reisen Sie ...?	**Are you travelling ...?**
a·lain	allein	on your own
in ai·ner gru·pe	in einer Gruppe	in a group
mit ee·rer	mit Ihrer	with your
fa·mee·li·e	Familie	family

at customs

I have nothing to declare.
Ich habe nichts
zu verzollen.

ikh *hah*·be nikhts
tsoo fer·*tso*·len

I have something to declare.
Ich habe etwas
zu verzollen.

ikh *hah*·be *et*·vas
tsoo fer·*tso*·len

I didn't know I had to declare it.
Ich wusste nicht, dass ich
das verzollen muss.

ikh *vus*·te nikht das ikh
das fer·*tso*·len mus

That's (not) mine.
Das ist (nicht) meins.

das ist (nikht) mains

For phrases on payments and receipts, see **money**, page 33.

---

bureaucabulary

Although Germany has a reputation for being a well-organised country, you may find your spontaneity as a traveller hampered by endless red tape. Learning some of these words can help you get on your way:

Abschrift f	*ahb*·shrift	copy/extract
Abstammungs-	ahb·*shta*·mungs·	birth
urkunde f	ur·kun·de	certificate
Bekenntnis n	be·*kent*·nis	religion
Familienname m	fa·*mee*·li·en·nah·me	surname
Familienstand m	fa·*mee*·li·en·shtant	marital status
geborene	ge·*baw*·re·ne	maiden name
geboren am	ge·*baw*·ren am	born on
Geburtsdatum n	ge·*burts*·da·tum	date of birth
Heirats-	*hai*·rahts·	marriage
urkunde f	ur·kun·de	certificate
Staatsange-	shtahts·an·ge·	citizenship/
hörigkeit f	*her*·rikh·kait	nationality
Urkunde f	ur·kun·de	document
Vorname m	*for*·nah·me	first name
Wohnort m	*vawn*·ort	place of residence

finding accommodation

eine unterkunft finden

Where's a/an ...?	Wo ist ...?	vaw ist ...
bed & breakfast	*eine Pension*	ai·ne pahng·*zyawn*
camping ground	*ein Campingplatz*	ain *kem*·ping·plats
guesthouse	*eine Pension*	ai·ne pahng·*zyawn*
hotel	*ein Hotel*	ain ho·*tel*
inn	*ein Gasthof*	ain *gast*·hawf
room in a private home	*ein Privatzimmer*	ain pri·*vaht*·tsi·mer
youth hostel	*eine Jugendherberge*	ai·ne yoo·gent·her·ber·ge

Can you recommend somewhere ...?	Können Sie etwas ... empfehlen?	ker·nen zee et·vas ... emp·*fay*·len
cheap	*Billiges*	bi·li·ges
good	*Gutes*	goo·tes
luxurious	*Luxuriöses*	luk·su·ri·er·ses
nearby	*in der Nähe*	in dair nay·e
romantic	*Romantisches*	ro·*man*·ti·shes

farm stay	*Landgasthof* m	*lant*·gast·hawf
ski resort	*Skiort* m	*shee*·ort
spa	*Kurbad* f	*koor*·baht
wellness centre	*Spa* n	shpah

What's the address? *Wie ist die Adresse?* vee ist dee a·*dre*·se

For responses, see **directions**, page 59.

> booking ahead & checking in

I'd like to book a room, please.
Ich möchte bitte ein Zimmer reservieren.
ikh *merkh*·te *bi*·te ain tsi·mer re·zer·vee·ren

I have a reservation.
Ich habe eine Reservierung.
ikh *hah*·be ai·ne re·zer·vee·rung

For (three) nights/weeks.
Für (drei) Nächte/Wochen.   für (drai) *nekh*·te/*vo*·khen

From (July 2) to (July 6).
Vom (2. Juli) bis   vom (*tsvai*·ten *yoo*·li) bis
zum (6. Juli).   tsum (*zeks*·ten *yoo*·li)

Do you offer (long-stay) discounts?
Bieten Sie Rabatte (für   *bee*·ten zee ra·*ba*·te (für
längere Aufenthalte) an?   *lairng*·e·re *owf*·ent·hal·te) an

Is breakfast included?
Ist das Frühstück inklusive?   ist das *frü*·shtük in·kloo·*zee*·ve

How much	*Wie viel kostet*	vee feel *kos*·tet
is it per ...?	*es pro ...?*	es praw ...
night	*Nacht*	nakht
person	*Person*	per·*zawn*
week	*Woche*	*vo*·khe

Do you have	*Haben Sie ein ...?*	*hah*·ben zee ain ...
a ... room?		
double	*Doppelzimmer*	*do*·pel·tsi·mer
	mit einem	mit *ai*·nem
	Doppelbett	*do*·pel·bet
single	*Einzelzimmer*	*ain*·tsel·tsi·mer
twin	*Doppelzimmer*	*do*·pel·tsi·mer
	mit zwei	mit tsvai
	Einzelbetten	*ain*·tsel·be·ten

---

listen for ...

dair *shlü*·sel ist an dair re·tsep·*tsyawn*
Der Schlüssel ist   **The key is at reception.**
an der Rezeption.

ee·ren pas *bi*·te
Ihren Pass, bitte.   **Your passport, please.**

es toot meer lait veer *hah*·ben *kai*·ne *tsi*·mer frai
Es tut mir Leid, wir   **I'm sorry, we're full.**
haben keine Zimmer frei.

für vee *fee*·le *nekh*·te
Für wie viele Nächte?   **For how many nights?**

Can I see it?
Kann ich es sehen?   kan ikh es *zay*·en

Is there parking?
Gibt es Parkplätze?   geept es *park*·ple·tse

Is there hot water all day?
Gibt es den ganzen   gipt es dayn *gan*·tsen
Tag warmes Wasser?   tahk *var*·mes *va*·ser

It's fine. I'll take it.
Es ist gut, ich nehme es.   es ist goot ikh *nay*·me es

Do I need to pay upfront?
Muss ich im Voraus   mus ikh im *faw*·rows
bezahlen?   be·*tsah*·len

Can I pay by credit card?
Nehmen Sie Kreditkarten?   *nay*·men zee kre·*deet*·kar·ten

For other methods of payment, see **money**, page 33.

> requests & queries

When/Where is breakfast served?
Wann/Wo gibt es Frühstück?   van/vaw gipt es *frü*·shtük

Please wake me at (seven).
Bitte wecken Sie mich   *bi*·te ve·ken zee mikh
um (sieben) Uhr.   um (*zee*·ben) oor

Can I use the ...?	*Kann ich ...*	kan ikh ...
	benutzen?	be·*nu*·tsen
Internet	*das Internet*	das *in*·ter·net
kitchen	*die Küche*	dee *kü*·khe
laundry	*eine*	*ai*·ne
	Waschmaschine	*vash*·ma·shee·ne
telephone	*das Telefon*	das te·le·*fawn*

Do you have a ...?	*Haben Sie ...?*	*hah*·ben zee ...
laundry service	*einen*	*ai*·nen
	Wäscheservice	*ve*·she·ser·vis
lift/elevator	*einen Aufzug*	*ai*·nen *owf*·tsook
message board	*ein Nachrichten-*	ain *nahkh*·rikh·ten·
	brett	bret
safe	*einen Safe*	*ai*·nen sayf
swimming pool	*ein Schwimmbad*	ain *shvim*·baht

Do you arrange tours here?
Arrangieren Sie hier Touren?   a·rang·zhee·ren zee heer too·ren

Do you change money here?
Wechseln Sie hier Geld?   vek·seln zee heer gelt

Can I leave a message for someone?
Kann ich eine Nachricht für jemanden hinterlassen?   kan ikh ai·ne nahkh·rikht für yay·man·den hin·ter·la·sen

Is there a message for me?
Haben Sie eine Nachricht für mich?   hah·ben zee ai·ne nahkh·rikht für mikh

I'm locked out of my room.
Ich habe mich aus meinem Zimmer ausgesperrt.   ikh hah·be mikh ows mai·nem tsi·mer ows·ge·shpert

There's no hot water.
Es gibt kein warmes Wasser.   es geept kain var·mes va·ser

signs

Aufzug	owf·tsook	**Lift/Elevator**
Fahrstuhl	fahr·shtool	**Lift/Elevator**
Fernsehzimmer	fern·zay·tsi·mer	**TV Room**
Frühstücksraum	frü·shtüks·rowm	**Breakfast Room**
Notausgang	nawt·ows·gang	**Emergency Exit**

Could I have ..., please?	*Könnte ich bitte ... haben?*	kern·te ikh bi·te ... hah·ben
my key	*meinen Schlüssel*	mai·nen shlü·sel
a receipt	*eine Quittung*	ai·ne kvi·tung
It's too ...	*Es ist zu ...*	es ist tsoo ...
cold	*kalt*	kalt
dark	*dunkel*	dung·kel
expensive	*teuer*	toy·er
light/bright	*hell*	hel
noisy	*laut*	lowt
small	*klein*	klain

The ... doesn't work.	... funktioniert nicht.	... fungk·tsyaw·neert nikht
air-conditioning	Die Klimaanlage	dee klee·ma·an·lah·ge
fan	Der Ventilator	dair ven·ti·lah·tor
heater	Das Heizgerät	das haits·ge·rayt
toilet	Die Toilette	dee to·a·le·te

The (bathroom) door is locked.

Die (Badezimmer)Tür ist abgeschlossen.	dee (bah·de·tsi·mer·)tür ist ap·ge·shlo·sen

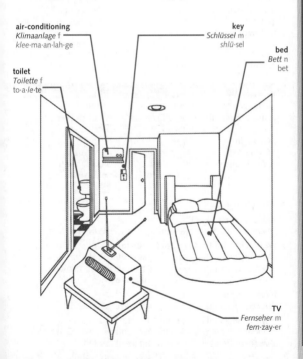

air-conditioning
Klimaanlage f
klee·ma·an·lah·ge

key
Schlüssel m
shlü·sel

bed
Bett n
bet

toilet
Toilette f
to·a·*le*·te

TV
Fernseher m
fern·zay·er

The window won't open/close.
Das Fenster lässt sich   das *fens*·ter lest zikh
nicht öffnen/schließen.   nikht *erf*·nen/*shlee*·sen

This (sheet) isn't clean.
Dieses (Bettlaken)   dee·zes (*bet*·lah·ken)
ist nicht sauber.   ist nikht *zow*·ber

Can I get	*Kann ich noch*	kan ikh nokh
another ...?	*einen/eine/ein ...*	ai·nen/ai·ne/ain ...
	bekommen? m/f/n	be·ko·men
blanket	*Decke* f	de·ke
duvet cover	*Bettbezug* m	bet·be·tsook
pillow	*Kopfkissen* n	kopf·ki·sen
pillowcase	*Kopfkissen-*	kopf·ki·sen·
	bezug m	be·tsook
sheet	*Bettlaken* n	bet·lah·ken
towel	*Handtuch* n	hant·tookh

a knock at the door

Who is it?	*Wer ist da?*	vair ist dah
Just a moment.	*Einen Augenblick,*	ai·nen ow·gen·*blik*
	bitte!	*bi*·te
Come in.	*Herein!*	he·*rain*
Come back	*Kommen Sie*	*ko*·men zee
later, please.	*bitte später*	*bi*·te shpay·ter
	noch einmal.	nokh *ain*·mahl

> checking out

What time is checkout?
Wann muss ich auschecken?   van mus ikh *ows*·che·ken

How much extra to stay until (six o'clock)?
Was kostet es extra, wenn   vas *kos*·tet es *eks*·tra ven
ich bis (sechs Uhr) bleiben   ikh bis (zeks oor) *blai*·ben
möchte?   *merkh*·te

I'm leaving now.
Ich reise jetzt ab.   ikh *rai*·ze yetst ap

Can you call a taxi for me (for 11 o'clock)?
Können Sie mir (für 11 Uhr)   *ker*·nen zee meer (für elf oor)
ein Taxi rufen?   ain *tak*·si *roo*·fen

Can I leave my bags here until ...?	Kann ich meine Taschen bis ... hier lassen?	kan ikh *mai*·ne *ta*·shen bis ... heer *la*·sen
next week	nächste Woche	*naykhs*·te *vo*·khe
tonight	heute Abend	*hoy*·te *ah*·bent
Wednesday	Mittwoch	*mit*·vokh

Could I have my ..., please?	Könnte ich bitte ... haben?	*kern*·te ikh *bi*·te ... *hah*·ben
deposit	meine Anzahlung	*mai*·ne *an*·tsah·lung
passport	meinen Pass	*mai*·nen *pas*
valuables	meine Wertsachen	*mai*·ne *vert*·za·khen

There's a mistake in the bill.
Da ist ein Fehler in der Rechnung.
dah ist ain *fay*·ler in dair *rekh*·nung

I had a great stay, thank you.
Es hat mir hier sehr gut gefallen.
es hat meer heer zair goot ge·*fa*·len

I'll recommend it to my friends.
Ich werde Sie weiterempfehlen.
ikh *ver*·de zee *vai*·ter·emp·fay·len

camping

Where's the nearest ...?	Wo ist der nächste ...?	vaw ist dair *naykhs*·te ...
camp site	Zeltplatz	*tselt*·plats
shop	Laden	*lah*·den
shower facility	Duschraum	*doosh*·rowm
toilet block	Toilettenblock	to·a·*le*·ten·blok

Do you have ...?	Haben Sie ...?	*hah*·ben zee ...
electricity	Strom	shtrawm
shower facilities	Duschen	*doo*·shen
a site	einen Stellplatz	*ai*·nen *shtel*·plats
tents for hire	Zelte zu vermieten	*tsel*·te tsoo fer·*mee*·ten

Is it coin-operated?
Braucht man dafür Münzen? browkht man da·*für mün*·tsen

Is the water drinkable?
Kann man das Wasser trinken? kan man das va·ser *tring*·ken

Who do I ask to stay here?
Wen muss ich fragen, vayn mus ikh *frah*·gen
wenn ich hier zelten ven ikh heer *tsel*·ten
möchte? merkh·te

How much do	*Wie viel berechnen*	vee feel be·*rekh*·nen
you charge ...?	*Sie ...?*	zee ...
for a car	*für ein Auto*	für ain *ow*·to
for a caravan	*für einen*	für *ai*·nen
	Wohnwagen	*vawn*·vah·gen
for a tent	*für ein Zelt*	für ain tselt
per person	*pro Person*	praw per·*zawn*

Can I ...?	*Kann ich ...?*	kan ikh ...
camp here	*hier zelten*	heer *tsel*·ten
park next to	*neben meinem*	*nay*·ben *mai*·nem
my tent	*Zelt parken*	tselt *par*·ken

gas cylinder	*Gasflasche* f	*gahs*·fla·she
mallet	*Holzhammer* m	*holts*·ha·mer
peg	*Hering* m	*hay*·ring
rope	*Seil* n	zail
shower token	*Duschmünze* f	*doosh*·mün·tse
sleeping bag	*Schlafsack* m	*shlahf*·zak
spade	*Spaten* m	*shpah*·ten
tent	*Zelt* n	tselt
torch (flashlight)	*Taschenlampe* f	*ta*·shen·lam·pe

renting

I'm here about the ... for rent.	Ich komme wegen des/der/des zu ver- mietenden ... m/f/n	ikh ko·me vay·gen des/dair/des tsoo fer· mee·ten·den ...
apartment	Appartement n	a·part·ment
cabin	Hütte f	hü·te
holiday apartment	Ferienwohnung f	fay·ri·en·vaw·nung
house	Haus n	hows
room	Zimmer n	tsi·mer
villa	Villa f	vi·la

furnished	möbliert	mer·bleert
partly furnished	teilmöbliert	tail·mer·bleert
unfurnished	unmöbliert	un·mer·bleert

Do you have a/an ... for rent?
Haben Sie ... — hah·ben zee ...
zu vermieten? — tsoo fer·mee·ten

How many rooms does it have?
Wie viele — vee fee·le
Zimmer hat es? — tsi·mer hat es

I want something near the ...	Ich möchte etwas in der Nähe ...	ikh merkh·te et·vas in dair nay·e ...
beach	des Strandes	des shtran·des
city centre	des Stadt- zentrums	des shtat· tsen·trums
shops	der Geschäfte	dair ge·shef·te

How much is it for ...?	Was kostet es für ...?	vas kos·tet es für ...
(one) week	(eine) Woche	(ai·ne) vo·khe
(two) months	(zwei) Monate	(tsvai) maw·na·te

Who is my ...?	Wer ist ...?	vair ist ...
agent	mein Makler	main mahk·ler
contact person	meine Kontaktperson	mai·ne kon·takt·per·zawn

I want to rent it from (July 2) to (July 6).
Ich möchte es vom   ikh *merkh*·te es fom
(2. Juli) bis zum   (*tsvai*·ten *yoo*·li) bis tsum
(6. Juli) mieten.   (*zeks*·ten *yoo*·li) *mee*·ten

Is there a bond?
Gibt es eine Kaution?   gipt es *ai*·ne kow·*tsyawn*

Are bills extra?
Kommen noch   *ko*·men nokh
Nebenkosten dazu?   *nay*·ben·kos·ten da·*tsoo*

staying with locals

bei einheimischen übernachten

Can I stay at your place?
Kann ich bei Ihnen/dir   kan ikh bai *ee*·nen/deer
übernachten? pol/inf   ü·ber·*nakh*·ten

Is there anything I can do to help?
Kann ich Ihnen/dir   kan ikh *ee*·nen/deer
irgendwie helfen? pol/inf   *ir*·gent·vee *hel*·fen

I have my own ...	*Ich habe ...*	ikh *hah*·be ...
mattress	*meine eigene*	*mai*·ne *ai*·ge·ne
	Matratze	ma·*tra*·tse
sleeping bag	*meinen eigenen*	*mai*·nen *ai*·ge·nen
	Schlafsack	*shlahf*·zak

Can I ...?	*Kann ich ...?*	kan ikh ...
bring anything	*etwas für das*	et·vas für das
for the meal	*Essen mitbringen*	e·sen *mit*·bring·en
do the dishes	*abwaschen*	*ap*·va·shen
set/clear	*den Tisch decken/*	dayn tish *de*·ken/
the table	*abräumen*	*ap*·roy·men
take out the	*den Müll*	dayn mül
rubbish	*rausbringen*	*rows*·bring·en

Thanks for your hospitality.
Vielen Dank für Ihre/deine   *fee*·len dangk für *ee*·re/*dai*·ne
Gastfreundschaft. pol/inf   *gast*·froynt·shaft

To compliment your host's cooking, see **eating out**, page 143.

Where's (a bank)?
Wo ist (eine Bank)?   vaw ist (*ai*·ne bangk)

I'm looking for (the cathedral).
Ich suche (den Dom).   ikh *zoo*·khe (dayn dawm)

Which way is a public toilet)?
In welcher Richtung ist   in *vel*·kher *rikh*·tung ist
(eine öffentliche Toilette)?   (*ai*·ne er·*fent*·li·khe to·a·*le*·te)

listen for ...

es ist ...	*Es ist ...*	**It's ...**
an dair *e*·ke	*an der Ecke*	**on the corner**
dort	*dort*	**there**
fawr ...	*vor ...*	**in front of ...**
gay·gen·*ü*·ber ...	*gegenüber ...*	**opposite ...**
ge·rah·de·*ows*	*geradeaus*	**straight ahead**
heer	*hier*	**here**
hin·ter ...	*hinter ...*	**behind ...**
lingks	*links*	**left**
nah·e	*nahe*	**near**
nay·ben ...	*neben ...*	**next to ...**
rekhts	*rechts*	**right**
vait vek	*weit weg*	**far away**
bee·gen zee ... ap	*Biegen Sie ... ab.*	**Turn ...**
an dair *e*·ke	*an der Ecke*	**at the corner**
bai dair *am*·pel	*bei der Ampel*	**at the traffic lights**
lingks/rekhts	*links/rechts*	**left/right**
es ist ... ent·*fernt*	*Es ist ... entfernt.*	**It's ...**
(tsayn) *may*·ter	*(10) Meter*	**(10) metres**
(fünf) mi·*noo*·ten	*(fünf) Minuten*	**(five) minutes**
nor·den	*Norden* m	**north**
zü·den	*Süden* m	**south**
os·ten	*Osten* m	**east**
ves·ten	*Westen* m	**west**

How can I get there?
Wie kann ich da hinkommen?   vee kan ikh dah *hin*·ko·men

Can you show me (on the map)?
Können Sie es mir   *ker*·nen zee es meer
(auf der Karte) zeigen?   (owf dair *kar*·te) *tsai*·gen

What's the address?
Wie ist die Adresse?   vee ist dee a·*dre*·se

How far is it?
Wie weit ist es?   vee *vait* ist es

by bus	*mit dem Bus*	mit daym *bus*
by taxi	*mit dem Taxi*	mit daym *tak*·si
by train	*mit dem Zug*	mit daym *tsook*
on foot	*zu Fuß*	tsoo *foos*

avenue	*Allee* f	a·*lay*
lane	*Gasse* f	*ga*·se
square	*Platz* m	*plats*
street	*Straße/Weg* f/m	*shtrah*·se/*vayk*

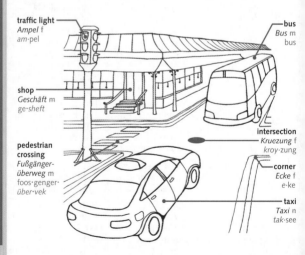

traffic light
Ampel f
am·pel

bus
Bus m
bus

shop
Geschäft m
ge·*sheft*

pedestrian crossing
Fußgängerüberweg m
foos·*genger*·*über*·vek

intersection
Kruezung f
kroy·zung

corner
Ecke f
e·ke

taxi
Taxi n
tak·see

looking for ...

Where's (a/the supermarket)?
Wo ist (ein/der Supermarkt)?
vaw ist (ain/dair zoo·per·markt)

Where can I buy ...?
Wo kann ich ... kaufen?
vaw kan ikh ... kow·fen

For phrases on getting there, see **directions**, page 59, and for additional shops and services, see the **dictionary**.

making a purchase

I'd like to buy ...
Ich möchte ... kaufen.
ikh merkh·te ... kow·fen

I'm just looking.
Ich schaue mich nur um.
ikh show·e mikh noor um

What is this made of?
Woraus ist das gemacht?
vaw·rows ist das ge·makht

How much is this?
Wie viel kostet das?
vee feel kos·tet das

Can you write down the price?
Können Sie den Preis aufschreiben?
ker·nen zee dayn prais owf·shrai·ben

Do you have any others?
Haben Sie noch andere?
hah·ben zee nokh an·de·re

Can I look at it?
Können Sie es mir zeigen?
ker·nen zee es meer tsai·gen

Do you accept ...? *Nehmen Sie ...?* nay·men zee ...
  credit cards *Kreditkarten* kre·deet·kar·ten
  debit cards *Debitkarten* day·bit·kar·ten

Could I have ..., please?	Könnte ich ... bekommen?	kern·te ikh ... be·ko·men
a bag	eine Tüte	ai·ne tü·te
a receipt	eine Quittung	ai·ne kvi·tung
it wrapped	es eingepackt	es ain·ge·pakt

I don't need a bag, thanks.
Ich brauche keine Tüte, danke.	ikh brow·khe kai·ne tü·te dang·ke

Does it have a guarantee?
Gibt es darauf Garantie?	gipt es da·rowf ga·ran·tee

Can I have it sent overseas?
Kann ich es ins Ausland verschicken lassen?	kan ikh es ins ows·lant fer·shi·ken la·sen

Can you order it for me?
Können Sie es für mich bestellen?	ker·nen zee es für mikh be·shte·len

Can I pick it up later?
Kann ich es später abholen?	kan ikh es shpay·ter ap·haw·len

It's faulty/broken.
Es ist fehlerhaft/kaputt.	es ist fay·ler·haft/ka·put

I'd like ..., please.	Ich möchte bitte ...	ikh merkh·te bi·te ...
my change	mein Wechselgeld	main vek·sel·gelt
my money back	mein Geld zurückhaben	main gelt tsu·rük·hah·ben
to return this	dieses zurückgeben	dee·zes tsu·rük·gay·ben

local talk

bargain	Schnäppchen n	shnep·khen
bargain hunter	Schnäppchenjäger m	shnep·khen·yay·ger
rip-off	Nepp m	nep
sale	Ausverkauf m	ows·fer·kowf
specials	Sonderangebote n pl	zon·der·an·ge·baw·te

bargaining

That's too expensive.
Das ist zu teuer.   das ist tsoo *toy*·er

Can you lower the price?
Können Sie mit dem   *ker*·nen zee mit dem
Preis heruntergehen?   prais he·*run*·ter·gay·en

Do you have something cheaper?
Haben Sie etwas Billigeres?   *hah*·ben zee *et*·vas *bi*·li·ge·res

I'll give you ...
Ich gebe Ihnen ...   ikh *gay*·be ee·nen ...

clothes

Can I try it on?
Kann ich es anprobieren?   kan ikh es *an*·pro·bee·ren

My size is ...
Ich habe Größe ...   ikh *hah*·be *grer*·se ...

It doesn't fit.
Es passt nicht.   es past nikht

small	*klein*	klain
medium	*mittelgroß*	*mi*·tel·graws
large	*groß*	graws

For clothes items see the **dictionary**, and for sizes see **numbers & amounts**, page 27.

repairs

Can I have my ... repaired here?
Kann ich hier mein ...   kan ikh heer main ...
reparieren lassen?   re·pa·*ree*·ren *la*·sen

When will my shoes be ready?
Wann sind meine   van zint *mai*·ne
Schuhe fertig?   *shoo*·e *fer*·tikh

When will my ... be ready?	*Wann ist mein/ meine ... fertig?* m/f	van ist main/ *mai*·ne ... *fer*·tikh
backpack	*Rucksack* m	*ruk*·zak
camera	*Kamera* f	*ka*·me·ra
(sun)glasses	*(Sonnen)Brille* f	(zo·nen·)*bri*·le

darn holes		
buttons	*Knöpfe* m pl	*knerp*·fe
needle	*Nadel* f	*nah*·del
scissors	*Schere* f	*shair*·re
thread	*Faden* m	*fah*·den

hairdressing

I'd like (a) ...	*Ich möchte ...*	ikh *merkh*·te ...
blow wave	*eine Fönwelle*	*ai*·ne *fern*·ve·le
colour	*mir die Haare färben lassen*	meer dee *hah*·re *fer*·ben *la*·sen
foils	*Folien*	*faw*·li·en
haircut	*mir die Haare schneiden lassen*	meer dee *hah*·re *shnai*·den *la*·sen
my beard trimmed	*mir den Bart stutzen lassen*	meer dayn bart *shtu*·tsen *la*·sen
shave	*mich rasieren lassen*	mikh ra·*zee*·ren *la*·sen
streaks	*Strähnchen*	*shtrayn*·khen
trim	*mir die Haare nachschneiden lassen*	meer dee *hah*·re *nahkh*·shnai·den *la*·sen

Please use a new blade.
Benutzen Sie bitte   be·*nu*·tsen zee *bi*·te
eine neue Klinge.   *ai*·ne *noy*·e *kling*·e

Don't cut it too short.
Schneiden Sie es   shnai·den zee es
nicht zu kurz.   nikht tsoo kurts

Shave it all off!
Rasieren Sie alles ab!   ra·zee·ren zee a·les ap

I should never have let you near me!
Ich hätte Sie nie an mein   ikh he·te zee nee an main
Haar lassen dürfen!   hahr la·sen dür·fen

For colours, see the **dictionary**.

books & reading

bücher und lesen

Is there a/an (English-language) ...?	*Gibt es ...? (für englische Bücher)*	gipt es ... (für eng·li·she bü·kher)
bookshop	*einen Buchladen*	ai·nen bookh·lah·den
section	*eine Abteilung*	ai·ne ap·tai·lung

Do you have Lonely Planet guidebooks?
Haben Sie Lonely-Planet-   hah·ben zee lohn·li·ple·net·
Reiseführer?   rai·ze·fü·rer

I'm looking for something by (Herman Hesse).
Ich suche nach etwas von   ikh zoo·khe nahkh et·vas fon
(Herman Hesse).   (her·man he·se)

---

listen for ...

kan ikh ee·nen hel·fen
  Kann ich Ihnen helfen?   **Can I help you?**
merkh·ten zee nokh et·vas
  Möchten Sie noch   **Would you like anything**
  etwas?   **else?**
nain (hah·ben veer) lai·der nikht
  Nein, (haben wir)   **No, we don't have any.**
  leider nicht.

music & DVD

I'd like (a) ...	Ich hätte gern ...	ikh *he*·te gern ...
CD	eine CD	*ai*·ne tsay·*day*
DVD	eine DVD	*ai*·ne day·fow·*day*
headphones	Kopfhörer	*kopf*·her·rer

What's their best recording?
Was ist ihre beste CD?   vas ist *ee*·re *bes*·te tsay·*day*

Can I listen to this?
Kann ich mir das anhören?   kan ikh meer das *an*·her·ren

Is this a pirated copy?
Ist das eine Raubkopie?   ist das *ai*·ne *rowp*·ko·pee

Will this work on any DVD player?
Funktioniert die auf   fungk·tsyaw·*neert* dee owf
jedem DVD-Player?   *yay*·dem day·fow·*day*·play·er

What region is this DVD for?
Für welche Region ist   für *vel*·khe re·*gyawn* ist
diese DVD?   *dee*·ze day·fow·*day*

video & photography

I need a ... film	Ich brauche einen	ikh *brow*·khe *ai*·nen
for this camera.	... für diese Kamera.	... für *dee*·ze *ka*·me·ra
B&W	Schwarzweißfilm	shvarts·*vais*·film
colour	Farbfilm	*farp*·film
slide	Diafilm	*dee*·a·film
(200) speed	(200)-ASA-Film	(tsvai·hun·dert)·*ah*·za·film

Can you ...?	Können Sie ...?	*ker*·nen zee ...
develop this film	diesen Film	*dee*·zen film
	entwickeln	ent·*vi*·keln
load my film	mir den Film	meer dayn film
	einlegen	*ain*·lay·gen

Can you ...?	Können Sie ...?	ker·nen zee ...
print digital photos	digitale Fotos drucken	dee·gee·*tah*·le *faw*·tos *dru*·ken
recharge the battery for my digital camera	den Akku meiner Digitalkamera aufladen	dayn *a*·koo *mai*·ner dee·gee·*tahl*·kah·me·ra *owf*·lah·den
transfer my photos from camera to CD	Fotos von meiner Kamera auf CD brennen	*faw*·tos fon *mai*·ner *kah*·me·ra owf tsay·*day* bre·nen

Do you have a ... for this camera?	Haben Sie ... für diese Kamera?	*hah*·ben zee ... für *dee*·ze *kah*·me·ra
batteries	Akkus	*a*·koos
flash (bulb)	eine Blitzröhre	*ai*·ne *blits*·rer·re
light meter	einen Belichtungs- messer	*ai*·nen be·*likh*·tungs· me·ser
memory cards	Speicherkarten	*shpai*·kher·kar·ten
zoom (lens)	ein Zoom- Objektiv	ain *zoom*· op·yek·teef

digital camera	Digitalkamera f	dee·gee·*tahl*·kah·me·ra
disposable camera	Wegwerfkamera f	*vek*·verf·kah·me·ra
video camera	Videokamera f	*vee*·dyaw·kah·me·ra

How much is it to develop this film?
Was kostet es, diesen Film entwickeln zu lassen?
vas *kos*·tet es *dee*·zen film ent·*vi*·keln tsoo *la*·sen

I need a passport photo taken.
Ich möchte ein Passfoto machen lassen.
ikh *merkh*·te ain *pas*·faw·to *ma*·khen *la*·sen

I need a cable to connect my camera to a computer.
Ich brauche ein Kabel, um meine Kamera an einem Computer anzuschließen.
ikh *brow*·khe ain *kah*·bel um *mai*·ne *kah*·me·ra an *ai*·nem kom·*pyoo*·ter an·tsoo·shlee·sen

I need a cable to recharge this battery.
Ich brauche ein Ladekabel für diesen Akku.
ikh *brow*·khe ain *lah*·de·kah·bel für *dee*·zen *a*·koo

I need a video cassette for this camera.
Ich brauche eine Videokassette für diese Kamera.
ikh *brow*·khe *ai*·ne *vee*·dyaw·ka·se·te für *dee*·ze *kah*·me·ra

cheers for beers & souvenirs

Aachen: *Aachener Printen* (gingerbread)

Austria: chocolates like *Mozartkugeln,* fruit brandies

Bavarian Forest: crystal glassware

Harz Mountains: puppets and marionettes, glassware

Lübeck: marzipan

Meissen: modern and antique porcelain
Nuremberg: toys, *Lebkuchen* (gingerbread)

Rhine and Moselle Rivers: renowned for their white wines

Rothenburg ob der Tauber: wooden toys, Christmas decorations

Switzerland: cuckoo clocks, chocolate, cow bells

The Black Forest: cuckoo clocks, dolls, fruit brandies

Thuringia: wooden figures, Christmas decorations

beer stein	*Bierkrug* m	*beer*·krook
chocolate	*Schokolade* f	sho·ko·*lah*·de
chocolates	*Pralinen* n pl	pra·*lee*·nen
Christmas decorations	*Weihnachts- schmuck* m	*vai*·nakhts· shmuk
clock	*Uhr* f	oor
cow bell	*Kuhglocke* f	koo·*glo*·ke
crystal glassware	*Kristallglas* n	kris·*tal*·glahs
cuckoo clock	*Kuckucksuhr* f	ku·kuks·oor
doll	*Puppe* f	*pu*·p e
fruit brandy	*Obstler* m	*awpst*·ler
glassware	*Glaswaren* pl	*glahs*·vah·ren
gingerbread	*Lebkuchen* m	*layp*·koo·khen
marionette	*Marionette* f	ma·ri·o·*ne*·te
marzipan	*Marzipan* n	*mar*·tsi·pahn
porcelain	*Porzellan* n	por·tse·*lahn*
puppet	*Puppe* f	*pu*·pe
tin toys	*Blechspielzeug* n	*blekh*·shpeel·tsoyk
white wine	*Weißwein* m	*vais*·vain
witch	*Hexe* f	*hek*·se
wooden figure	*Holzfigur* f	*holts*·fi·goor
wooden toys	*Holzspielzeug* n	*holts*·shpeel·tsoyk

post office

post

I want to send a ...	Ich möchte ... senden.	ikh *merkh*·te ... *zen*·den
fax	ein Fax	ain faks
parcel	ein Paket	ain pa·*kayt*
postcard	eine Postkarte	*ai*·ne *post*·kar·te
I want to buy a/an...	Ich möchte ... kaufen.	ikh *merkh*·te ... *kow*·fen
aerogram	ein Aerogramm	ain air·ro·*gram*
envelope	einen Umschlag	*ai*·nen *um*·shlahk
stamp	eine Briefmarke	*ai*·ne *breef*·mar·ke

airmail	Luftpost f	*luft*·post
customs declaration	Zollerklärung f	*tsol*·er·klair·rung
domestic	Inlands-	*in*·lants·
express mail	Expresspost f	eks·*pres*·post
fragile	zerbrechlich	tser·*brekh*·likh
international	international	in·ter·na·tsyo·*nahl*
mail box	Briefkasten m	*breef*·kas·ten
PO box	Postfach n	*post*·fakh
postal address	Postanschrift f	*post*·an·shrift
postcode	Postleitzahl f	*post*·lait·tsahl
registered mail	Einschreiben n	*ain*·shrai·ben
sea mail	Schiffspost f	*shifs*·post
surface mail	Landbeförderung f	*lant*·be·fer·de·rung

Please send it by (airmail) to ...
Bitte schicken Sie das per   *bi·te shi·ken zee das per*
(Luftpost) nach ...   *(luft·post) nahkh ...*

It contains ...
Es enthält ...   es ent·*helt* ...

Where's the poste restante section?
Wo ist der Schalter für   vaw ist dair *shal·*ter für
postlagernde Briefe?   *post·*lah·gern·de *bree·*fe

Is there any mail for me?
Ist Post für mich da?   ist post für mikh dah

listen for ...

vas ist dah drin
   Was ist da drin?   **What does it contain?**

*vaw·*hin *merkh·*ten zee das *shi·*ken
   Wohin möchten   **Where are you**
   Sie das schicken?   **sending it?**

phone

telefon

I want to make ...	*Ich möchte ...*	ikh *merkh·*te ...
a call to	*nach (Singapur)*	nahkh (*zing·*a·poor)
(Singapore)	*telefonieren*	te·le·fo·*nee·*ren
an Internet call	*einen Anruf über*	*ai·*nen *an·*roof ü·ber
	das Internet	das *in·*ter·net
	machen	*ma·*khen
a local call	*ein Ortsgespräch*	ain *orts·*gesh·prairkh
	führen	*fü·*ren
a reverse-charge/	*ein R-Gespräch*	ain *air·*ge·shpraykh
collect call	*führen*	*fü·*ren
How much is ...?	*Wie viel kostet ...?*	vee feel *kos·*tet ...
a (three)-	*ein (drei)-*	ain (drai)·
minute call	*minutiges*	mi·*noo·*ti·ges
	Gespräch	ge·*shpraykh*
each extra	*jede zusätzliche*	*yay·*de tsu·*zayts·*li·khe
minute	*Minute*	mi·*noo·*te

What's your phone number?
> *Wie ist Ihre/deine*   vee ist *ee·re/dai·*ne
> *Telefonnummer?* pol/inf   te·le·*fawn·*nu·mer

Where's the nearest public phone?
> *Wo ist das nächste*   vaw ist das *naykhs·*te
> *öffentliche Telefon?*   er·fent·li·khe te·le·*fawn*

Can I look at a phone book?
> *Haben Sie ein*   *hah·*ben zee ain
> *Telefonbuch?*   tay·lay·*fawn·*bookh

I want to buy a phone card.
> *Ich möchte eine*   ikh *merkh·*te *ai·*ne
> *Telefonkarte kaufen.*   te·le·*fawn·*kar·te *kow·*fen

Do you have international prepaid phone cards?
> *Haben Sie internationale*   *hah·*ben zee in·ter·na·tsyo·*nah·*le
> *Prepaid-Telefonkarten?*   pree·payd·tay·lay·fawn·kar·ten

I'd like to know the number for ...
> *Ich möchte gerne die*   ikh *merkh·*te gern dee
> *Nummer für ... wissen.*   *nu·*mer für ... *vi·*sen

The number is ...
> *Die Nummer ist ...*   dee *nu·*mer ist ...

What's the area/country code for ...?
> *Was ist die Vorwahl für ...?*   vas ist dee *fawr·*vahl für ...

It's engaged.
> *Es ist besetzt.*   es ist be·*zetst*

The connection's bad.
> *Die Verbindung ist schlecht.*   dee fer·*bin·*dung ist shlekht

I've been cut off.
> *Ich bin unterbrochen worden.*   ikh bin un·ter·*bro·*khen *vor·*den

Can I speak to ...?
> *Kann ich mit ... sprechen?*   kan ikh mit ... *shpre·*khen

Can I leave a message?
> *Kann ich eine Nachricht*   kan ikh *ai·*ne *nahkh·*rikht
> *hinterlassen?*   hin·ter·*la·*sen

---

phone numbers

To avoid confusion with *drei* drai (three) on the phone, Germans use *zwo* tsoo instead of *zwei* tsvai, for 'two' (see also **numbers & amounts**, page 27).

ai·nen ow·gen·*blik bi*·te
Einen Augenblick, bitte.   **One moment, please.**

es toot meer lait (air/zee) ist nikht heer
Es tut mir Leid, (er/sie)   **I'm sorry, (he/she)**
ist nicht hier.   **is not here.**

mit vaym *merkh*·ten zee *shpre*·khen
Mit wem möchten   **Who do you want**
Sie sprechen?   **to speak to?**

toot meer lait zee *hah*·ben dee *fal*·she *nu*·mer
Tut mir Leid, Sie haben   **Sorry, wrong number.**
die falsche Nummer.
vair ist am a·pa·*raht*
Wer ist am Apparat?   **Who's calling?**

yah (air/zee) ist heer
Ja, (er/sie) ist hier.   **Yes, (he/she) is here.**

Please tell him/her I called.
Bitte sagen Sie ihm/ihr,   *bi*·te *zah*·gen zee eem/eer
dass ich angerufen habe.   das ikh *an*·ge·roo·fen *hah*·be

I'll call back later.
Ich rufe später   ikh *roo*·fe *shpay*·ter
nochmal an.   *nokh*·mahl an

What time should I call?
Wann kann ich am   van kan ikh am
besten anrufen?   *bes*·ten *an*·roo·fen

My number is ...
Meine Nummer ist ...   *mai*·ne *nu*·mer ist ...

I don't have a contact number.
Ich habe keine Nummer,   ikh *hah*·be *kai*·ne *nu*·mer
unter der Sie mich   *un*·ter dair zee mikh
erreichen können.   er·*rai*·khen *ker*·nen

> mobile/cell phone

What are the rates?
Wie hoch sind   vee hawkh zint
die Gebühren?   dee ge·*bü*·ren

I'd like a/an ...	*Ich hätte gern ...*	ikh *he*·te gern ...
adaptor plug	*einen Adapter für die Steckdose*	*ai*·nen a·*dap*·ter für dee *shtek*·daw·ze
charger for my phone	*ein Ladegerät für mein Handy*	ain *lah*·de·ge·rayt für main *hen*·di
mobile/cell phone for hire	*ein Miethandy*	ain *meet*·hen·di
prepaid mobile/ cell phone	*ein Handy mit Prepaidkarte*	ain *hen*·di mit pree·payd·*kar*·te
prepaid recharge card	*eine Karte mit Prepaid- Guthaben*	*ai*·ne *kar*·te mit pree·payd· goot·hah·ben
SIM card for your network	*eine SIM-Karte für Ihr Netz*	*ai*·ne *zim*·kar·te für eer nets

the internet

das internet

Where's the local Internet cafe?
Wo ist hier ein Internet-Café?
vaw ist heer ain *in*·ter·net·ka·fay

Do you have public Internet access here?
Haben Sie hier einen öffentlichen Internetzugang?
hah·ben zee heer *ai*·nen *er*·fent·li·khen *in*·ter·net·tsoo·gang

Is there wireless Internet access here?
Gibt es hier einen WLAN-Zugang?
geept es heer *ai*·nen *vay*·lahn·tsoo·gang

Can I connect my laptop here?
Kann ich meinen Laptop hier anschließen?
kan ikh *mai*·nen *lep*·top heer *an*·shlee·sen

Do you have PCs/Macs?
Haben Sie PCs/Macs?
hah·ben zee pay·*tsays*/meks

How much per hour/page?
Was kostet es pro Stunde/Seite?
vas *kos*·tet es praw *shtun*·de/*zai*·te

Do you have headphones (with a microphone)?
Haben Sie Kopfhörer (mit einem Mikrofon)?
hah·ben zee *kopf*·her·rer (mit *ai*·nem *mee*·kro·fawn)

How do I log on?
Wie logge ich mich ein?   vee *law*·ge ikh mikh ain

What's the password?
Wie lautet das Passwort?   vee *low*·tet das *pas*·vort

It's crashed.
Es ist abgestürzt.   es ist *ap*·ge·shtürtst

I've finished.
Ich bin fertig.   ikh bin *fer*·tikh

I'd like to buy a card/USB for prepaid mobile Internet.
Ich möchte gerne eine   ikh *merkh*·te gern *ai*·ne
Prepaid-Karte/einen   pree·payd·*kar*·te/*ai*·nen
USB-Stick für mobiles   oo·es·*bay*·shtik für mo·*bee*·les
Internet kaufen.   *in*·ter·net *kow*·fen

I'd like to ...	Ich möchte ...	ikh *merkh*·te ...
burn a CD	eine CD brennen	*ai*·ne tse de *bre*·nen
check my email	meine E-Mails checken	*mai*·ne ee·mayls *che*·ken
download my photos	meine Fotos herunterladen	*mai*·ne *faw*·tos he·*run*·ter·lah·den
get Internet access	Internetzugang haben	*in*·ter·net·tsoo·gang *hah*·ben
use a printer	einen Drucker benutzen	*ai*·nen *dru*·ker be·*nu*·tsen
use a scanner	einen Scanner benutzen	*ai*·nen *ske*·ner be·*nu*·tsen
use Skype	Skype benutzen	skaip be·*nu*·tsen

Can I connect my ... to this computer?	Kann ich ... an diesen Computer anschließen?	kan ikh ... an *dee*·zen kom·*pyoo*·ter *an*·shlee·sen
camera	meine Kamera	*mai*·ne *kah*·me·ra
iPhone	mein iPhone	main *ai*·fawn
iPod	meinen iPod	*mai*·nen *ai*·pod
media player (MP3)	meinen MP3-Player	*mai*·nen em·pay·*drai*·play·er
portable hard drive	meine tragbare Festplatte	*mai*·ne *trahk*·bah·re *fest*·pla·te
PSP	meine PSP	*mai*·ne pay·es·*pay*
USB flash drive (memory stick)	meinen USB-Stick	*mai*·nen oo·es·*bay*·shtik

Where's the ...?	Wo ist ...?	vaw ist ...
business centre	das Tagungs-zentrum	das tah·gungks·tsen·trum
conference	die Konferenz	dee kon·fe·rents
meeting	das Meeting	das mee·ting

I'm attending a ...	Ich nehme an ... teil.	ikh nay·me an ... tail
conference	einer Konferenz	ai·ner kon·fe·rents
course	einem Kurs	ai·nem kurs
meeting	einem Meeting	ai·nem mee·ting

I'm with ...	Ich bin ...	ikh bin ...
(company ...)	bei (Firma ...)	bai (fir·ma ...)
my colleague	mit meinem Kollegen hier m	mit mai·nem ko·lay·gen heer
	mit meiner Kollegin hier f	mit mai·ner ko·lay·gin heer
my colleagues	mit meinen Kollegen hier m pl	mit mai·nen ko·lay·gen heer
	mit meinen Kolleginnen hier f pl	mit mai·nen ko·lay·gi·nen heer
(two) others	mit (zwei) anderen hier	mit (tsvai) an·de·ren heer

I'm visiting a trade fair.
Ich besuche eine Messe. ikh be·zoo·khe ai·ne me·se

I'm here for (three) days/weeks.
Ich bin für (drei) ikh bin für (drai)
Tage/Wochen hier. tah·ge/vo·khen heer

I'm staying at ..., room ...
Ich wohne im ..., Zimmer ...   ikh *vaw*·ne im ... *tsi*·mer ...

I'm alone.
Ich bin allein.   ikh bin a·*lain*

I have an appointment with ...
Ich habe einen   ikh *hah*·be *ai*·nen
Termin bei ...   ter·*meen* bai ...

Here's my business card.
Hier ist meine Karte.   heer ist *mai*·ne *kar*·te

Can I have your business card?
Kann ich Ihre/deine   kan ikh *ee*·re/*dai*·ne
Karte bekommen? pol/inf   *kar*·te be·*ko*·men

That went very well.
Das war sehr gut.   das vahr zair goot

Thank you for your interest.
Danke für Ihr/dein   *dang*·ke für eer/dain
Interesse. pol/inf   in·te·*re*·se

Thank you for your time.
Danke für Ihre/deine   *dang*·ke für *ee*·re/*dai*·ne
Zeit. pol/inf   tsait

Shall we go for a drink/meal?
Sollen wir noch etwas   *zo*·len veer nokh *et*·vas
trinken/essen gehen?   *tring*·ken/e·sen *gay*·en

It's on me.
Ich lade Sie ein.   ikh *lah*·de zee ain

See also the box **titles and addressing people**, page 88.

See also the box **titles and addressing people**, page 88.

body language

Shaking hands is customary for both men and women in Germany, Austria and Switzerland. Always give a firm handshake and look people in the eye. Never keep your other hand in your pocket, as this is considered impolite.

PRACTICAL

76

Where can I ...?	Wo kann ich ...?	vaw kan ikh ...
I'd like to ...	Ich möchte ...	ikh merkh·te ...
arrange a transfer	einen Transfer tätigen	ai·nen trans·fer tay·ti·gen
cash a cheque	einen Scheck einlösen	ai·nen shek ain·ler·zen
change money	Geld umtauschen	gelt um·tow·shen
change travellers cheques	Reiseschecks einlösen	rai·ze·sheks ain·ler·zen
get a cash advance	eine Barauszahlung	ai·ne bahr·ows·tsah·lung
get change for this note	diesen Schein wechseln	dee·zen shain vek·seln
withdraw money	Geld abheben	gelt ap·hay·ben

Where's the nearest ...?	Wo ist der/die nächste ...? m/f	vaw ist dair/dee naykhs·te ...
automatic teller machine	Geldautomat m	gelt·ow·to·maht
foreign exchange office	Geldwechsel- stube f	gelt·vek·sel· shtoo·be

What time does the bank open?
Wann macht die Bank auf?   van makht dee bangk owf

The automatic teller machine took my card.
Der Geldautomat hat   dair gelt·ow·to·maht hat
meine Karte einbehalten.   mai·ne kar·te ain·be·hal·ten

I've forgotten my PIN.
Ich habe meine   ikh hah·be mai·ne
Geheimnummer vergessen.   ge·haim·nu·mer fer·ge·sen

Can I use my credit card to withdraw money?
Kann ich mit meiner   kan ikh mit mai·ner
Kreditkarte Geld abheben?   kre·deet·kar·te gelt ap·hay·ben

What's the ...?	*Wie ...?*	vee ...
charge for that	*hoch sind die*	hawkh zint dee
	Gebühren dafür	ge·*bü*·ren da·*für*
commission	*hoch ist*	hawkh ist
	die Kommission	dee ko·mi·*syawn*
exchange rate	*ist der*	ist dair
	Wechselkurs	*vek*·sel·kurs

Has my money arrived yet?

Ist mein Geld schon — ist main gelt shawn
angekommen? — an·ge·ko·men

How long will it take to arrive?

Wie lange dauert es, — vee *lang*·e *dow*·ert es
bis es da ist? — bis es dah ist

For other useful phrases, see **money**, page 33.

---

listen for ...

*bi·*te *shrai*·ben zee es owf
Bitte schreiben Sie es auf. **Please write it down.**

*bi·*te un·ter·*shrai*·ben zee heer
Bitte unterschreiben Sie hier. **Please sign here.**

das *ker*·nen veer nikht *ma*·khen
Das können wir **We can't do that.**
nicht machen.

es gipt dah ain pro·*blaym* mit *ee*·rem *kon*·to
Es gibt da ein Problem **There's a problem**
mit Ihrem Konto. **with your account.**

eer *kon*·to ist ü·ber·*tsaw*·gen
Ihr Konto ist überzogen. **You're overdrawn.**

in *ai*·ner *vo*·khe
In einer Woche. **In one week.**

in (feer) *ar*·baits·tah·gen
In (vier) Arbeitstagen. **In (four) working days.**

kan ikh *bi*·te *ai*·nen *ows*·vais zay·en
Kann ich bitte einen **Can I see some ID**
Ausweis sehen? **please?**

I'd like a/an ...	Ich hätte gern ...	ikh *he*·te gern ...
audio set	einen	*ai*·nen
	Audioführer	ow·di·o·fü·rer
catalogue	einen Katalog	*ai*·nen ka·ta·*lawg*
guide	einen Reiseführer	*ai*·nen rai·ze·fü·rer
guidebook in	einen Reiseführer	*ai*·nen rai·ze·fü·rer
English	auf Englisch	owf *eng*·lish
(local) map	eine Karte	*ai*·ne *kar*·te
	(von hier)	(fon heer)

Do you have	Haben Sie	*hah*·ben zee
information	Informationen	in·for·ma·*tsyaw*·nen
on ... sights?	über ... Sehens-	*ü*·ber ... zay·ens·
	würdigkeiten?	vür·dikh·kai·ten
architectural	architektonische	ar·khi·tek·*taw*·ni·she
cultural	kulturelle	kul·tu·re·le
historical	historische	his·*taw*·ri·she
local	örtliche	*ert*·li·khe
natural	natürliche	na·*tür*·li·khe
religious	religiöse	re·li·*gyer*·ze
unique	einzigartige	*ain*·tsikh·ar·ti·ge

We only have (one day).
Wir haben nur (einen Tag).   veer *hah*·ben noor (*ai*·nen tahk)

I'd like to see ...
Ich möchte ... sehen.   ikh *merkh*·te ... zay·en

I'd like to hire a local guide.
Ich würde gerne einen   ikh *vür*·de gern *ai*·nen
Fremdenführer anheuern.   *frem*·den·fü·rer an·ho·yern

What's that?
Was ist das? vas ist das

Who made it?
Wer hat das gemacht? vair hat das ge·*makht*

How old is it?
Wie alt ist es? vee alt ist es

Could you take a photograph of me?
Könnten Sie ein Foto kern·ten zee ain *faw*·to
von mir machen? fon meer *ma*·khen

Can I take photographs (of you)?
Kann ich (Sie/du) kan ikh (zee/doo)
fotografieren? pol/inf fo·to·gra·*fee*·ren

I'll send you the photograph.
Ich schicke Ihnen/dir ikh *shi*·ke ee·nen/deer
das Foto. pol/inf das *faw*·to

getting in

eintritt

What time does it open/close?
Wann macht es auf/zu? van makht es owf/tsoo

What's the admission charge?
Was kostet der Eintritt? vas *kos*·tet dair *ain*·trit

It costs ...
Er kostet ... air *kos*·tet ...

Is there a	*Gibt es eine*	gipt es *ai*·ne
discount for ...?	*Ermäßigung für ...?*	er·*may*·si·gung für ...
children	*Kinder*	*kin*·der
families	*Familien*	fa·*mee*·li·en
groups	*Gruppen*	*gru*·pen
older people	*Senioren*	zay·*nyaw*·ren
pensioners	*Rentner*	*rent*·ner
students	*Studenten*	shtu·*den*·ten

tours

Are there (organised) walking tours?
Gibt es (organisierte) geept es (or·ga·ni·zeer·te)
Wandertouren? van·der·too·ren

I'd like to do cooking/language classes.
Ich würde gerne eine ikh vür·de gern ai·ne
Kochkurs/Sprachkurs kokh·kurs/shprahkh·kurs
machen. ma·khen

Can you recommend a ...?
Können Sie ein ... ker·nen zee ain ...
empfehlen? emp·fay·len

When's the next ...?	*Wann ist der/die nächste ...?* m/f	van ist dair/dee naykhs·te ...
boat-trip	*Bootsrundfahrt* f	bawts·runt·fahrt
daytrip	*Tagesausflug* m	tah·ges·ows·flook
excursion	*Ausflug* m	ows·flook
tour	*Tour* f	toor

Is ... included?	*Ist ... inbegriffen?*	ist ... in·be·gri·fen
accommodation	*die Unterkunft*	dee un·ter·kunft
equipment	*die Ausrüstung*	dee ows·rüs·tung
food	*das Essen*	das e·sen
transport	*die Beförderung*	dee be·fer·de·rung

Do I need to take ... with me?
Muss ich ... mitnehmen?   mus ikh ... *mit*·nay·men

The guide will pay.
Der Reiseleiter bezahlt.   dair *rai*·ze·lai·ter be·*tsahlt*

The guide has paid.
Der Reiseleiter hat bezahlt.   dair *rai*·ze·lai·ter hat be·*tsahlt*

How long is the tour?
Wie lange dauert   vee *lang*·e dow·ert
die Führung?   dee *fü*·rung

What time should we be back?
Wann sollen wir zurück sein?   van zo·len veer tsu·*rük* zain

Be back here at (10) o'clock.
Seien Sie um (zehn)   *zai*·en zee um (tsayn)
Uhr zurück.   oor tsu·*rük*

I'm with them.
Ich gehöre zu ihnen.   ikh ge·*her*·re tsoo *ee*·nen

I've lost my group.
Ich habe meine   ikh *hah*·be *mai*·ne
Gruppe verloren.   *gru*·pe fer·*law*·ren

Have you seen a group of (Australians)?
Haben Sie eine Gruppe   *hah*·ben zee *ai*·ne *gru*·pe
(Australier) gesehen?   (ows·*trah*·li·er) ge·*zay*·en

signs

Ausgang	*ows*·gang	**Exit**
Damen	*dah*·men	**Women**
Eingang	*ain*·gang	**Entrance**
Geschlossen	ge·*shlo*·sen	**Closed**
Heiß	hais	**Hot**
Herren	*hair*·en	**Men**
Kalt	kalt	**Cold**
Kein Zutritt	kain *tsu*·trit	**No Entry**
Offen	*o*·fen	**Open**
Rauchen	*row*·khen	**No Smoking**
Verboten	fer·*baw*·ten	
Toiletten (WC)	to·a·*le*·ten (vee·*tsee*)	**Toilets**
Verboten	fer·*baw*·ten	**Prohibited**

senior & disabled travellers
senioren und behinderte reisende

I'm deaf.
Ich bin taub. ikh bin towp

I'm hard of hearing.
Ich höre schlecht. ikh *her*·re shlekht

I have a hearing aid.
Ich habe ein Hörgerät. ikh *hah*·be ain *her*·ge·rayt

Speak more loudly, please.
Ich habe ein Hörgerät. ikh *hah*·be ain *her*·ge·rayt

My companion is blind.
Mein Begleiter ist blind. main be·*glai*·ter ist blint

I have a disability.
Ich bin behindert. ikh bin be·*hin*·dert

I need assistance.
Ich brauche Hilfe. ikh *brow*·khe *hil*·fe

Are guide dogs permitted?
Sind Blindenhunde erlaubt? zint *blin*·den·hun·de er·*lowpt*

What services do you have for people with a disability?
Was für Leistungen gibt vas für *lais*·tung·en gipt
es für behinderte Reisende? es für be·*hin*·der·te *rai*·zen·de

Is there wheelchair access?
Gibt es eine Rollstuhlrampe? gipt es *ai*·ne rol·shtool·ram·pe

Are there parking spaces for people with a disability?
Gibt es Behinderten- geept es be·*hin*·der·ten·
parkplätze? park·ple·tse

Are there rails in the bathroom?
Ist das Bad ist das baht
behindertengerecht? be·*hin*·der·ten·ge·rekht

Are there toilets for people with a disability?
Gibt es Toiletten für gipt es to·a·*le*·ten für
Behinderte? be·*hin*·der·te

How wide are the doors?
Wie breit sind die Türen? vee brait sind dee *tü*·ren

How many steps are there?
Wieviele Stufen sind es?   vee·*fee*·le *shtoo*·fen sind es

Is there a lift?
Gibt es einen Aufzug?   gipt es *ai*·nen owf·*tsook*

Is there an induction loop for the hard of hearing?
Gibt es eine Induktions-   gipt es *ai*·ne in·duk·*tsyawns*·
schleife für Schwerhörige?   shlai·fe für shver·*her*·ri·ge

Is there somewhere I can sit down?
Kann ich mich hier   kan ikh mikh heer
irgendwo hinsetzen?   ir·gent·*vaw* hin·ze·tsen

Could you help me cross this street safely?
Könnten Sie mich sicher   *kern*·ten zee mikh *zi*·kher
über diese Straße bringen?   *ü*·ber *dee*·ze *shtrah*·se *bring*·en

Could you call me a taxi for the disabled?
Könnten Sie mir ein Taxi   *kern*·ten zee meer ain *tak*·si
für Behinderte rufen?   für be·*hin*·der·te *roo*·fen

Braille library	*Blindenbibliothek* f	*blin*·den·bi·bli·o·tayk
crutches	*Krücke* f pl	*krü*·ke
guide dog	*Blindenhund* m	*blin*·den·hunt
person with a	*Behinderter* m	be·*hin*·der·ter
disability	*Behinderte* f	be·*hin*·der·te
senior person	*Senior(in)* m/f	*zay*·nyaw/
		zay·nyaw·rin
walking frame	*Gehwagen* m	*gay*·vah·gen
walking stick	*Gehstock* m	*gay*·shtok
wheelchair	*Rollstuhl* m	*rol*·shtool
wheelchair ramp	*Rollstuhlrampe* f	*rol*·shtool·ram·pe
wheelchair space	*Rollstuhlplatz* m	*rol*·shtool·plats

Is there a/an...?	Gibt es ...?	gipt es ...
baby change room	einen Wickelraum	ai·nen vi·kel·rowm
(English-speaking) babysitter	einen (englisch-sprachigen) Babysitter	ai·nen (eng·lish·shprah·khi·gen) bay·bi·si·ter
child discount	eine Kinder-ermäßigung	ai·ne kin·der·er·may·si·gung
child-minding service	einen Babysitter-Service	ai·nen bay·bi·si·ter·ser·vis
children's menu	eine Kinderkarte	ai·ne kin·der·kar·te
family discount	eine Familien-ermäßigung	ai·ne fa·mee·li·en·er·may·si·gung
highchair	einen Kinderstuhl	ai·nen kin·der·shtool
park	einen Park	ai·nen park
playground nearby	einen Spielplatz in der Nähe	ai·nen shpeel·plats in dair nay·e
theme park	einen Freizeitpark	ai·nen frai·tsait·park

I need a ...	Ich brauche ...	ikh brow·khe ...
baby seat	einen Babysitz	ai·nen bay·bi·zits
child seat	einen Kindersitz	ai·nen kin·der·zits
cot	ein Kinderbett	ain kin·der·bet
potty	ein Kinder-töpfchen	ain kin·der·terpf·khen
stroller	einen Kinderwagen	ai·nen kin·der·vah·gen

Do you sell ...?	*Verkaufen Sie ...?*	fer·*kow*·fen zee ...
baby wipes	*feuchte Tücher*	*foykh*·te tü·kher
disposable nappies/ diapers	*Einweg-Windeln*	*ain*·vek·vin·deln
milk formula	*Muttermilch-ersatz*	*mu*·ter·milkh·er·zats
painkillers for infants	*Schmerzmittel für Kinder*	*shmerts*·mi·tel für *kin*·der

Can I breastfeed here?
Kann ich meinem Kind hier die Brust geben? — kan ikh *mai*·nem kint heer dee brust *gay*·ben

Are children allowed?
Sind Kinder erlaubt? — zint *kin*·der er·*lowpt*

Is this suitable for (three)-year-old children?
Ist das für (drei) Jahre alte Kinder geeignet? — ist das für (drai) *yah*·re *al*·te *kin*·der ge·*aig*·net

What's your name?
Wie heißt du? inf — vee haist doo

How old are you?
Wie alt bist du? inf — vee alt bist doo

If your child is sick, see **health**, page 177. For more on talking to children, see **meeting people**, page 95.

signs

When travelling with children, keep an eye out for the following signs:

Junioren bis 5 Jahre frei	yoo·*nyaw*·ren bis fünf *yah*·re frai	**Children up to the age of 5 free**
Junioren bis 15 Jahre halber Preis	yoo·*nyaw*·ren bis fünf·tsayn *yah*·re *hal*·per prais	**Children up to the age of 15 half price**
Wickeltisch	*vi*·kel·tish	**Change Room**
Spielplatz	*shpeel*·plats	**Playground**

SOCIAL > meeting people

basics

grundlagen

Yes.	*Ja.*	yah
No.	*Nein.*	nain
Please.	*Bitte.*	*bi*·te
Thank you.	*Danke.*	*dang*·ke
Thank you very much.	*Vielen Dank.*	*fee*·len dangk
You're (very) welcome.	*Bitte (sehr).*	*bi*·te (zair)
Excuse me.	*Entschuldigung.*	ent·*shul*·di·gung
Sorry.	*Entschuldigung.*	ent·*shul*·di·gung
Don't worry.	*Macht nichts.*	makht nikhts

greetings

grüsse

Hello.		
(all of Germany)	*Guten Tag.*	*goo*·ten tahk
(southern Germany)	*Grüß Gott.*	grüs got
(Switzerland)	*Grüezi.*	*grü*·e·tsi
(Austria)	*Servus.*	*zer*·vus
Good ...	*Guten ...*	*goo*·ten ...
morning	*Morgen*	*mor*·gen
day/afternoon	*Tag*	tahk
evening	*Abend*	*ah*·bent
Hi.	*Hallo.*	*ha*·lo
See you later.	*Bis später.*	bis *shpay*·ter
Good night.	*Gute Nacht.*	*goo*·te nakht
Goodbye.	*Auf Wiedersehen.*	owf *vee*·der·zay·en
Bye.	*Tschüss/Tschau.*	chüs/chow

How are you?

Wie geht es
Ihnen/dir? pol/inf

vee gayt es
ee·nen/deer

Fine. And you?

Danke, gut.
Und Ihnen/dir? pol/inf

dang·ke goot
unt ee·nen/deer

What's your name?

Wie ist Ihr Name? pol
Wie heißt du? inf

vee ist eer nah·me
vee haist doo

My name is ...

Mein Name ist ... pol
Ich heiße ... inf

main nah·me ist ...
ikh hai·se ...

I'd like to introduce you to ...

Darf ich Ihnen/dir
... vorstellen? pol/inf

darf ikh ee·nen/dir
... fawr·shte·len

I'm pleased to meet you.

Angenehm.

an·ge·naym

---

titles & addressing people

In the past *Fräulein* froy·lain was used to address all unmarried women regardless of age, but today the term is only used to address girls (and sometimes female waiters). All other women should be addressed using *Frau* frow. There's no equivalent of the English 'Ms' – use *Frau*. The equivalents of Sir and Madam, *Mein Herr* main her and *Meine Dame* mai·ne dah·me, are very old-fashioned.

If you want to include academic titles when addressing somebody, these are combined with *Herr* and *Frau*, eg, *Frau Professor* frow pro·fe·sor or *Herr Doktor* her dok·tor.

Mr	*Herr*	her
Mrs	*Frau*	frow
Miss	*Frau/Fräulein*	frow/froy·lain

making conversation

Do you live here?
Wohnen Sie hier? pol	*vaw·nen zee heer*
Wohnst du hier? inf	vawnst doo heer

Where are you going?
Wohin fahren Sie? pol	*vaw·hin fah·ren zee*
Wohin fährst du? inf	vaw·hin fairst doo

What are you doing?
Was machen Sie? pol	vas *ma·khen zee*
Was machst du? inf	vas makhst doo

Are you waiting (for a bus)?
Warten Sie (auf einen Bus)? pol	*var·ten zee (owf ai·nen bus)*
Wartest du (auf einen Bus)? inf	*var·test doo (owf ai·nen bus)*

Are you also travelling (on this train)?
Fahren Sie auch (mit diesem Zug)? pol	*fah·ren zee owkh (mit dee·zem tsook)*
Fährst du auch (mit diesem Zug)? inf	fairst doo owkh (mit *dee·zem tsook)*

Can I have a light?
Haben Sie Feuer? pol	*hah·ben zee foy·er*
Hast du Feuer? inf	hast doo *foy·er*

Nice day, isn't it?
Schönes Wetter heute!	*sher·nes we·ter hoy·te*

Terrible weather today!
Furchtbares Wetter heute!	*furkht·bah·res we·ter hoy·te*

Just joking!
Das war nur ein Scherz!	das vahr noor ain sherts

meeting people

89

This is my ...	Das ist mein/meine/ mein ... m/f/n	das ist main/mai·ne/ main ...
child	Kind n	kint
colleague	Kollege/ Kollegin m/f	ko·lay·ge/ ko·lay·gin
friend	Freund(in) m/f	froynt/froyn·din
husband	Mann m	man
partner	Partner(in) m/f	part·ner/part·ne·rin
wife	Frau f	frow

Do you like it here?
Gefällt es Ihnen/ ge·*felt* es ee·nen/
dir hier? pol/inf deer heer

I love it here.
Mir gefällt es hier sehr gut. meer ge·*felt* es heer zair goot

What do you think (about ...)?
Was denken Sie (über ...)? pol vas *deng*·ken zee (*ü*·ber ...)
Was denkst du (über ...)? inf vas dengkst doo (*ü*·ber ...)

What's this called?
Wie heißt das? vee haist das

What a beautiful baby!
Was für ein schönes Baby! vas für ain *sher*·nes *bay*·bi

Can I take a photo (of you)?
Kann ich ein Foto kan ikh ain *faw*·to
(von Ihnen/dir) (fon ee·nen/deer)
machen? pol/inf *ma*·khen

That's (beautiful), isn't it?
Ist das nicht (schön)? ist das nikht (shern)

Are you here on holiday?
Sind Sie hier im Urlaub? pol zint zee heer im *oor*·lowp
Bist du hier im Urlaub? inf bist doo heer im *oor*·lowp

I'm here ...	*Ich bin hier ...*	ikh bin heer ...
for a holiday	*im Urlaub*	im *oor*·lowp
on business	*auf Geschäfts-reise*	owf ge·*shefts*·rai·ze
to study	*zum Studieren*	tsum shtu·*dee*·ren
with my family	*mit meiner Familie*	mit *mai*·ner fa·*mee*·li·e
with my partner	*mit meinem Partner* m	mit *mai*·nem *part*·ner
	mit meiner Partnerin f	mit *mai*·ner *part*·ne·rin

How long are you here for?

Für wie lange sind Sie hier? pol		für vee *lang*·e zint zee heer
Für wie lange bist du hier? inf		für vee *lang*·e bist doo heer

I'm here for (four) weeks/days.

Ich bin für (vier) Tage/Wochen hier.		ikh bin für (feer) *tah*·ge/*vo*·khen heer

local talk

Hey!	*Hi/Hey!*	hai/hei
Great!	*Toll/Geil!/ Super!/Spitze!*	tol/gail/ zoo·per/*shpi*·tse
No problem.	*Kein Problem.*	kain pro·*blaym*
Sure.	*Klar!*	klahr
Maybe.	*Vielleicht.*	fi·*laikht*
No way!	*Auf keinen Fall!*	owf *kai*·nen fal
It's OK.	*Das ist OK.*	das ist o·*kay*
I'm OK.	*Alles klar.*	a·les klahr
Look!	*Guck mal!*	guk mahl
Listen!	*Hör mal!*	her mahl
Listen to this!	*Hör dir das an!*	her deer das an
I'm ready.	*Ich bin so weit.*	ikh bin zaw vait
Are you ready?	*Bist du so weit?*	bist doo zaw vait
Just a minute.	*Einen Augenblick.*	*ai*·nen *ow*·gen·*blik*

nationalities

Where are you from?
  Woher kommen Sie? pol   *vaw*·hair *ko*·men zee
  Woher kommst du? inf   *vaw*·hair komst doo

I'm from …	*Ich komme aus …*	ikh *ko*·me ows …
Australia	*Australien*	ows·*trah*·li·en
Canada	*Kanada*	*ka*·na·da
England	*England*	*eng*·lant
New Zealand	*Neuseeland*	noy·*zay*·lant
the USA	*den USA*	dayn oo·es·*ah*

For more countries, see the **dictionary**.

age

How old …?	*Wie alt …?*	vee alt …
are you	*sind Sie* pol	zint zee
	bist du inf	bist doo
is your daughter	*ist Ihre/deine*	ist *ee*·re/*dai*·ne
	Tochter pol/inf	*tokh*·ter
is your son	*ist Ihr/dein*	ist eer/dain
	Sohn pol/inf	zawn

I'm … years old.
  Ich bin … Jahre alt.   ikh bin … *yah*·re alt

He's/She's … years old.
  Er/Sie ist … Jahre alt.   air/zee ist … *yah*·re alt

Too old!
  Zu alt!   tsoo alt

I'm younger than I look.
  Ich bin jünger als   ikh bin *yüng*·er als
  ich aussehe.   ikh *ows*·zay·e

For your age, see **numbers & amounts**, page 27.

SOCIAL

occupations & studies

What's your occupation?

Als was arbeiten Sie? pol		als vas *ar*·bai·ten zee
Als was arbeitest du? inf		als vas *ar*·bai·test doo

I'm a ...	*Ich bin ein/eine ...* m/f	ikh bin ain/ain·e ...
farmer	*Bauer* m	*bow*·er
	Bäuerin f	*boy*·e·rin
student	*Student* m	shtu·*dent*
	Studentin f	shtu·*den*·tin
teacher	*Lehrer* m	*lay*·rer
	Lehrerin f	*lay*·re·rin
writer	*Schriftsteller* m	*shrift*·shte·ler
	Schriftstellerin f	*shrift*·shte·le·rin

I work in ...	*Ich arbeite ...*	ikh *ar*·bai·te ...
administration	*in der Verwaltung*	in dair fer·*val*·tung
IT	*in der*	in dair
	IT-Branche	ai·*tee*·brang·she
sales &	*im Verkauf*	im fer·*kowf*
marketing	*und Marketing*	unt *mar*·ke·ting

I'm ...	*Ich bin ...*	ikh bin ...
retired	*Rentner* m	*rent*·ner
	Rentnerin f	*rent*·ne·rin
self-employed	*selbstständig*	*zelpst*·shten·dikh
unemployed	*arbeitslos*	*ar*·baits·laws

What are you studying?

Was studieren Sie? pol		vas shtu·*dee*·ren zee
Was studierst du? inf		vas shtu·*deerst* doo

I'm studying ...	*Ich studiere ...*	ikh shtu·*dee*·re ...
engineering	*Ingenieurwesen*	in·zhe·*nyer*·vay·zen
German	*Deutsch*	doytsh
medicine	*Medizin*	me·di·*tseen*

For more occupations and fields of study, see the **dictionary**.

family

Do you have a ...?
Haben Sie einen/eine ...? m/f pol — hah·ben zee ai·nen/ai·ne ...
Hast du einen/eine ...? m/f inf — hast doo ai·nen/ai·ne ...

I (don't) have a ...
Ich habe (k)einen/
(k)eine ... m/f — ikh hah·be (k)ai·nen/
(k)ai·ne ...

Do you live with (your parents)?
Leben Sie bei — lay·ben zee bai
(Ihren Eltern)? pol — (ee·ren el·tern)
Lebst du bei — laypst doo bai
(deinen Eltern)? inf — (dai·nen el·tern)

I live with my ...
Ich lebe bei meinem/ — ikh lay·be bai mai·nem/
meiner/meinen ... m/f/pl — mai·ner/mai·nen ...

This is my ...
Das ist mein/meine ... m/f — das ist main/mai·ne ...

Are you married?
Sind Sie verheiratet? pol — zint zee fer·hai·ra·tet
Bist du verheiratet? inf — bist doo fer·hai·ra·tet

I live with someone.
Ich lebe mit jemandem — ikh lay·be mit yay·man·dem
zusammen. — tsu·za·men

I'm ... — *Ich bin ...* — ikh bin ...
  married — *verheiratet* — fer·hai·ra·tet
  separated — *getrennt* — ge·trent
  single — *ledig* — lay·dikh

children

When's your birthday?
Wann hast du Geburtstag? van hast doo ge·*burts*·tahk

Do you go to school or kindergarten?
Gehst du in die Schule gayst doo in dee *shoo*·le
oder in den Kindergarten? aw·der in dayn *kin*·der·gar·ten

What grade are you in?
In welcher Klasse bist du? in *vel*·kher *kla*·se bist doo

What do you do after school?
Was machst du vas makhst doo
nach der Schule? nahkh dair *shoo*·le

Do you learn English?
Lernst du Englisch? lernst doo *eng*·lish

I come from very far away.
Ich komme von sehr weit her. ikh *ko*·me fon zair vait hair

Are you lost?
Hast du dich verlaufen? hast doo dikh fer·*low*·fen

farewells

Tomorrow is my last day here.
Morgen ist mein *mor*·gen ist main
letzter Tag hier. *lets*·ter tahk heer

Here's my ...	*Hier ist meine ...*	heer ist *mai*·ne ...
What's your...?	*Wie ist Ihre/*	vee ist *ee*·re/
	deine ...? pol/inf	*dai*·ne ...
address	*Adresse*	a·*dre*·se
email address	*E-mail-Adresse*	ee·mayl·a·dre·se
fax number	*Faxnummer*	faks·nu·mer
mobile number	*Handynummer*	hen·di·nu·mer
pager number	*Pagernummer*	pay·dzher·nu·mer
work number	*Nummer bei*	nu·mer bai
	der Arbeit	dair *ar*·bait

For more on addresses, see **directions**, page 59.

meeting people

95

Are you on Facebook?

Sind Sie auf Facebook? pol	zint zee owf *fays*·buk
Bist du auf Facebook? inf	bist doo owf *fays*·buk

If you ever visit (Scotland), come and visit us.

Wenn Sie jemals nach	ven zee *yay*·mahls nahkh
(Schottland) kommen,	(*shot*·lant) *ko*·men
besuchen Sie uns	be·*zoo*·khen zee uns
doch mal. pol	dokh mahl
Wenn du jemals nach	ven doo *yay*·mahls nahkh
(Schottland) kommst,	(*shot*·lant) komst
besuche uns doch mal. inf	be·*zoo*·khe uns dokh mahl

Keep in touch!

Melden Sie sich	*mel*·den zee zikh
doch mal! pol	dokh mahl
Melde dich mal! inf	*mel*·de dikh mahl

It's been great meeting you.

Es war schön, Sie/dich	es vahr shern zee/dikh
kennen zu lernen. pol/inf	*ke*·nen tsoo *ler*·nen

---

local talk

Bless you! (when sneezing)	*Gesundheit!*	ge·*zunt*·hait
Bon voyage!	*Gute Reise!*	*goo*·te *rai*·ze
Cheers!	*Prost!*	prawst
Good luck!	*Viel Glück!*	feel glük
Happy birthday!	*Herzlichen*	*herts*·li·khen
	Glückwunsch	*glük*·vunsh
	zum Geburtstag!	tsum ge·*burts*·tahk
What a pity!	*Schade!*	*shah*·de
Congratulations!	*Gratuliere!*	gra·too·*lee*·re

common interests

gemeinsame interessen

What do you do in your spare time?

Was machen Sie in	vas *ma*·khen zee in
Ihrer Freizeit? pol	ee·rer *frai*·tsait
Was machst du in	vas makhst doo in
deiner Freizeit? inf	*dai*·ner *frai*·tsait

Do you like ...?	*Mögen Sie ...?* pol	*mer*·gen zee ...
	Magst du ...? inf	mahkst doo ...
I (don't) like ...	*Ich mag (keinen/*	ikh mahk (*kai*·nen/
	keine) ... m/f	*kai*·ne) ...
art	*Kunst* f	kunst
sport	*Sport* m	shport

I (don't) like ...	*Ich ... (nicht) gern.*	ikh ... (nikht) gern
cooking	*koche*	*ko*·khe
dancing	*tanze*	*tan*·tse
drawing	*zeichne*	*tsaikh*·ne
hiking	*wandere*	*van*·de·re
painting	*male*	*mah*·le
photography	*fotografiere*	fo·to·gra·*fee*·re
reading	*lese*	*lay*·ze
travelling	*reise*	*rai*·ze

I (don't) like ...	*Ich ... (nicht) gern ...*	ikh ... (nikht) gern ...
films	*sehe ... Filme*	*zay*·e ... *fil*·me
gardening	*arbeite ...*	ar·*bai*·te ...
	im Garten	im *gar*·ten
shopping	*kaufe ... ein*	*kow*·fe ... ain
socialising	*gehe ... aus*	*gay*·e ... ows

And you?	*Und Sie/du?* pol/inf	unt zee/doo

For sporting interests, see **sports**, page 123, and the **dictionary**.

music

Do you like to ...?

listen to music	*Hören Sie gern*	*her·ren zee gern*
	Musik? pol	mu·*zeek*
	Hörst du gern	herst doo gern
	Musik? inf	mu·*zeek*
dance	*Tanzen Sie*	*tan·tsen zee*
	gern? pol	gern
	Tanzt du gern? inf	tantst doo gern
go to concerts	*Gehen Sie gern*	*gay·en zee gern*
	in Konzerte? pol	in kon·*tser·*te
	Gehst du gern	gayst doo gern
	in Konzerte? inf	in kon·*tser·*te
sing	*Singen Sie*	*zing·en zee*
	gern? pol	gern
	Singst du gern? inf	zingkst doo gern

Do you play an instrument?

Spielen Sie ein	*shpee·len zee ain*
Instrument? pol	in·stru·*ment*
Spielst du ein	shpeelst doo ain
Instrument? inf	in·stru·*ment*

Which ... do	*Welche ...*	*vel·*khe ...
you like?	*mögen Sie?* pol	*mer·*gen zee
	Welche ...	*vel·*khe ...
	magst du? inf	mahkst doo
bands	*Bands*	*bents*
music	*Art von Musik*	art fon mu·*zeek*
singers	*Sänger*	*zeng·*er

classical music	klassische Musik f	kla·si·she mu·zeek
electronic music	elektronische	e·lek·traw·ni·she
	Musik f	mu·zeek
metal	Metal m	me·tel
pop	Popmusik f	pop·mu·zeek
rock	Rockmusik f	rok·mu·zeek
traditional music	traditionelle	tra·di·tsyo·ne·le
	Musik f	mu·zeek
world music	Weltmusik f	velt·mu·zeek

Planning to go to a concert? See **buying tickets**, page 36, and **going out**, page 107.

cinema & theatre

kino und theater

I feel like	Ich hätte Lust,	ikh he·te lust
going to a ...	ins... zu gehen.	ins... tsoo gay·en
film	Kino	kee·no
play	Theater	te·ah·ter

Did you like it?
Hat es Ihnen/dir   hat es ee·nen/deer
gefallen? pol/inf   ge·fa·len

What's showing at the cinema/theatre tonight?
Was gibt es heute im   vas gipt es hoy·te im
Kino/Theater?   kee·no/te·ah·ter

Is it in English?
Ist es auf Englisch?   ist es owf eng·lish

Is it dubbed?
Ist er synchronisiert?   ist air zün·kro·nee·zeert

Does it have subtitles?
Hat es Untertitel?   hat es un·ter·tee·tel

Are those seats taken?
Sind diese Plätze besetzt?   zint dee·ze ple·tse be·zetst

Have you seen ...?
Haben Sie ... gesehen? pol   hah·ben zee ... ge·zay·en
Hast du ... gesehen? inf   hast doo ... ge·zay·en

Who's in it?
Wer spielt da mit?   vair shpeelt dah mit

It stars ...
Es ist mit ...   es ist mit ...

I thought it was ...	*Ich fand es ...*	ikh fant es ...
excellent	*ausgezeichnet*	ows·ge·*tsaikh*·net
long	*lang*	lang
OK	*okay*	o·*kay*

I (don't) like ...	*Ich mag ...*	ikh mahk ...
action movies	*(keine)*	(*kai*·ne)
	Actionfilme	ek·shen·fil·me
animated	*(keine)*	(*kai*·ne)
films	*Zeichentrickfilme*	tsai·khen·trik·fil·me
classical	*(kein) klassisches*	(kain) *kla*·si·shes
theatre	*Theater*	te·*ah*·ter
comedies	*(keine)*	(*kai*·ne)
	Komödien	ko·*mer*·di·en
documentaries	*(keine)*	(*kai*·ne)
	Dokumentarfilme	do·ku·men·*tahr*·fil·me
drama	*(keine)*	(*kai*·ne)
	Schauspiele	*show*·shpee·le
German	*(keine) deutsche(n)*	(*kai*·ne) *doyt*·she(n)
cinema	*Filme*	*fil*·me
horror	*(keine)*	(*kai*·ne)
movies	*Horrorfilme*	*ho*·ror·fil·me
period	*(keine)*	(*kai*·ne)
dramas	*Historienfilme*	his·*taw*·ri·en·fil·me
realism	*(keinen) Realismus*	(*kai*·nen) re·a·*lis*·mus
sci-fi	*(keinen)*	(*kai*·nen)
	Sciencefiction	sai·ens·*fik*·shen
short films	*(keine) Kurzfilme*	(*kai*·ne) *kurts*·fil·me
war movies	*(keine) Kriegsfilme*	(*kai*·ne) *kreeks*·fil·me

feelings

gefühle

I'm (not) ...	Ich bin (nicht) ...	ikh bin (nikht) ...
Are you ...?	Sind Sie ...? pol	zint zee ...
	Bist du ...? inf	bist doo ...
annoyed	verärgert	fer·er·gert
disappointed	enttäuscht	en·toysht
happy	glücklich	glük·likh
sad	traurig	trow·rikh
tired	müde	mü·de

I'm (not) ...	Ich habe (kein) ...	ikh hah·be (kain) ...
Are you ...?	Haben Sie ...? pol	hah·ben zee ...
	Hast du ...? inf	hast doo ...
hungry	Hunger	hung·er
thirsty	Durst	durst

I'm (not) ...	Mir ist (nicht)	meer ist (nikht) ...
Are you ...?	Ist Ihnen/	ist ee·nen/
	dir ...? pol/inf	deer ...
cold	kalt	kalt
hot	heiß	hais

I'm (not) ...		
embarrassed	Das ist mir (nicht) peinlich.	das ist meer (nikht) pain·likh
worried	Ich mache mir (keine) Sorgen.	ikh ma·khe meer (kai·ne) zor·gen

If you're not feeling well, see **health**, page 180.

Are you …?

embarrassed	*Ist Ihnen/dir* *das peinlich?* pol/inf	ist *ee*·nen/deer das *pain*·likh
worried	*Machen Sie* *sich Sorgen?* pol *Machst du dir* *Sorgen?* inf	*ma*·khen zee zikh *zor*·gen makhst doo deer *zor*·gen

mixed feelings

a little I'm a little sad.	*ein bisschen* *Ich bin ein* *bisschen traurig.*	ain *bis*·khen ikh bin ain *bis*·khen *trow*·rikh
terribly I'm terribly sorry.	*furchtbar* *Es tut mir* *furchtbar Leid.*	*furkht*·bahr es toot meer *furkht*·bahr lait
very I feel very lucky.	*sehr* *Ich schätze mich* *sehr glücklich.*	zair ikh *she*·tse mikh zair *glük*·likh
completely not at all profoundly quite totally	*völlig* *überhaupt nicht* *abgrundtief* *ziemlich* *total*	*fer*·likh ü·ber·*howpt* nikht *ap*·grun·teef *tseem*·likh to·*tahl*

opinions

meinungen

Did you like it?
Hat es Ihnen/dir   hat es *ee*·nen/deer
gefallen? pol/inf   ge·*fa*·len

What did you think of it?
Wie hat es Ihnen/dir   vee hat es *ee*·nen/deer
gefallen? pol/inf   ge·*fa*·len

It is/was ...	Es ist/war ...	es ist/vahr ...
awful	schrecklich	shrek·likh
beautiful	schön	shern
boring	langweilig	lang·vai·likh
great	toll	tol
interesting	interessant	in·tre·sant
OK	okay	o·kay
too expensive	zu teuer	tsoo toy·er

politics & social issues

politische und soziale fragen

I support the	Ich unterstütze	ikh un·ter·shtü·tse
... party.	die ... Partei.	dee ... par·tai
communist	kommunistische	ko·mu·nis·ti·she
conservative	konservative	kon·zer·va·tee·ve
democratic	demokratische	de·mo·krah·tish·e
green	grüne	grün·e
liberal	liberale	li·be·rahl·e
social democratic	sozial-demokratische	zo·tsyahl·de·mo·krah·tish·e
socialist	sozialistische	zo·tsya·lis·tish·e

I support the labour party.
Ich unterstütze die Arbeiterpartei.
ikh un·ter·shtü·tse dee ar·bai·ter·par·tai

Who do you vote for?
Wen wählen Sie? pol
vayn vay·len zee
Wen wählst du? inf
vayn vaylst doo

Did you hear about ...?
Haben Sie von ... gehört? pol
hah·ben zee fon ... ge·hert
Hast du von ... gehört? inf
hast doo fon ... ge·hert

Do you agree with it?
Sind Sie damit einverstanden? pol
zint zee dah·mit ain·fer·shtan·den
Bist du damit einverstanden? inf
bist doo dah·mit ain·fer·shtan·den

I (don't) agree with that.
Ich bin damit (nicht)   ikh bin dah·*mit* (nikht)
einverstanden.   *ain*·fer·shtan·den

Are you against ... ?
Sind Sie gegen ...? pol   zint zee *gay*·gen ...
Bist du gegen ...? inf   bist doo *gay*·gen ...

Are you in favour of ...?
Sind Sie für ...? pol   zint zee für ...
Bist du für ...? inf   bist doo für ...

How do people feel about ...?
Was denken die   vas *deng*·ken dee
Leute über ...?   *loy*·te ü·ber ...

abortion	*Abreibung* f	*ap*·trai·bung
animal rights	*Tierschutz* m	*teer*·shuts
corruption	*Korruption* f	ko·rup·*tsyawn*
crime	*Verbrechen* n	fer·*bre*·khen
discrimination	*Diskriminierung* f	dis·kri·mi·*nee*·rung
drugs	*Drogen* f pl	*draw*·gen
the economy	*die Wirtschaft* f	dee *virt*·shaft
education	*Bildung* f	*bil*·dung
the environment	*die Umwelt* f	dee *um*·velt
equal opportunity	*Gleichberech-tigung* f	*glaikh*·be·rekh·ti·gung
EU expansion	*EU–Erweiterung* f	ay·oo·er·vai·te·rung
euthanasia	*Euthanasie* f	oy·ta·na·zee
globalisation	*Globalisierung* f	glaw·ba·li·zee·rung
health care	*Gesundheitswesen* n	ge·zunt·haits·vay·zen
human rights	*Menschenrechte* n pl	*men*·shen·rekh·te
immigration	*Einwanderung* f	*ain*·van·de·rung
military service	*Wehrdienst* m	*vayr*·deenst
racism	*Rassismus* m	ra·*sis*·mus
sexism	*Sexismus* m	sek·*sis*·mus
social welfare	*Wohlfahrtsstaat* m	*vawl*·fahrts·shtaht
taxes	*Steuern* f	*shtoy*·ern
terrorism	*Terrorismus* m	te·ro·*riz*·mus
unemployment	*Arbeitslosigkeit* f	*ar*·baits·law·zikh·kait
war in ...	*Krieg* m *in* ...	kreek in ...

the environment

Is there a ... problem here?
Gibt es hier ein Problem mit ...?
gipt es heer ain pro·*blaym* mit ...

What should be done about ...?
Was sollte man gegen ... tun?
vas *zol*·te man gay·gen ... toon

alternative energy sources	*alternative Energiequellen* f pl	al·ter·na·*tee*·ve ay·ner·*gee*·kve·len
biodegradable	*biologisch abbaubar*	bi·o·*law*·gish ap·bow·bahr
carbon dioxide emissions	*Kohlendioxid- Emissionen* f pl	kaw·len·dee·ok·seet· ay·mee·syaw·nen
climate change	*Klimawandel* m	klee·ma·wan·del
conservation	*Schutz* m	shuts
deforestation	*Abholzung* f	ap·hol·tsung
drought	*Trockenheit* f	tro·ken·hait
ecosystem	*Ökosystem* n	er·ko·züs·taym
endangered species	*gefährdete Arten* f pl	ge·*fair*·de·te ar·ten
floods	*Überschwem- mungen* f pl	ü·ber·*shve*· mung·en
genetically modified food/crops	*genmanipuliertes Essen/Getreide* n/n	gayn·ma·ni·pu·leer·tes e·sen/ge·*trai*·de
global warming	*globale Erwärmung* f	glo·*bah*·le er·*ver*·mung
hunting	*Jagd* f	yahkt
hydroelectricity	*Strom* m aus *Wasserkraft*	shtrawm ows va·ser·kraft
nuclear energy	*Atomenergie* f	a·*tawm*·e·ner·gee
nuclear testing	*Atomtests* m pl	a·*tawm*·tests
nuclear waste	*Atommüll* m	a·*tawm*·mül
ozone layer	*Ozonschicht* f	o·*tsawn*·shikht
pesticides	*Pestizide* n pl	pes·ti·*tsee*·de
pollution	*Umweltver- schmutzung* f	um·velt·fer· shmu·tsung
sustainable energy	*nachhaltige Energie* f	nahkh·hal·ti·ge ay·ner·gee
toxic waste	*Giftmüll* m	gift·mül
water supply	*Wasserversorgung* f	va·ser·fer·zor·gung

Is this a protected ...?	*Ist das ...?*	ist das ...
forest	*ein geschützter Wald*	ain ge-*shüts*-ter valt
species	*eine geschützte Art*	*ai*-ne ge-*shüts*-te art

the final say

If you'd like to underline your opinions with some colourful language and impress your new German-speaking acquaintances, try your hand at these sayings:

That goes without saying.
Das versteht sich von selbst.
das ver-*shtet* zikh fon zelbst

That cuts no ice with me.
Damit können Sie bei mir nicht landen.
da-mit *ker*-nen zee bai meer nikht *lan*-den

Nobody cares two hoots about it.
Danach kräht kein Hahn.
da-*nakh* krayt kain han

There's the rub.
Da liegt der Hund begraben.
da leegt dair hunt be-*grab*-en

Stick to the facts!
Bleiben Sie sachlich!
blai-ben zee *zakh*-likh

That will get you nowhere.
Das führt zu nichts.
das fürt tsu nikhts

Tell us another one!
Das können Sie uns nicht erzählen!
das *kern*-en zee uns nikht er-*tsay*-len

to have the final say
das letzte Wort haben
das *lets*-te vort *hab*-en

where to go

What's there to do in the evenings?
Was kann man abends   vas kan man *ah*·bents
unternehmen?   un·ter·*nay*·men

What's on ...?	*Was ist ... los?*	vas ist ... laws
locally	*hier*	heer
this weekend	*dieses*	*dee*·zes
	Wochenende	*vo*·khen·en·de
today	*heute*	*hoy*·te
tonight	*heute Abend*	*hoy*·te *ah*·bent

Where are the ...?	*Wo sind die ...?*	vaw zint dee ...
clubs	*Klubs*	klups
gay venues	*Schwulen- und*	*shvoo*·len unt
	Lesbenkneipen	*les*·ben·knai·pen
places to eat	*Restaurants*	res·to·*rangs*
pubs	*Kneipen*	*knai*·pen

Is there a local entertainment guide?
Gibt es einen   gipt es *ai*·nen
Veranstaltungskalender?   fer·*an*·shtal·tungks·ka·len·der

Is there a local gay guide?
Gibt es einen Führer für die   gipt es *ai*·nen *fü*·rer für dee
Schwulen- und Lesbenszene?   *shvoo*·len unt *les*·bens·tsay·ne

I feel like going out somewhere.
Ich hätte Lust, auszugehen.   ikh *he*·te lust ows·tsu·*gay*·en

I feel like going to a/the ...	Ich hätte Lust, ... zu gehen.	ikh he·te lust ... tsoo gay·en
ballet	zum Ballett	tsum ba·let
bar/pub	in eine Kneipe	in ai·ne knai·pe
cafe	in ein Café	in ain ka·fay
concert	in ein Konzert	in ain kon·tsert
movies	ins Kino	ins kee·no
nightclub	in einen Nachtklub	in ai·nen nakht·klup
opera	in die Oper	in dee aw·per
restaurant	in ein Restaurant	in ain res·to·rang
theatre	ins Theater	ins te·ah·ter

For more on bars, drinks and partying, see **eating out**, page 148.

invitations

einladungen

What are you doing ...?	Was machst du ...?	vas makhst doo ...
right now	jetzt gerade	jetst ge·rah·de
this evening	heute Abend	hoy·te ah·bent
this weekend	am Wochenende	am vo·khen·en·de

Would you like to go (for a) ...?	Möchtest du ... gehen?	merkh·test doo ... gay·en
coffee	einen Kaffee trinken	ai·nen ka·fay tring·ken
dancing	tanzen	tan·tsen
drink	etwas trinken	et·vas tring·ken
meal	essen	e·sen

Do you want to come to the ... concert with me?
Möchtest du mit mir zum ...-konzert gehen?   merkh·test doo mit meer tsum ...·kon·tsert gay·en

We're having a party.
Wir machen eine Party.   veer ma·khen ai·ne par·ti

Would you like to come?
Hättest du Lust zu kommen?   he·test doo lust tsoo ko·men

responding to invitations

auf einladungen reagieren

Sure!	*Klar!*	klahr
Yes, I'd love to.	*Ja, gerne.*	yah *ger*·ne
That's very kind of you.	*Das ist sehr nett von dir/euch.* sg/pl	das ist zair net fon deer/oykh
Where shall we go?	*Wo sollen wir hingehen?*	vaw *zo*·len veer *hin*·gay·en
No, I'm afraid I can't.	*Nein, es tut mir Leid, aber ich kann nicht.*	nain es toot meer lait *ah*·ber ikh kan nikht
What about tomorrow?	*Wie wäre es mit morgen?*	vee *vair*·re es mit *mor*·gen

local talk

There's nothing going on there.
  Da ist nichts los.   dah ist nikhts laws

It's a hole.
  Da ist tote Hose.   dah ist *taw*·te *haw*·ze
  (lit: there is dead trousers)

It's all happening there.
  Da ist die Sau los.   da ist dee zow laws
  (lit: there is the sow loose)
  Da boxt der Papst.   dah bokst dair pahpst
  (lit: there boxes the pope)

arranging to meet

einen treffpunkt verabreden

Where/When shall we meet?
  Wo/Wann sollen wir   vaw/van *zo*·len veer
  uns treffen?   uns *tre*·fen

Let's meet at ...	*Wir treffen uns ...*	veer *tre*·fen uns ...
(eight) o'clock	*um (acht) Uhr*	um (akht) oor
the entrance	*am Eingang*	am *ain*·gang

I'll see you then.
Bis dann! — bis dan

I'll pick you up.
Ich hole dich ab. — ikh *haw*·le dikh ap

I'll be coming later. Where will you be?
Ich komme später. — ikh *ko*·me *shpay*·ter
Wo wirst du sein? — vaw virst doo zain

If I'm not there by (nine), don't wait for me.
Wenn ich bis (neun) — ven ikh bis (noyn)
Uhr nicht da bin, — oor nikht dah bin
warte nicht auf mich. — *var*·te nikht owf mikh

See you later/tomorrow.
Bis später/morgen. — bis *shpay*·ter/*mor*·gen

I'm looking forward to it.
Ich freue mich darauf. — ikh *froy*·e mikh da·*rowf*

Sorry I'm late.
Es tut mir Leid, dass — es toot meer lait das
ich zu spät komme. — ikh tsoo shpayt *ko*·me

Never mind.
Macht nichts. — makht nikhts

drugs

I don't take drugs.
Ich nehme keine Drogen. — ikh *nay*·me *kai*·ne *draw*·gen

I take ... occasionally.
Ich nehme ab und zu ... — ikh *nay*·me ap unt tsoo ...

Do you want to have a smoke?
Wollen wir einen — *vo*·len veer *ai*·nen
Joint rauchen? — dzhoynt *row*·khen

Do you have a light?
Haben Sie Feuer? pol — *hah*·ben zee *foy*·er
Hast du Feuer? inf — hast doo *foy*·er

If the police are talking to you about drugs, see **police**, page 174, for useful phrases.

asking someone out

sich verabreden

Would you like to do something ...?	*Hättest du Lust,* *... was zu unternehmen?*	he·test doo lust ... vas tsoo un·ter·nay·men
Where would you like to go ...?	*Wo würdest du* *... gerne hingehen?*	vaw vür·dest doo ... ger·ne hin·gay·en
tomorrow	*morgen*	mor·gen
tonight	*heute Abend*	hoy·te ah·bent
on the weekend	*am Wochenende*	am vo·khen·en·de

Yes, I'd love to.
Ja, gerne.   yah ger·ne
Sure, thanks.
Klar! Das wäre nett.   klahr das vair·re net
I'm busy.
Ich habe keine Zeit.   ikh hah·be kai·ne tsait
Forget it!
Vergiss es!   fer·gis es

local talk

He's/She's a ...	*Er/Sie ist ...*	air/zee ist ...
babe	*eine Schönheit*	ai·ne shern·hait
bitch	*eine Zicke*	ai·ne tsi·ke
hot guy	*ein heißer Typ*	ain hai·ser tüp
hot girl	*eine heiße Frau*	ai·ne hai·se frow
prick	*ein Depp*	ain dep

He/She looks really great.
Er/Sie sieht echt geil aus.   air/zee zeet ekht gail ows

He/She gets around.
Er/Sie lässt nichts   air/zee lest nikhts
anbrennen.   an·bre·nen
(lit: he/she lets nothing burn)

pick-up lines

Haven't we met before?
Kennen wir uns nicht   ke·nen veer uns nikht
von irgendwoher?   fon ir·gent·vo·hair

Would you like a drink?
Möchtest du etwas trinken?   merkh·test doo et·vas tring·ken

What star sign are you?
Was für ein Sternzeichen   vas für ain shtern·tsai·khen
bist du?   bist doo

Shall we get some fresh air?
Sollen wir ein bisschen an   zo·len veer ain bis·khen an
die frische Luft gehen?   dee fri·she luft gay·en

You have a beautiful personality.
Du hast eine wundervolle   doo hast ai·ne vun·der·vo·ler
Persönlichkeit.   per·zern·likh·kait

You have (a) beautiful ...	*Du hast ...*	doo hast ...
body	*einen schönen Körper*	ai·nen sher·nen ker·per
eyes	*schöne Augen*	sher·ne ow·gen
hands	*schöne Hände*	sher·ne hen·de
laugh	*ein schönes Lachen*	ain sher·nes la·khen

rejections

I'm here with ...	*Ich bin mit ... hier.*	ikh bin mit ... heer
my boyfriend	*meinem Freund*	mai·nem froynt
my girlfriend	*meiner Freundin*	mai·ner froyn·din

Excuse me, I have to go now.
Tut mir Leid, ich   toot meer lait ikh
muss jetzt gehen.   mus yetst gay·en

No, thank you.
  Nein, danke.   nain *dang*·ke

I'd rather not.
  Lieber nicht.   *lee*·ber nikht

Perhaps some other time.
  Vielleicht ein andermal.   fi·*laikht* ain *an*·der·mahl

**Before this goes any further, I must be upfront.
I'm (an accountant).**
  Bevor wir uns näher   be·*fawr* veer uns *nay*·er
  kennen lernen, muss   *ke*·nen *ler*·nen mus
  ich etwas klarstellen.   ikh *et*·vas *klahr*·shte·len
  Ich bin (Buchhalter/   ikh bin (*bookh*·hal·ter/
  Buchhalterin). m/f   *bookh*·hal·te·rin)

Your ego is out of control.
  Du leidest wohl unter   doo *lai*·dest vawl *un*·ter
  Größenwahn.   *grer*·sen·wahn

I'd rather you left me alone.
  Es wäre mir lieber,   es *vair*·re meer *lee*·ber
  du würdest mich in   doo *vür*·dest mikh in
  Frieden lassen.   *free*·den *la*·sen

Leave me alone!
  Lass mich zufrieden!   las mikh tsu·*free*·den

You're (really) getting on my nerves!
  Du nervst (echt   doo nerfst (ekht
  verstärkt)!   fer·*shterkt*)

Piss off!
  Verpiss dich!   fer·*pis* dikh

I'm not interested.
  Ich bin nicht interessiert.   ikh bin nikht in·tre·*seert*

getting closer

Will you take me home?
Kannst du mich nach   kanst doo mikh nahkh
Hause bringen?   how·ze bring·en

Do you want to come inside for a while?
Möchtest du noch   merkh·test doo nokh
kurz mit reinkommen?   kurts mit rain·ko·men

You're very nice.
Du bist sehr nett.   doo bist zair net

I like you very much.
Ich mag dich sehr.   ikh mahk dikh zair

Do you like me too?
Magst du mich auch?   mahkst doo mikh owkh

You're very attractive.
Du bist sehr attraktiv.   doo bist zair a·trak·teef

I'm interested in you.
Ich interessiere mich   ikh in·tre·see·re mikh
für dich.   für dikh

You're great.
Du bist toll.   doo bist tol

sex

Kiss me.	*Küss mich.*	küs mikh
I want you.	*Ich will dich.*	ikh vil dikh
Take this off.	*Zieh das aus!*	tsee das ows
Oh yeah!	*Oh ja!*	aw yah
That's great.	*Das ist geil.*	das ist gail
Easy tiger!	*Sachte!*	zakh·te

Touch me here.
Berühr mich hier!   be·*rür* mikh heer

Do you like this?
Magst du das?   mahkst doo das

I (don't) like that.
Das mag ich (nicht).   das mahk ikh (nikht)

I want to make love to you.
Ich möchte mit dir schlafen.   ikh *merkh*·te mit deer *shlah*·fen

Let's go to bed!
Gehen wir ins Bett!   *gay*·en veer ins bet

Do you have (a condom)?
Hast du (ein Kondom)?   hast doo (ain kon·*dawm*)

Let's use a (condom).
Lass uns (ein Kondom)   las uns (ain kon·*dawm*)
benutzen.   be·*nu*·tsen

I won't do it without protection.
Ohne Kondom mache   *aw*·ne kon·*dawm* ma·khe
ich es nicht.   ikh es nikht

Please (don't) stop!
Bitte hör (nicht) auf.   *bi*·te her (nikht) owf

I think we should stop now.
Ich denke, wir sollten   ikh *deng*·ke veer *zol*·ten
jetzt aufhören.   yetst *owf*·her·ren

It's my first time.
Das ist mein erstes Mal.   das ist main *ers*·tes mahl

It helps to have a sense of humour.
Mit Humor geht   mit hu·*mawr* gayt
alles besser.   *a*·les *be*·ser

---

m before f

In this book, masculine forms appear before the feminine forms. If letters have been added to the masculine word to form the feminine word (often -*in*), these will appear in parentheses. Where the change involves more than the addition of -*in*, two words are given, separated by a slash. The neuter form – where applicable – is mentioned last. See also **gender** in the **grammar** chapter, page 17.

AIDS	*AIDS* n	aydz
contraception	*Empfängnis-*	emp·*feng*·nis·
	verhütung f	fer·hü·tung
dental dam	*Dental Dam* m	*den*·tel dem
HIV	*HIV* n	hah·ee·*fow*
IUD	*Intrauterin-*	in·tra·u·te·*reen*·
	pessar m	pe·sahr
the Pill	*die Pille* f	dee *pi*·le
spermicide	*Spermizid* n	shper·mi·*tseet*

> afterwards

That was ...	*Das war ...*	das vahr ...
amazing	*fantastisch*	fan·*tas*·tish
weird	*seltsam*	*zelt*·zahm

Can I ...?	*Kann ich ...?*	kan ikh ...
call you	*dich anrufen*	dikh *an*·roo·fen
meet you	*dich morgen*	dikh *mor*·gen
tomorrow	*treffen*	*tre*·fen
see you again	*dich wiedersehen*	dikh *vee*·der·zay·en
stay over	*hier übernachten*	heer ü·ber·*nakh*·ten

I'll ...	*Ich ...*	ikh ...
call you	*rufe dich*	*roo*·fe dikh
tomorrow	*morgen an*	*mor*·gen an
never forget	*werde das nie*	*ver*·de das nee
this	*vergessen*	fer·*ge*·sen
see you	*sehe dich morgen*	*zay*·e dikh *mor*·gen
tomorrow		

love

I love you.
Ich liebe dich.   ikh *lee*·be dikh

I think we're good together.
Ich glaube, wir passen   ikh *glow*·be veer *pa*·sen
gut zueinander.   goot tsu·ai·*nan*·der

Will you ...?	*Willst du ...?*	vilst doo ...
go out with me	*mit mir gehen*	mit meer *gay*·en
live with me	*mit mir*	mit meer
	zusammenleben	tsu·za·men·*lay*·ben
marry me	*mich heiraten*	mikh *hai*·ra·ten

problems

Are you seeing someone else?
Gibt es da einen anderen? m   gipt es dah *ai*·nen *an*·de·ren
Gibt es da eine andere? f   gipt es dah *ai*·ne *an*·de·re

I never want to see you again.
Ich will dich nie   ikh vil dikh nee
mehr wiedersehen.   mair *vee*·der·zay·en

We'll work it out.
Wir finden schon   veer *fin*·den shawn
eine Lösung.   *ai*·ne *ler*·zung

He's just a friend.
Er ist nur ein Freund. m   air ist noor ain froynt

She's just a friend.
Sie ist nur eine Freundin. f   zee ist noor *ai*·ne *froyn*·din

I want to ...	*Ich möchte ...*	ikh *merkh*·te ...
end the	*Schluss*	shlus
relationship	*machen*	*ma*·khen
stay friends	*dass wir Freunde*	das veer *froyn*·de
	bleiben	*blai*·ben

leaving

I have to leave tomorrow.
Ich muss morgen los.   ikh mus *mor*·gen laws

I'll ...	*Ich ...*	ikh ...
come and	*komme dich*	*ko*·me dikh
visit you	*besuchen*	be·*zoo*·khen
miss you	*werde dich*	*ver*·de dikh
	vermissen	fer·*mi*·sen

on heat

Some German expressions might seem similar to English expressions, but have a very different meaning – beware of the following:

Ich bin heiss.
  ikh bin hais
  (lit: I am hot)   **I'm feeling sexy.**

Ich bin kalt.
  ikh bin kalt
  (lit: I am cold)   **I'm frigid/I have an**
                               unfriendly personality.

To say you're feeling physically hot or cold, use:

Mir ist heiss.
  mir ist hais   **I'm hot.**
  (lit: to me is hot)

Mir ist kalt.
  mir ist kalt   **I'm cold.**
  (lit: to me is cold)

Similarly, be careful not to mix up these:

Ich bin voll.
  ikh bin fol   **I'm drunk.**
  (lit: I am full)

Ich bin satt.
  ikh bin zat.   **I've had enough to eat.**
  (lit: I am full)

religion

religion

What's your religion?
Was ist Ihre/deine   vas ist ee·re/*dai*·ne
Religion? pol/inf   re·li·*gyawn*

I'm (not) religious.
Ich bin (nicht) religiös.   ikh bin (nikht) re·li·*gyers*

I'm (not) ...	*Ich bin (kein/ keine) ...* m/f	ikh bin (kain/ *kai*·ne) ...
agnostic	*Agnostiker(in)* m/f	a·*gnos*·ti·ker/ a·*gnos*·ti·ke·rin
Buddhist	*Buddhist(in)* m/f	bu·*dist*/bu·*dis*·tin
Catholic	*Katholik(in)* m/f	ka·to·*leek*/ ka·to·*lee*·kin
Christian	*Christ(in)* m/f	krist/*kris*·tin
(Eastern) Orthodox	*Orthodox* m&f	or·taw·*doks*
Hindu	*Hindu* m&f	*hin*·du
Jewish	*Jude/Jüdin* m/f	*yoo*·de/*yü*·din
Muslim	*Moslem/ Moslime* m/f	*mos*·lem/ mos·*lee*·me
practising	*praktizierender/ praktizierende* m/f	prak·ti·*tsee*·ren·der/ prak·ti·*tsee*·ren·de
Protestant	*Protestant(in)* m/f	pro·tes·*tant*/ pro·tes·*tan*·tin

I (don't) believe in ...	*Ich glaube (nicht) an ...*	ikh *glow*·be (nikht) an ...
God	*Gott*	got
destiny/fate	*das Schicksal*	das *shik*·zahl

Where can I ...?	Wo kann ich ...?	vaw kan ikh ...
attend mass	eine Messe	ai·ne me·se
	besuchen	be·zoo·khen
attend service	einen	ai·nen
	Gottesdienst	go·tes·deenst
	besuchen	be·zoo·khen
make confession	(auf Englisch)	(owf eng·lish)
(in English)	beichten	baikh·ten
pray	beten	bay·ten
receive	das Abendmahl	das ah·bent·mahl
communion	empfangen	emp·fang·en
worship	meine Andacht	mai·ne an·dakht
	verrichten	fer·rikh·ten

cultural differences

kulturelle unterschiede

Is this a local or national custom?
Ist das ein örtlicher oder ist das ain ert·li·kher aw·der
landesweiter Brauch? lan·des·vai·ter browkh

I'm not used to this.
Das ist ganz ungewohnt das ist gants un·ge·vawnt
für mich. für mikh

I don't mind watching, but I'd rather not join in.
Ich sehe gerne zu, ikh zay·e ger·ne tsoo
würde aber lieber nicht vür·de ah·ber lee·ber nikht
selbst mitmachen. zelpst mit·ma·khen

I'll try it.
Ich versuche es. ikh fer·zoo·khe es

I'm sorry, I didn't mean to do/say anything wrong.
Es tut mir Leid, ich wollte es toot meer lait ikh vol·te
nichts Falsches tun/sagen. nikhts fal·shes toon/zah·gen

I'm sorry, | *Es tut mir Leid,* | es toot meer lait
it's against my ... | *das ist gegen* | das ist gay·gen
| *meine ...* | mai·ne ...
beliefs | *Anschauungen* | an·show·ung·en
culture | *Kultur* | kul·toor
religion | *Religion* | re·li·gyawn

Where's (the museum)?
Wo ist (das Museum)?   vaw ist (das mu·zay·um)

When's (the gallery) open?
Wann hat (die Galerie)   van hat (dee ga·le·ree)
geöffnet?   ge·erf·net

What kind of art are you interested in?
Für welche Art von Kunst   für vel·khe art fon kunst
interessieren Sie sich? pol   in·tre·see·ren zee zikh
Für welche Art von Kunst   für vel·khe art fon kunst
interessierst du dich? inf   in·tre·seerst doo dikh

What's in the collection?
Was gibt es in der   vas gipt es in dair
Sammlung?   zam·lung

What do you think of ...?
Was halten Sie von ...? pol   vas hal·ten zee fon ...
Was hältst du von ...? inf   vas heltst doo fon ...

artistic styles

art nouveau	*Jugendstil* m	*yoo·gent·shteel*
baroque art	*barocke Kunst* f	*ba·ro·ke kunst*
Bauhaus art	*Bauhaus-Kunst* f	*bow·hows·kunst*
expressionist art	*expressionistische Kunst* f	*eks·pre·syo·nis·ti·she kunst*
Gothic art	*gotische Kunst* f	*gaw·ti·she kunst*
impressionist art	*impressionistische Kunst* f	*im·pre·syo·nis·ti·she kunst*
modernist art	*moderne Kunst* f	*mo·der·ne kunst*
Renaissance art	*Renaissance-Kunst* f	*re·ne·sangs·kunst*
Romanesque art	*romanische Kunst* f	*ro·mah·ni·she kunst*

It's a/an ... exhibition.
Es ist eine ...-Ausstellung.   es ist *ai*·ne ...·ows·shte·lung

I'm interested in ...
Ich interessiere mich für ...   ikh in·tre·*see*·re mikh für ...

I like the works of ...
Ich mag die Arbeiten von ...   ikh mahk dee *ar*·bai·ten fon ...

It reminds me of ...
Es erinnert mich an ...   es er·*i*·nert mikh an ...

---

tongue twisters

If you're feeling pretty comfortable with the language and
want to impress the locals, try these tongue twisters:

**Blaukraut bleibt Blaukraut und Brautkleid bleibt
Brautkleid.**
blow·krowt blaipt *blow*·krowt unt *browt*·klait blaipt
browt·klait
(Red cabbage remains red cabbage and a wedding
dress remains a wedding dress.)

**Der Potsdamer Postkutscher putzt den Potsdamer
Postkutschkasten.**
dair *pots*·dah·mer *post*·ku·cher putst dayn
pots·dah·mer *post*·kuch·kah·sten
(The Potsdam mailcoach driver cleans the Potsdam
mailcoach postboxes.)

**Der Dachdecker deckt dein Dach, drum dank dem
Dachdecker, der dein Dach deckt.**
dair *dakh*·de·ker dekt dain dakh drum dank daym
dakh·de·ker dair dain dakh dekt
(The roofer roofs your roof, for that thank the roofer,
who roofs your roof.)

sporting interests

sportarten

What sport do you play?
   Was für Sport treiben Sie? pol   vas für shport *trai*·ben zee
   Was für Sport treibst du? inf   vas für shport traipst doo

What sport do you follow?
   Für welche Sportarten   für *vel*·khe *shport*·ar·ten
   interessieren Sie sich? pol   in·tre·*see*·ren zee zikh
   Für welche Sportarten   für *vel*·khe *shport*·ar·ten
   interessierst du dich? inf   in·tre·*seerst* doo dikh

I play ...	*Ich spiele ...*	ikh *shpee*·le ...
I do ...	*Ich mache ...*	ikh *ma*·khe ...
I follow ...	*Ich interessiere*	ikh in·tre·*see*·re
	mich für ...	mikh für ...
athletics	*Leichtathletik*	*laikht*·at·lay·tik
basketball	*Basketball*	*bahs*·ket·bal
football (soccer)	*Fußball*	*foos*·bal
handball	*Handball*	*hant*·bal
ice hockey	*Eishockey*	*ais*·ho·ki
skiing	*Skifahren*	*shee*·fah·ren
tennis	*Tennis*	*te*·nis

For more sports, see the **dictionary**.

Do you like (sport)?
   Mögen Sie (Sport)? pol   *mer*·gen zee (shport)
   Magst du (Sport)? inf   mahkst doo (shport)

Yes, very much.
   Ja, sehr.   yah zair

Not really.
   Nicht besonders.   nikht be·*zon*·ders

I like watching it.
   Ich sehe es mir gerne an.   ikh *zay*·e es meer *ger*·ne an

Only as a spectator.
Nur als Zuschauer.   noor als *tsoo*·show·er

Who's your favourite sportsperson?
Wer ist Ihr/dein   vair ist eer/dain
Lieblingssportler? pol/inf   *leep*·lingks·shport·ler

Who's your favourite team?
Was ist Ihre/deine   vas ist *ee*·re/*dai*·ne
Lieblingsmannschaft? pol/inf   *leep*·lingks·man·shaft

Can you play (soccer)?
Spielen Sie (Fußball)? pol   *shpee*·len zee (*foos*·bal)
Spielst du (Fußball)? inf   *shpeelst* doo (*foos*·bal)

going to a game

zu einem spiel gehen

Would you like to go to a game?
Möchten Sie zu einem   *merkh*·ten zee tsoo *ai*·nem
Spiel gehen? pol   shpeel *gay*·en
Möchtest du zu einem   *merkh*·test doo tsoo *ai*·nem
Spiel gehen? inf   shpeel *gay*·en

Who are you supporting?
Wen unterstützen Sie? pol   vayn un·ter·*shtü*·tsen zee
Wen unterstützt du? inf   vayn un·ter·*shtütst* doo

Who's ...?	*Wer ...?*	vair ...
playing	*spielt*	speelt
winning	*gewinnt*	ge·*vint*

---

sports talk

What a ...!	*Was für ...!*	vas für ...
goal	*ein Tor*	ain tawr
hit	*ein Treffer*	ain *tre*·fer
kick	*ein Schuss*	ain shus
pass	*ein Pass*	ain pas
performance	*eine Leistung*	*ai*·ne *lais*·tung

What was the final score?
Was war das Endergebnis?   vas vahr das *ent*·er·gayp·nis

It was a draw.
Es ging unentschieden aus.   es ging *un*·ent·shee·den ows

That was a	*Das war ein*	das vahr ain
... game!	*... Spiel!*	... shpeel
bad	*schlechtes*	*shlekh*·tes
boring	*langweiliges*	*lang*·vai·li·ges
great	*tolles*	*to*·les

scoring

What's the score?	*Wie steht es?*	vee shtayt es
draw/even	*unentschieden*	*un*·ent·shee·den
love (zero)	*null*	nul
match-point	*Matchball*	*mech*·bal
nil (zero)	*null*	nul
3–1	*3:1 (drei zu eins)*	drai tsoo ains

playing sport

sport treiben

Do you want to play?
Möchten Sie mitspielen? pol   *merkh*·ten zee *mit*·shpee·len
Möchtest du mitspielen? inf   *merkh*·test doo *mit*·shpee·len

Can I join in?
Kann ich mitspielen?   kan ikh *mit*·shpee·len

Yes, that'd be great.
Ja, das wäre toll.   yah das *vair*·re tol

I'm sorry, I can't.
Es tut mir Leid,   es toot meer lait
ich kann nicht.   ikh kan nikht

I have an injury.
Ich habe eine Verletzung.   ikh *hah*·be *ai*·ne fer·*le*·tsung

Your point.
Ihr/Dein Punkt. pol/inf   eer/dain pungkt

My point.
Mein Punkt.   main pungkt

Kick/Pass it to me!
Hierher!   heer·hair

You're a good player.
Sie sind   zee zint
ein guter Spieler/   ain *goo*·ter *shpee*·ler/
eine gute Spielerin. m/f pol   *ai*·ne *goo*·te *shpee*·le·rin

You're a good player.
Du bist   doo bist
ein guter Spieler/   ain *goo*·ter *shpee*·ler/
eine gute Spielerin. m/f inf   *ai*·ne *goo*·te *shpee*·le·rin

Thanks for the game.
Vielen Dank für das Spiel.   *fee*·len dangk für das shpeel

Where's the nearest ...?	*Wo ist ...?*	vaw ist ...
gym	*das nächste Fitness-Studio*	das *naykhs*·te *fit*·nes·shtoo·di·o
swimming pool	*das nächste Schwimmbad*	das *naykhs*·te *shvim*·baht
tennis court	*der nächste Tennisplatz*	dair *naykhs*·te *te*·nis·plats

Where's the best place to jog/run around here?
Wo kann man hier am   vaw kan man heer am
besten joggen/laufen?   *bes*·ten *dzho*·gen/*low*·fen

Do I have to be a member to attend?
Muss ich Mitglied sein,   mus ikh *mit*·gleet zain
um mitzumachen?   um *mit*·tsu·ma·khen

Is there a women-only session?
Gibt es eine Session   gipt es *ai*·ne ses·yawn
nur für Frauen?   noor für *frow*·en

Is there a women-only pool?
Gibt es ein Schwimmbecken   gipt es ain *shvim*·be·ken
nur für Frauen?   noor für *frow*·en

Where are the change rooms?
Wo sind die   vaw zint dee
Umkleideräume?   *um*·klai·de·roy·me

What's the	*Wie viel kostet*	vee feel *kos*·tet
charge per ...?	*es pro ...?*	es praw ...
day	*Tag*	tahk
game	*Spiel*	shpeel
hour	*Stunde*	*shtun*·de
visit	*Besuch*	be·*zookh*

Can I hire a ...?	*Kann ich ...?*	kan ikh ...
ball	*einen Ball leihen*	*ai*·nen bal *lai*·en
bicycle	*ein Fahrrad leihen*	ain *fahr*·raht *lai*·en
court	*einen Platz*	*ai*·nen plats
	mieten	*mee*·ten
racquet	*einen Schläger*	*ai*·nen *shlay*·ger
	leihen	*lai*·en

cycling

radsport

Where does the race finish?
Wo endet das Rennen?   vaw en·det das *re*·nen

Where does the race pass through?
Wo führt das Rennen lang?   vaw fürt das *re*·nen lang

Who's winning?
Wer gewinnt?   vair ge·*vint*

Is today's leg very hard?
Ist die Etappe heute   ist dee e·*ta*·pe *hoy*·te
sehr schwer?   zair shvair

How many kilometres is today's (leg)?
> *Wie viel Kilometer ist* — vee feel ki·lo·*may*·ter ist
> *(die Etappe) heute?* — (dee e·*ta*·pe) *hoy*·te

My favourite cyclist is ...
> *Mein Lieblings-* — main *leep*·lingks·
> *radfahrer ist ...* — *raht*·fah·rer ist ...

climbing stage	*Bergetappe* f	*berk*·e·ta·pe
cyclist	*Radfahrer(in)* m/f	*raht*·fah·rer/
		raht·fah·re·rin
the (yellow) jersey	*das (gelbe) Trikot* n	das (*gel*·be) tri·*kaw*
leg (in race)	*Etappe* f	e·*ta*·pe
	(des Rennens)	(des *re*·nens)
racing cyclist	*Radrenn-*	*raht*·ren·fah·rer/
	fahrer(in) m/f	*raht*·ren·fah·re·rin
time trial	*Zeitfahren* n	*tsait*·fah·ren
winner	*Sieger(in)* m/f	*zee*·ger/*zee*·ge·rin
winner of a leg	*Etappen-*	e·*ta*·pen·*zee*·ger/
	sieger(in) m/f	e·*ta*·pen·*zee*·ge·rin

For phrases on getting around by bicycle, see **transport**, page 45.

extreme sports

extremsportarten

Are you sure this is safe?
> *Sind Sie sicher, dass das* — zint zee *zi*·kher das das
> *ungefährlich ist?* pol — *un*·ge·fair·likh ist
> *Bist du sicher, dass das* — bist doo *zi*·kher das das
> *ungefährlich ist?* inf — *un*·ge·fair·likh ist

Is the equipment secure?
> *Ist die Ausrüstung sicher?* — ist dee *ows*·rüs·tung *zi*·kher

This is insane.
> *Das ist verrückt!* — das ist fer·*rükt*

abseiling	*Abseilen* n	*ap*·zai·len
bungy-jumping	*Bungyjumping* n	*ban*·dzhi·dzham·ping
caving	*Höhlenerforschung* f	*her*·len·er·for·shung
hanggliding	*Drachenfliegen* n	*dra*·khen·flee·gen
mountain biking	*Mountainbiken* n	*mown*·ten·bai·ken
parachuting	*Fallschirmspringen* n	*fal*·shirm·shpring·en
parasailing	*Parasailing* n	*pah*·ra·say·ling
rock-climbing	*Klettern* n	*kle*·tern
skydiving	*Skydiving* n	*skai*·dai·ving
snowboarding	*Snowboarden* n	*snoh*·bor·den
white-water rafting	*Wildwasser-fahrten* f pl	*vilt*·va·ser·fahr·ten

For phrases on hiking, see **outdoors**, page 133, and **camping**, page 55.

soccer/football

fußball

Who plays for (Bayern München)?
Wer spielt für (Bayern München)? — vair shpeelt für (*bai*·ern *mün*·khen)

What a terrible team!
Was für eine furchtbare Mannschaft! — vas für *ai*·ne *furkht*·bah·re *man*·shaft

Which team is at the top of the league?
Welcher Verein steht an der Tabellenspitze? — *vel*·kher fer·*ain* shtayt an dair ta·*be*·len·shpi·tse

She's a great player.
Sie ist eine tolle Spielerin. — zee ist *ain*·e *to*·le *shpee*·ler·in

He played brilliantly in the match against (Italy).
Im Spiel gegen (Italien) hat er fantastisch gespielt. — im shpeel *gay*·gen (i·*tah*·li·en) hat air fan·*tas*·tish ge·*shpeelt*

She scored (three) goals.
Sie hat (drei) Tore geschossen. — zee hat (drai) *taw*·re ge·*sho*·sen

corner	*Ecke* f	*e·ke*
free kick	*Freistoß* m	*frai·shtaws*
goalkeeper	*Torhüter(in)* m/f	*tawr·hü·ter/*
		tawr·hü·te·rin
offside	*Abseits* n	*ap·zaits*
penalty	*Strafstoß* m	*shtrahf·shtaws*

skiing

skifahren

How much is a pass?
Was kostet ein Skipass?   vas *kos·*tet ain *shee·*pas

Can I take lessons?
Kann ich Unterricht nehmen?   kan ikh *un·*ter·rikht *nay·*men

I'd like to hire (a) ...	*Ich möchte ... leihen.*	ikh *merkh·*te ... *lai·*en
boots	*Skistiefel*	*shee·shtee·*fel
goggles	*eine Skibrille*	*ai·*ne *shee·*bri·le
poles	*Skistöcke*	*shee·*shter·ke
skis	*Skier*	*shee·*er
ski suit	*einen Skianzug*	*ai·*nen *shee·*an·tsook

Is it possible to go ... here/there?	*Kann man hier/da ...?*	kan man heer/dah ...
Alpine skiing	*Abfahrtsski fahren*	*ap·*fahrts·shee *fah·*ren
cross-country skiing	*Skilanglauf machen*	shee·*lang·*lowf *ma·*khen
snowboarding	*snowboarden*	*snoh·*bor·den
tobogganing	*Schlitten fahren*	*shli·*ten *fah·*ren

What are the skiing conditions like ...?	Wie sind die Schneebedingungen ...?	vee zint dee shnay·be·ding·ung·en ...
at (Lauberhorn)	am (Lauberhorn)	am (low·ber·horn)
higher up	weiter oben	vai·ter aw·ben
on that run	an dieser Abfahrt	an dee·zer ap·fahrt

Which are the ... slopes?	Welches sind die ...?	vel·khes zint dee ...
beginner	Anfängerhänge	an·feng·er·heng·e
intermediate	mittelschweren Hänge	mi·tel·shvair·ren heng·e
advanced	Fortgeschrittenenhänge	fort·ge·shri·te·nen·heng·e

What level is that slope?
Wie schwierig ist dieser Hang? — vee shvee·rikh ist dee·zer hang

cable car	Seilbahn f	zail·bahn
chairlift	Sessellift m	ze·sel·lift
instructor	Skilehrer m	shee·lair·rer
resort	Ort m	ort
ski-lift	Skilift m	shee·lift
sled	Schlitten m	shli·ten

tennis

Would you like to play tennis?
Möchten Sie Tennis spielen? pol — merkh·ten zee te·nis shpee·len
Möchtest du Tennis spielen? inf — merkh·test doo te·nis shpee·len

Can we play at night?
Können wir abends spielen? — ker·nen veer ah·bents shpee·len

ace	*Ass* n	as
advantage	*Vorteil* m	*fawr*·tail
clay court	*Sandplatz* m	*zant*·plats
fault	*Fehler* m	*fay*·ler
game, set, match	*Spiel, Satz und Sieg*	shpeel *zats* unt zeek
grass court	*Rasenplatz* m	*rah*·zen·plats
hard court	*Hartplatz* m	*hart*·plats
play doubles	*ein Doppel spielen*	ain *do*·pel *shpee*·len
serve	*Aufschlag* m	*owf*·shlahk
set	*Satz* m	zats

könig fußball

The king of German amateur and professional sports is *König Fußball* ker·nikh *foos*·bal (king football). Football (or soccer, as it's known in the US and Australia) is played at thousands of amateur clubs known as *Fußballvereine* foos·bal·fe·rai·ne. Germans are passionate about the game and professional games draw an average 25,000 fans. One of the longest words in the German language is also from the football sphere. Try getting your tongue around this: *Fußballweltmeisterschaftsqualifikationsspiel* foos·bal·*velt*·mais·ter·shafts·kva·li·fi·ka·*tsyawns*·shpeel (Soccer World Cup qualifying game).

hiking

Where can I ...?	*Wo kann ich ...?*	vaw kan ikh ...
buy supplies	*Vorräte*	fawr·ray·te
	einkaufen	ain·kow·fen
find out about	*Informationen*	in·for·ma·tsyaw·nen
hiking trails	*über Wanderwege*	ü·ber van·der·vay·ge
	bekommen	be·ko·men
find someone	*jemanden*	yay·man·den
who knows	*finden, der die*	fin·den dair dee
this area	*Gegend kennt*	gay·gent kent
get a map	*eine Karte*	ai·ne kar·te
	bekommen	be·ko·men
hire hiking gear	*Wanderaus-*	van·der·ows-
	rüstung leihen	rüs·tung lai·en
Do we need	*Müssen wir ...*	mü·sen veer ...
to take ...?	*mitnehmen?*	mit·nay·men
bedding	*Bettzeug*	bet·tsoyk
food	*Essen*	e·sen
water	*Wasser*	va·ser

How long is the trail?
Wie lang ist der Weg?   vee lang ist dair vayk

How high is the climb?
Wie hoch führt die   vee hawkh fürt dee
Klettertour hinauf?   kle·ter·toor hi·nowf

Do we need a guide?
Brauchen wir einen Führer?   brow·khen veer ai·nen fü·rer

Are there guided treks?
Gibt es geführte   gipt es ge·für·te
Wanderungen?   van·de·rung·en

Is it safe?
Ist es ungefährlich?   ist es un·ge·fair·likh

Is there a hut there?
Gibt es dort eine Hütte?   gipt es dort ai·ne hü·te

When does it get dark?
Wann wird es dunkel?   van virt es dung·kel

Is the track ...?	*Ist der Weg ...?*	ist dair vayk ...
(well-)marked	*(gut) markiert*	(goot) mar·keert
open	*offen*	o·fen
scenic	*schön*	shern
Which is the	*Welches ist die ...*	vel·khes ist dee ...
... route?	*Route?*	roo·te
easiest	*einfachste*	ain·fakhs·te
most interesting	*interessanteste*	in·te·re·san·tes·te
shortest	*kürzeste*	kür·tses·te roo·te
Where's a/the ...?	*Wo ...?*	vaw ...
camp site	*ist ein Zeltplatz*	ist ain tselt·plats
nearest village	*ist das*	ist das
	nächste Dorf	naykhs·te dorf
showers	*sind die Duschen*	zint dee doo·shen
toilets	*sind die*	zint dee
	Toiletten	to·a·le·ten

Where have you come from?

Wo kommen Sie		vaw *ko*·men zee
gerade her? pol		ge·*rah*·de hair
Wo kommst du		vaw komst doo
gerade her? inf		ge·*rah*·de hair

How long did it take?

Wie lange hat	vee *lang*·e hat
das gedauert?	das ge·*dow*·ert

Does this path go to ...?

Führt dieser Weg nach ...?	fürt *dee*·zer vayk nahkh ...

Can we go through here?

Können wir hier	*ker*·nen veer heer
durchgehen?	*durkh*·gay·en

Is the water OK to drink?

Kann man das	kan man das
Wasser trinken?	*va*·ser *tring*·ken

I'm lost.

Ich habe mich verlaufen.	ikh *hah*·be mikh fer·*low*·fen

at the beach

am strand

Where's the ...	*Wo ist der ...*	vaw ist dair ...
beach?	*Strand?*	shtrant
best	*beste*	*bes*·te
nearest	*nächste*	*naykhs*·te
nudist	*FKK-*	ef·kah·*kah*·
public	*öffentliche*	*er*·fent·li·khe

signs

Schwimmen	shvi·men	**No Swimming!**
Verboten!	fer·*baw*·ten	
Sturmwarnung!	shturm *var*·nunk	**Storm Warning!**

135

Is it safe to dive/swim here?
Kann man hier gefahrlos tauchen/ schwimmen?
kan man heer ge·fahr·laws tow·khen/ shvi·men

What time is high/low tide?
Wann ist Flut/Ebbe?
van ist floot/e·be

Do we have to pay?
Müssen wir bezahlen?
mü·sen veer be·tsah·len

How much for a/an ...?	*Was kostet ein ...?*	vas kos·tet ain ...
canopied wicker beach-chair	*Strandkorb*	shtrant·korp
chair	*Stuhl*	shtool
hut	*Hut*	hoot
umbrella	*Schirm*	shirm

weather

What's the weather like?
Wie ist das Wetter? vee ist das ve·ter

What's the weather forecast?
Wie ist der Wetterbericht? vee ist dair ve·ter·be·rikht

It's snowing.
Es schneit. es shnait

Will it be snowing tomorrow?
Wird es morgen schneien? virt es mor·gen shnai·en

It's ...	*Es ist ...*	es ist ...
Will it be ...	*Wird es morgen*	virt es mor·gen
tomorrow?	*... sein?*	... zain
cloudy	*wolkig*	vol·kikh
cold	*kalt*	kalt
freezing	*eiskalt*	ais·kalt
hot	*heiß*	hais
raining	*regnerisch*	rayg·ne·rish
sunny	*sonnig*	zo·nikh
warm	*warm*	varm
windy	*windig*	vin·dikh

Where can I	*Wo kann ich*	vaw kan ikh
buy a/an ...?	*... kaufen?*	... kow·fen
rain jacket	*eine Regenjacke*	ai·ne ray·gen·ya·ke
umbrella	*einen Regenschirm*	ai·nen ray·gen·shirm

flora & fauna

flora und fauna

What ... is that?	*Wie heißt ...?*	vee haist ...
animal	*dieses Tier*	dee·zes teer
bird	*dieser Vogel*	dee·zer faw·gel
flower	*diese Blume*	dee·ze bloo·me
plant	*diese Pflanze*	dee·ze pflan·tse
tree	*dieser Baum*	dee·zer bowm

Is it ...?	Ist es ...?	ist es ...
common	weit verbreitet	vait fer·brai·tet
dangerous	gefährlich	ge·fair·likh
endangered	vom Aussterben	fom ows·shter·ben
	bedroht	be·drawt
poisonous	giftig	gif·tikh
protected	geschützt	ge·shütst

What's it used for?
Wofür wird es benutzt?   vaw·für virt aes be·nutst

Can you eat it?
Kann man es essen?   kan man es e·sen

For geographical and agricultural terms and names of animals and plants, see the **dictionary**.

---

anyone for a dip?

Aquatic pursuits are popular in Germany and it's hard to find a town that doesn't have a public *Schwimmbad* shvim·baht (swimming pool). Often there's a *Hallenbad* ha·len·baht (indoor pool) alongside the *Freibad* frai·baht (outdoor pool). Spas are popular too, with people seeking to cure a variety of conditions. The most famous spa town in Germany is called *Baden Baden* bah·den bah·den. This double-barrelled name represents both the name of the surrounding region and the German word for bathing.

key language

wichtige wörter

breakfast	*Frühstück* n	frü·shtük
lunch	*Mittagessen* n	mi·tahk·e·sen
dinner	*Abendessen* n	ah·bent·e·sen
snack	*Snack* m	snek
eat	*essen*	e·sen
drink	*trinken*	tring·ken
daily special	*Gericht* n *des Tages*	ge·rikht des tah·ges
set menu	*Menü* n	may·nü
I'd like ...	*Ich möchte ...*	ikh merkh·te ...
Enjoy your meal!	*Guten Appetit!*	goo·ten a·pay·teet
I'm starving!	*Ich bin am Verhungern!*	ikh bin am fer·hung·ern

finding a place to eat

ein restaurant suchen

Can you recommend a ...	*Können Sie ... empfehlen?* pol	ker·nen zee ... emp·fay·len
	Kannst du ... empfehlen? inf	kanst doo ... emp·fay·len
bar/pub	*eine Kneipe*	ai·ne knai·pe
coffee bar	*eine Espressobar*	ai·ne es·pre·so·bahr
restaurant	*ein Restaurant*	ain res·to·rang
Where would you go for (a) ...?	*Wo kann man hingehen, um ...?*	vaw kan man hin·gay·en um ...
celebration	*etwas zu feiern*	et·vas tsoo fai·ern
cheap meal	*etwas Billiges zu essen*	et·vas bi·li·ges tsoo e·sen
local specialities	*örtliche Spezialitäten zu essen*	ert·li·khe shpe·tsya·li·tay·ten tsoo e·sen

I'd like to reserve a table for ...	*Ich möchte einen Tisch für ... reservieren.*	ikh *merkh*·te *ai*·nen tish für ... re·zer·*vee*·ren
(two) people	*(zwei) Personen*	(tsvai) per·*zaw*·nen
(eight) o'clock	*(acht) Uhr*	(akht) oor
I'd like ..., please.	*Ich hätte gern ..., bitte.*	ikh *he*·te gern ... *bi*·te
a table for (five)	*einen Tisch für (fünf) Personen*	*ai*·nen tish für (fünf) per·*zaw*·nen
the non-smoking section	*einen Nichtrauchertisch*	*ai*·nen *nikht*· row·kher·tish
the smoking section	*einen Rauchertisch*	*ai*·nen *row*·kher· tish
Do you have ...?	*Haben Sie ...?*	*hah*·ben zee ...
children's meals	*Kinderteller*	*kin*·der·te·ler
a menu in English	*eine englische Speisekarte*	*ai*·ne *eng*·li·she *shpai*·ze·kar·te

FOOD

140

Are you still serving food?
Gibt es noch etwas   gipt es nokh *et*·vas
zu essen?   tsoo e·sen

How long is the wait?
Wie lange muss man   vee *lang*·e mus man
warten?   *var*·ten

at the restaurant

im restaurant

I'd like the	*Ich hätte gern*	ikh *he*·te gern
..., please.	*die ..., bitte.*	dee ... *bi*·te
drink list	*Getränkekarte*	ge·*treng*·ke·kar·te
menu	*Speisekarte*	*shpai*·ze·kar·te

What would you recommend?
Was empfehlen Sie?   vas emp·*fay*·len zee

I'll have what they're having.
Ich nehme das   ikh *nay*·me das
gleiche wie sie.   *glai*·khe vee zee

I'd like a local speciality.
Ich möchte etwas   ikh *merkh*·te *et*·vas
Typisches aus der Region.   *tü*·pi·shes ows dair re·*gyawn*

---

listen for ...

ikh emp·*fay*·le *ee*·nen ...
Ich empfehle Ihnen ...   **I suggest the ...**

mer·gen zee ...
Mögen Sie ...?   **Do you like ...?**

vee *merkh*·ten zee das tsoo·be·*rai*·tet *hah*·ben
Wie möchten Sie das   **How would you**
zubereitet haben?   **like that cooked?**

merkh·ten zee *et*·vas *tring*·ken *vair*·rent zee *var*·ten
Möchten Sie etwas trinken,   **Would you like a drink**
während Sie warten?   **while you wait?**

What's in that dish?
Was ist in diesem Gericht?   vas ist in *dee*·zem ge·*rikht*

Does it take long to prepare?
Dauert das lange?   *dow*·ert das *lang*·e

Is it self-serve?
Ist das Selbstbedienung?   ist das *zelpst*·be·dee·nung

Is service included in the bill?
Ist die Bedienung   ist dee be·*dee*·nung
inbegriffen?   *in*·be·gri·fen

Are these complimentary?
Sind die gratis?   zint dee *grah*·tis

We're just having drinks.
Wir möchten nur   veer *merkh*·ten noor
etwas trinken.   *et*·vas *tring*·ken

look for ...

Vorspeisen	*fawr*·shpai·zen	Appetisers
Suppen	*zu*·pen	Soups
Salate	za·*lah*·te	Salads
Hauptgerichte	*howpt*·ge·rikh·te	Main Courses
Beilagen	*bai*·lah·gen	Side Dishes
Nachspeisen	*nahkh*·shpai·zen	Desserts
Aperitifs	a·pe·ri·*teefs*	Aperitifs
Alkoholfreie	al·ko·*hawl*·frai·e	Soft Drinks
Getränke	ge·*treng*·ke	
Spirituosen	shpi·ri·tu·*aw*·zen	Spirits
Bier	beer	Beers
Schaumweine	*showm*·vai·ne	Sparkling Wines
Weißweine	*vais*·vai·ne	White Wines
Rotweine	*rawt*·vai·ne	Red Wines
Dessertweine	de·*sair*·vai·ne	Dessert Wines
Digestifs	di·zhes·*teefs*	Digestifs

For more words you might see on a menu, see the
culinary reader, page 163.

FOOD

at the table

Please bring ...	Bitte bringen Sie ...	bi·te bring·en zee ...
the bill	die Rechnung	dee rekh·nung
a cloth	eine Tischdecke	ai·ne tish·de·ke
a glass	ein Glas	ain (vain·)glahs

I didn't order this.
 Das habe ich nicht bestellt.   das hah·be ikh nikht be·shtelt

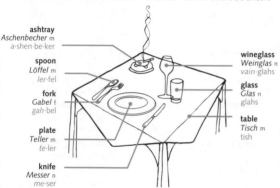

ashtray
Aschenbecher m
a·shen·be·ker

spoon
Löffel m
ler·fel

fork
Gabel f
gah·bel

plate
Teller m
te·ler

knife
Messer n
me·ser

wineglass
Weinglas n
vain·glahs

glass
Glas n
glahs

table
Tisch m
tish

talking food

übers essen sprechen

I love this dish.
 Ich mag dieses Gericht.   ikh mahk dee·zes ge·rikht

I love the local cuisine.
 *Ich mag die
 regionale Küche.*   ikh mahk dee
re·gyo·nah·le kü·khe

That was delicious!
 *Das hat hervorragend
 geschmeckt!*   das hat her·fawr·rah·gent
ge·shmekt

know your wurst

One of Germany's favourite and most famous foods is the not-so-humble *Wurst* (sausage). There are over 1500 types, some of the more common of which are listed below:

Blutwurst f	*bloot*·vurst	blood sausage
Bockwurst f	*bok*·vurst	pork sausage
Bratwurst f	*braht*·vurst	fried pork sausage
Bregenwurst f	*bray*·gen·vurst	brain sausage
Cervelatwurst f	ser·ve·*laht*·vurst	sausage made of a spicy pork and beef mixture
Katenwurst f	*kah*·ten·vurst	country-style smoked sausage
Knackwurst f	*knak*·vurst	mildly garlic-flavoured sausage
Krakauer f	*krah*·kow·er	thick, paprika-spiced sausage of Polish origin
Landjäger m	*lant*·yay·ger	thin, long, hard spicy sausage
Leberwurst f	*lay*·ber·vurst	liver sausage
Regensburger m	*ray*·gens·bur·ger	highly spiced smoked sausage
Rotwurst f	*rawt*·vurst	black pudding
Thüringer f	*tü*·ring·er	long, thin spicy sausage
Wiener Würstchen n	*vee*·ner *vürst*·khen	frankfurter (small smoked sausage)
Weißwurst f	*vais*·vurst	veal sausage
Würstchen n	*vürst*·khen	small sausage
Zwiebelwurst f	*tsvee*·bel·vurst	liver and onion sausage

This is ...	*Das ist ...*	das ist ...
(too) cold	*(zu) kalt*	(tsoo) kalt
spicy	*scharf*	sharf
superb	*exzellent*	ek·se·*lent*

My compliments to the chef.
*Mein Kompliment
an den Koch.*
main kom·pli·*ment*
an dayn kokh

I'm full.
Ich bin satt.
ikh bin zat

meals

> breakfast

What's a typical breakfast in (Bavaria)?
*Was ißt man in (Bayern)
normalerweise zum
Frühstück?*
vas ist man in (*bai*·ern)
nor·*mah*·ler·vai·ze tsum
frü·shtük

---

when is a roll not a roll?

Bread rolls can be called many different things, depending on which area you're in. Below are five of the most common terms and where you'll hear them used:

Brötchen n	*brert*·khen	in Germany
Schrippe f	*shri*·pe	in Berlin
Semmel f	*ze*·mel	in Bavaria
Wecken m&f	*ve*·ken	in southern Germany and Austria
Weggli n	*veg*·li	in Switzerland

bread	*Brot* n	brawt
butter	*Butter* f	*bu*·ter
cereal	*Frühstücksflocken* f pl	*frü*·shtüks·flo·ken
cheese	*Käse* m	*kay*·ze
coffee	*Kaffee* m	*ka*·fay
cold cuts of meat/sausage	*Wurst* f/ *Aufschnitt* m	vurst/ *owf*·shnit
croissant	*Hörnchen* n	*hern*·khen
boiled egg	*gekochtes Ei* n	ge·*kokh*·tes ai
egg/eggs	*Ei/Eier* n sg/pl	ai/*ai*·er
fried egg	*Spiegelei* n	*shpee*·gel·ai
poached egg	*pochiertes Ei* n	po·*sheer*·tes ai
scrambled eggs	*Rührei* n	*rür*·ai
honey	*Honig* m	*haw*·nikh
jam	*Marmelade* f	mar·me·*lah*·de
milk	*Milch* f	milkh
muesli	*Müsli* n	*müs*·li
omelette	*Omelette* n	om·*let*
orange juice	*Orangensaft* m	o·*rang*·zhen·zaft
spreads	*Brotaufstrich* m	*brawt*·owf·shtrikh
tea	*Tee* m	tay
toast	*Toast* m	tawst

> light meals

What's that called?	*Wie heißt das?*	vee haist das
I'd like ..., please.	*Ich hätte gern ..., bitte.*	ikh *he*·te gern ... *bi*·te
one slice	*eine Scheibe*	*ai*·ne *shai*·be
a piece	*ein Stück*	ain shtük
a sandwich	*ein Sandwich*	ain *sent*·vich
that one	*dieses da*	*dee*·zes dah
two	*zwei*	tsvai

For typical dishes see the **culinary reader**, page 163, and for other food items see the **dictionary**.

> condiments

Is there any ...?	*Gibt es ...?*	gipt es ...
chilli sauce	*Chilisauce*	*chi*·li·zaw·se
ketchup	*Ketchup*	*ket*·chap
pepper	*Pfeffer*	*pfe*·fer
salt	*Salz*	zalts
tomato sauce	*Tomaten-*	to·*mah*·ten·
	ketchup	ket·chap
vinegar	*Essig*	e·sikh

methods of preparation

I'd like it ...	*Ich hätte es gern ...*	ikh *he*·te es gern ...
I don't want it ...	*Ich möchte*	ikh *merkh*·te
	es nicht ...	es nikht ...
boiled	*gekocht*	ge·*kokht*
broiled	*gegrillt*	ge·*grilt*
deep-fried	*frittiert*	fri·*teert*
fried	*gebraten*	ge·*brah*·ten
grilled	*gegrillt*	ge·*grilt*
mashed	*püriert*	pü·*reert*
medium	*halb durch*	halp durkh
rare	*englisch*	*eng*·lish
re-heated	*aufgewärmt*	*owf*·ge·vermt
steamed	*gedämpft*	ge·*dempft*
well-done	*gut durch-*	goot durkh·
	gebraten	ge·*brah*·ten
with the dressing	*mit dem Dressing*	mit daym *dre*·sing
on the side	*daneben*	da·*nay*·ben
without ...	*ohne ...*	*aw*·ne ...

For other specific meal requests, see **vegetarian & special meals**, page 159.

in the bar

Excuse me!	Entschuldigung!	ent·shul·di·gung
I'm next.	Ich bin dran.	ikh bin dran
I'll have ...	Ich hätte gern ...	ikh he·te gern ...

Same again, please.
  Dasselbe nochmal, bitte.   das·zel·be nokh·mahl bi·te

No ice, thanks.
  Kein Eis, bitte.   kain ais bi·te

How much alcohol does this contain?
  Wieviel Alkohol ist darin   vee·feel al·ko·hawl ist da·rin
  enthalten?   ent·hal·ten

I'll buy you a drink.
  Ich gebe Ihnen/dir   ikh gay·be ee·nen/deer
  einen aus. pol/inf   ai·nen ows

What would you like?
  Was möchten Sie? pol   vas merkh·ten zee
  Was möchtest du? inf   vas merkh·test doo

It's my round.
  Diese Runde geht auf mich.   dee·ze run·de gayt owf mikh

You can get the next one.
  Sie können die nächste   zee ker·nen dee naykhs·te
  Runde bestellen. pol   run·de be·shte·len
  Du kannst die nächste   doo kanst dee naykhs·te
  Runde bestellen. inf   run·de be·shte·len

---

listen for ...

vas merkh·ten zee (tring·ken)
  Was möchten Sie   **What are you having**
  (trinken)? pol   **(to drink)?**

ikh glow·be zee ha·ten ge·nook
  Ich glaube, Sie hatten   **I think you've**
  genug. pol   **had enough.**

Do you serve meals here?
Gibt es hier auch etwas zu essen?
gipt es heer owkh et·vas tsoo e·sen

nonalcoholic drinks

alkoholfreie getränke

boiled water	*heißes Wasser* n	*hai*·ses va·ser
coffee	*Kaffee* m	*ka*·fay
mineral water	*Mineralwasser* n	mi·ne·*rahl*·va·ser
soft drink	*Softdrink* m	*soft*·dringk
tea	*Tee* m	tay
water	*Wasser* n	va·ser
with (milk)	*mit (Milch)*	mit (milkh)
without (sugar)	*ohne (Zucker)*	*aw*·ne (*tsu*·ker)

what's in a name?

In Germany, *Softdrink* soft·dringk (soft drink) only designates sweet fizzy drinks, such as lemonade or cola. Mineral water is not known as *ein Softdrink* ain *soft*·dringk, but as *ein alkoholfreies Getränk* ain al·ko·*hawl*·frai·es ge·*trengk* (a nonalcoholic drink).

alcoholic drinks

beer	*Bier* n	beer
light beer	*Leichtbier* n	*laikht*·beer
nonalcoholic	*alkoholfreies*	al·ko·*hawl*·frai·es
beer	*Bier* n	beer
pilsner/lager	*Pils* n	pils
wheat beer	*Weißbier* n	*vais*·beer

brandy	*Weinbrand* m	*vain*·brant
(French)	*Champagner* m	sham·*pan*·yer
champagne		
cocktail	*Cocktail* m	*kok*·tayl
sparkling wine	*Sekt* m	zekt

a shot of ...	*einen ...*	*ai*·nen ...
gin	*Gin*	dzhin
rum	*Rum*	rum
tequila	*Tequila*	te·*kee*·la
vodka	*Wodka*	*vot*·ka
whisky	*Whisky*	*vis*·ki

a bottle of ... wine	*eine Flasche ...*	*ai*·ne *fla*·she ...
a glass of ... wine	*ein Glas ...*	ain glahs ...
dessert	*Dessertwein*	de·*sair*·vain
mulled	*Glühwein*	*glü*·vain
red	*Rotwein*	*rawt*·vain
rose	*Rosé*	ro·*zay*
sparkling	*Sekt*	zekt
white	*Weißwein*	*vais*·vain

a ... (of) beer	*ein ... Bier*	ain ... beer
glass	*Glas*	glahs
large	*großes*	*graw*·ses
pint	*halbes*	*halb*·es
small	*kleines*	*klai*·nes

| a beer on tap | *ein Bier vom Fass* | ain beer fom fas |

grape varieties

Germany is famous for its wines. There are three basic wine categories – *trocken* tro·ken (dry), *halbtrocken* halp·tro·ken (medium-dry), and *lieblich* leep·likh (sweet). Some of the more well-known grape varieties are listed below:

> **white**

Gewürztraminer m   ge·vürts·tra·mee·ner
very spicy with an intense bouquet

Müller-Thurgau m   mü·ler·toor·gow
early-ripening grape with a slight muscat flavour. Also called *Rivaner*, this wine is less acidic than *Riesling* and is best when young.

Riesling m   rees·ling
late-ripening grape with a fragrant, fruity bouquet, this wine can be drunk young or old

Ruländer/   roo·len·der/
Grauburgunder m   grow·bur·gun·der
robust, soft and full-bodied. Also known as *pinot gris* or *pinot grigio*.

Silvaner m   zil·vah·ner
full-bodied, mildly acidic wine with a neutral nose. Should be drunk young.

> **red**

Portugieser m   por·tu·gee·zer
light, mild red wine originally from Austria (not Portugal)

Spätburgunder m   shpayt·bur·gun·der
also known as Pinot Noir. A velvety and full-bodied wine – the best have an almond taste.

Trollinger m   tro·ling·er
hearty, full-bodied wine with a fragrant nose. *Trollinger* grapes ripen late and are only grown in Württemberg.

Alkoholfreies Bier n — al·ko·*hawl*·frai·es beer
nonalcoholic beer

Alster(wasser) n — *als*·ter(·va·ser)
mixture of pilsner and orange lemonade

Alt(bier) n — *alt*(·beer)
amber-coloured speciality beer from Düsseldorf, with
a strong taste of hops

Altbierbowle f — *alt*·beer·baw·le
Altbier with strawberries or other fruit

Alt-Schuss n — alt·*shus*
Altbier with a shot of syrup or *Malzbier*

Berliner Weiße f — ber·*lee*·ner *vai*·se
slightly fizzy and cloudy, often served with a shot of
raspberry (*rot*) or woodruff (*grün*) syrup

Bockbier n — *bok*·beer
light or dark beer with a high alcohol content

Eisbock m — *ais*·bok
Bockbier from which water has been extracted by
freezing thus increasing its alcoholic potency

Export n — eks·*port*
lager

Gose f — *gaw*·ze
wheat beer from Leipzig

Hefeweizen n — *hay*·fe·vai·tsen
cloudy wheat beer (with some yeast still in the
bottle) – comes in light (*hell*) or dark (*dunkel*) varieties

Helles n — *he*·les
lager (Bavaria)

Kölsch n — kerlsh
yellow-golden coloured beer from Cologne

Kräusen n — *kroy*·zen
unfiltered beer, gold-coloured or dark

Krefelder n — *kray*·fel·der
Altbier mixed with cola

Kristallweizen n — kris·*tal*·vai·tsen
clear light (*hell*) or dark (*dunkel*) wheat beer

Leichtbier n	*laikht*·beer
beer with half the alcohol content of normal beer	
Maibock m	*mai*·bok
special *Bockbier* brewed in May	
Malzbier n	*malts*·beer
nonalcoholic malt beer	
Märzen n	*mer*·tsen
special Bavarian beer brewed at the end of winter	
Pils/Pils(e)ner n	pils/*pil*·z(e·)ner
pilsner, similar to lager	
Radler n	*raht*·ler
mixture of pilsner or lager and sweet lemonade	
Rauchbier n	*rowkh*·beer
smoky-flavoured beer from Bamberg	
Schwarzbier n	*shvarts*·beer
stout (lit: black beer)	
Weizenbier/Weißbier n	*vai*·tsen·beer/*vais*·beer
wheat beer	

one too many?

einen über den durst?

Cheers!
Prost! — prawst

Thanks, but I don't feel like it.
Nein danke, ich möchte — nain *dang*·ke ikh *merkh*·te
jetzt nichts. — yetst nikhts

No thanks, I'm driving.
Nein danke, ich fahre. — nain *dang*·ke ikh *fah*·re

I don't drink alcohol.
Ich trinke keinen Alkohol. — ikh *tring*·ke *kai*·nen *al*·ko·hawl

I'm tired, I'd better go home.
Ich bin müde, ich sollte — ikh bin *mü*·de ikh *zol*·te
besser nach Hause gehen. — *be*·ser nahkh *how*·ze *gay*·en

This is hitting the spot.
Das kommt jetzt echt gut.   das komt yetst ekht goot

I'm feeling drunk.
Ich glaube, ich bin betrunken.   ikh *glow*·be ikh bin be·*trung*·ken

I feel fantastic!
Ich fühle mich fantastisch!   ikh *fü*·le mikh fan·*tas*·tish

I really, really love you.
Ich liebe dich echt total.   ikh *lee*·be dikh ekht to·*tahl*

I think I've had one too many.
Ich glaube, ich habe ein   ikh *glow*·be ikh *hah*·be ain
bisschen zu viel getrunken.   *bis*·khen tsoo feel ge·*trung*·ken

Can you call a taxi for me?
Können Sie mir ein   *ker*·nen zee meer ain
Taxi rufen? pol   *tak*·si *roo*·fen
Kannst du mir ein   kanst doo meer ain
Taxi rufen? inf   *tak*·si *roo*·fen

I don't think you should drive.
Ich glaube, Sie sollten   ikh *glow*·be zee *zol*·ten
nicht mehr fahren. pol   nikht mair *fah*·ren
Ich glaube, du solltest   ikh *glow*·be doo *zol*·test
nicht mehr fahren. inf   nikht mair *fah*·ren

There's still room for another!
Zwischen Leber und Milz   *tsvi*·shen *lay*·ber unt milts
ist noch Platz für ein Pils.   ist nokh plats für ain pils
(lit: between liver and spleen is still room for a beer)

Let's have a second drink.
Auf einem Bein steht   owf *ai*·nem bain shtayt
man schlecht.   man shlekht
(lit: on one leg stands one badly)

I feel ill.
Mir ist schlecht.   meer ist shlekht

I'm pissed.
Ich bin blau.   ikh bin blow
(lit: I am blue)

I have a hangover.
Ich habe einen Kater.   ikh *hah*·be *ai*·nen *kah*·ter
(lit: I have a tomcat)

key language

cooked	*gekocht*	ge·*kokht*
dried	*getrocknet*	ge·*trok*·net
fresh	*frisch*	frish
frozen	*eingefroren*	*ain*·ge·fraw·ren
raw	*roh*	raw
smoked	*geräuchert*	ge·*roy*·khert
A piece.	*Ein Stück.*	ain shtük
A slice.	*Eine Scheibe.*	*ai*·ne shai·be
That one.	*Dieses da.*	*dee*·zes dah
This.	*Dieses.*	*dee*·zes
A bit more.	*Ein bisschen mehr.*	ain *bis*·khen mair
Less.	*Weniger.*	*vay*·ni·ger
Enough.	*Genug.*	ge·*nook*

dining tips

The main meal of the day in the German-speaking countries is *das Mittagessen* das *mi*·tahk·e·sen or lunch.

It's good manners to say *Guten Appetit* goo·ten a·*pay*·teet or *Mahlzeit* mahl·tsait (Enjoy your meal) to your fellow diners. Observing German table etiquette is easy – it's enough to eat in a basically civilized manner. It's customary, however, to keep your hands on the table at all times.

To say you've really enjoyed your meal say *Das hat geschmeckt* das hat gesh·*mekt*. To get the attention of a waiter, call out *Herr Ober* her aw·ber (to a man) or *Fräulein* froy·lain (to a woman). To indicate that you want to pay your bill, say *Zahlen bitte!* tsah·len bi·te.

Germans are fond of toasts. If they break out the drink, wait until everyone is served. Then raise your glasses in unison, look your fellow toasters in the eye and give a hearty *Prost!* prawst or *Zum Wohl!* tsum vawl.

buying food

How much?
Wie viel?   vee feel

How much is (a kilo of cheese)?
Was kostet (ein Kilo Käse)?   vas kos·tet (ain kee·lo kay·ze)

What's the local speciality?
Was ist eine örtliche   vas ist ai·ne ert·li·khe
Spezialität?   shpe·tsya·li·tayt

What's that?
Was ist das?   vas ist das

Can I taste it?
Kann ich das probieren?   kan ikh das pro·bee·ren

Can I have a bag, please?
Könnte ich bitte eine   kern·te ikh bi·te ai·ne
Tüte haben?   tü·te hah·ben

I'd like ...	*Ich möchte ...*	ikh merkh·te ...
(200) grams	*(200) Gramm*	(tsvai·hun·dert) gram
(two) kilos	*(zwei) Kilo*	(tsvai) kee·lo
(three) pieces	*(drei) Stück*	(drai) shtük
(six) slices	*(sechs) Scheiben*	(zeks) shai·ben
some ...	*etwas ...*	et·vas ...
Do you have ...?	*Haben Sie ...?*	hah·ben zee ...
anything cheaper	*etwas Billigeres*	et·vas bi·li·ge·res
other kinds	*andere Sorten*	an·de·re zor·ten

For other useful amounts, see **numbers & amounts**, page 28.

Where can I find the ... section?	Wo kann ich die ... finden?	vaw kan ikh dee ... *fin*·den
dairy	Abteilung für Milchprodukte	ap·*tai*·lung für *milkh*·pro·duk·te
frozen goods	Abteilung für Tiefkühlprodukte	ap·*tai*·lung für *teef*·kül·pro·duk·te
fruit and vegetable	Obst- und Gemüse-abteilung	awpst· unt ge·*mü*·ze·ap·tai·lung
meat	Fleischabteilung	*flaish*·ap·tai·lung
poultry	Geflügel-abteilung	ge·*flü*·gel·ap·tai·lung

Where's the health-food section?

Wo ist die Nahrungsmittel-und Drogerie-Abteilung?
vaw ist dee *nah*·rungs·mi·tel· unt draw·ge·*ree*·ap·tai·lung

Where's the health-food store?

Wo ist ein Geschäft für Nahrungsmittel und Drogerie-Artikel?
vaw ist ain ge·*sheft* für *nah*·rungs·mi·tel unt draw·ge·*ree*·ar·tee·kel

For food items see the **culinary reader**, page 163, and the **dictionary**.

For food items see the **culinary reader**, page 163, and the **dictionary**.

listen for ...

kan ikh *ee*·nen *hel*·fen
Kann ich Ihnen helfen? **Can I help you?**

vas *merkh*·ten zee?
Was möchten Sie? **What would you like?**

das ist (*ai*·ne *brat*·vurst)
Das ist (eine Bratwurst). **That's (a bratwurst).**

das ist ows
Das ist aus. **There's none left.**

das *hah*·ben veer nikht
Das haben wir nicht. **I don't have any.**

merkh·ten zee nokh *et*·vas
Möchten Sie noch etwas? **Would you like anything else?**

das *kos*·tet (fünf *oy*·ro)
Das kostet (fünf Euro). **That's (five euros).**

self-catering

157

cooking utensils

Could I please borrow a ...?	*Könnte ich bitte ... ausleihen?*	kern·te ikh bi·te ... ows·lai·en
bottle opener	*einen Flaschenöffner*	ai·nen fla·shen·erf·ner
bowl	*eine Schüssel*	ai·ne shü·sel
can opener	*einen Dosenöffner*	ai·nen daw·zen·erf·ner
chopping board	*ein Schneidebrett*	ain shnai·de·bret
corkscrew	*einen Korkenzieher*	ai·nen kor·ken·tsee·er
cup	*eine Tasse*	ai·ne ta·se
fork	*eine Gabel*	ai·ne gah·bel
frying pan	*eine Bratpfanne*	ai·ne braht·pfa·ne
glass	*ein Glas*	ain glahs
knife	*ein Messer*	ain me·ser
plate	*einen Teller*	ai·nen te·ler
saucepan	*einen Kochtopf*	ai·nen kokh·topf
spoon	*einen Löffel*	ai·nen ler·fel
toaster	*einen Toaster*	ai·nen taws·ter
fridge	*Kühlschrank* m	kül·shrank
microwave	*Mikrowelle* f	mi·kro·ve·le
oven	*Ofen* m	aw·fen
stove	*Kochplatte* f	kokh·pla·te

For more cooking terminology, see the **dictionary**.

vegetarian & special meals
vegetarische und besondere gerichte

ordering

Is there a (vegetarian) restaurant near here?
Gibt es ein (vegetarisches)   gipt es ain vege·*tar*·ish·shes
Restaurant hier in der Nähe?   res·to·*rang* heer in dair *nay*·e

Do you have	*Haben Sie*	*hah*·ben zee
... food?	*... Essen?*	*... e·*sen
halal	*Halal-*	ha·*lal·*
kosher	*koscheres*	*kaw*·she·res
vegetarian	*vegetarisches*	ve·ge·*tah*·ri·shes

Is it cooked	*Ist es in/mit*	ist es in/mit
in/with ...?	*... zubereitet?*	*... tsoo*·be·rai·tet
butter	*Butter*	*bu*·ter
eggs	*Eiern*	*ai*·ern
meat stock	*Fleischbrühe*	*flaish*·brü·e

I don't eat ...
Ich esse kein ...   ikh *e*·se kain ...

Does this dish have ... in it?
Enthält dieses Gericht ...?   ent·*helt* dee·zes ge·*rikht* ...

Can I get this without ... in it?
Kann ich das ohne ...   kan ikh das *aw*·ne ...
bekommen?   be·*ko*·men

Could you prepare a meal without ...?
Können Sie ein Gericht   *ker*·nen zee ain ge·*rikht*
ohne ... zubereiten?   *aw*·ne ... *tsoo*·be·rai·ten

Is this ...?	Ist das ...?	ist das ...
free of animal produce	ohne tierische Produkte	aw·ne tee·ri·she pro·duk·te
free-range	von freilaufenden Tieren	fon frai·low·fen·den tee·ren
genetically modified	genmanipuliert	gayn·ma·ni·pu·leert
gluten-free	glutenfrei	gloo·ten·frai
halal	nach den Vorschriften des Koran zubereitet	nahkh dayn fawr·shrif·ten des ko·rahn tsoo·be·rai·tet
kosher	koscher	kaw·sher
low in sugar	zuckerarm	tsu·ker·arm
low-fat	fettarm	fet·arm
organic	organisch	or·gah·nish
salt-free	ohne Salz	aw·ne zalts

listen for ...

dah ist ü·ber·*al* (flaish) drin
Da ist überall (Fleisch) drin. **It all has (meat) in it.**

ikh *frah*·ge mahl in dair *kü*·khe
*Ich frage mal
in der Küche.* **I'll check with
the chef.**

ker·nen zee ... *e*·sen
Können Sie ... essen? **Can you eat ...?**

special diets & allergies

I'm (a) ...	Ich bin ...	ikh bin ...
Buddhist	*Buddhist(in)* m/f	bu·*dist*/bu·*dis*·tin
Hindu	*Hindu* m&f	*hin*·du
Jewish	*Jude/Jüdin* m/f	*yoo*·de/*yü*·din
Muslim	*Moslem/*	*mos*·lem/
	Moslime m/f	mos·*lee*·me
vegan	*Veganer(in)* m/f	ve·*gah*·ner/
		ve·*gah*·ne·rin
vegetarian	*Vegetarier(in)* m/f	ve·ge·*tah*·ri·er/
		ve·ge·*tah*·ri·e·rin

I'm allergic to ...	Ich bin allergisch gegen ...	ikh bin a·*lair*·gish gay·gen ...
animal products	*Tierprodukte*	*teer*·pro·duk·te
caffeine	*Koffein*	ko·fe·*een*
dairy produce	*Milchprodukte*	*milkh*·pro·duk·te
eggs	*Eier*	*ai*·er
fish	*Fisch*	fish
gelatin	*Gelatine*	zhe·la·*tee*·ne
genetically	*genmanipulierte*	*gayn*·ma·ni·pu·leer·te
modified food	*Speisen*	*shpai*·zen
gluten	*Gluten*	*gloo*·ten
honey	*Honig*	*haw*·nikh
MSG	*Natrium-*	*nah*·tri·um·
	glutamat	glu·ta·maht
nuts	*Nüsse*	*nü*·se
pork	*Schweinefleisch*	*shvai*·ne·flaish
poultry	*Geflügelfleisch*	ge·*flü*·gel·flaish
red meat	*Rind- und*	*rint*· unt
	Lammfleisch	*lam*·flaish
seafood	*Meeresfrüchte*	*mair*·res·frükh·te
shellfish	*Schaltiere*	*shahl*·tee·re

I'm on a special diet.
Ich bin auf einer Spezialdiät.
ikh bin owf *ai*·ner shpe·*tsyahl*·di·et

I can't eat it because I'm allergic.
Ich kann es nicht essen weil ich allergisch bin.
ikh kan es nikht ess·en vail ikh a·*lair*·gish bin

I can't eat it for …	*Ich kann es nicht essen aus …*	ikh kan es nikht ess·en ows …
health reasons	*Gesundheitsgründen*	ge·*zunt*·haits·grün·den
religious reasons	*religiösen Gründen*	re·li·*gyer*·zen *grün*·den
philosophical reasons	*philosophischen Gründen*	fi·lo·*zaw*·fi·shen *grün*·den

This miniguide to German cuisine is designed to help you navigate menus. German nouns, and adjectives affected by gender, have their gender indicated by ⓘ, ⓜ or ⓝ. If it's a plural noun, you'll also see pl.

A

Aachener Printen pl *ah·khe·ner print·ten* cakes with chocolate, nuts, fruit peel, honey & spices
Aal ⓜ *ahl* eel
 —suppe ⓘ *ahl·zu·pe* eel soup
 geräucherter Aal ⓜ *ge·roy·kher·ter ahl* smoked eel
Alpzirler ⓜ *alp·tsir·ler* cow's milk cheese from Austria
Apfel ⓜ *ap·fel* apple
 —strudel ⓜ *ap·fel·shtroo·del* apple strudel
Apfelsine ⓘ *ap·fel·zee·ne* orange
Aprikose ⓘ *a·pri·kaw·ze* apricot
 —nmarmelade ⓘ *a·pri·kaw·zen·mar·me·lah·de* apricot jam
Artischocke ⓘ *ar·ti·sho·ke* artichoke
Auflauf ⓜ *owf·lowf* souffle • casserole
Auster ⓘ *ows·ter* oyster

B

Bäckerofen ⓜ *be·ker·aw·fen* 'baker's oven' – pork & lamb bake from Saarland
Backhähnchen ⓝ *bak·hayn·khen* fried chicken
Backobst ⓝ *bak·awpst* dried fruit
Backpflaume ⓘ *bak·pflow·me* prune
Banane ⓘ *ba·nah·ne* banana
Barsch ⓜ *barsh* perch
Bauern
 —brot ⓝ *bow·ern·brawt* 'farmer's bread' – rye or wholemeal bread
 —frühstück ⓝ *bow·ern·frü·shtük* 'farmer's breakfast' – scrambled eggs, bacon, cooked diced potatoes, onions & tomatoes

 —schmaus ⓜ *bow·ern·shmows* 'farmer's feast' – sauerkraut garnished with bacon, smoked pork, sausages & dumpling or potatoes
 —suppe ⓘ *bow·ern·zu·pe* 'farmer's soup' – made of cabbage & sausage
Bayrisch Kraut ⓝ *bai·rish krowt* shredded cabbage cooked with sliced apples, wine & sugar
Beefsteak ⓝ *beef·stayk* hamburger patty
Berliner ⓜ *ber·lee·ner* jam doughnut
Beuschel ⓝ *boy·shel* heart, liver & kidney of a calf or lamb in a slightly sour sauce
Bienenstich ⓜ *bee·nen·shtikh* cake, baked on a tray with a coating of almonds & sugar
Birne ⓘ *bir·ne* pear
Bischofsbrot ⓝ *bi·shofs·brawt* fruit & nut cake
Blaubeere ⓘ *blow·bair·re* bilberry • blueberry
Blaukraut ⓝ *blow·krowt* red cabbage
Blumenkohl ⓜ *bloo·men·kawl* cauliflower
Blutwurst ⓘ *bloot·vurst* blood sausage
Bockwurst ⓘ *bok·vurst* pork sausage
Bohnen ⓘ pl *baw·nen* beans
Brat
 —huhn ⓝ *braht·hoon* roast chicken
 —kartoffeln ⓘ pl *braht·kar·to·feln* fried potatoes
 —wurst ⓘ *braht·vurst* fried pork sausage
Bregenwurst ⓘ *bray·gen·vurst* brain sausage, found mainly in Lower Saxony & Western Saxony-Anhalt
Brezel ⓘ *bray·tsel* pretzel

Brokkoli ⓜ pl bro·ko·li broccoli
Brombeere ① brom·bair·re blackberry
Brot ⓝ brawt bread
  belegtes Brot ⓝ be·layk·tes brawt
  open sandwich
Brötchen ⓝ brert·khen roll
Brühwürfel ⓜ brü·vür·fel stock cube
Bulette ① bu·le·te meatball (Berlin)
Butter ① bu·ter butter

C

Cervelatwurst ① ser·ve·laht·vurst
  spicy pork & beef sausage
Christstollen ① krist·shto·len
  spiced loaf with candied peel, traditionally eaten at Christmas
Cremespeise ① kraym·shpai·ze mousse

D

Damenkäse ① dah·men·kay·ze
  soft, buttery cheese
Dampfnudeln ⓜ pl dampf·noo·deln
  hot yeast dumplings with vanilla sauce
Dattel ① da·tel date
Dorsch ⓜ dorsh cod
Dotterkäse ⓜ do·ter·kay·ze cheese
  made from skimmed milk & egg yolk

E

Ei ⓝ ai egg
  gekochte Eier ⓜ pl ge·kokh·te ai·er
  boiled eggs
Eierkuchen ⓜ ai·er·koo·khen pancake
Eierschwammerln ⓜ pl
  ai·er·shva·merln
  chanterelle mushrooms (Austria)
Eierspeispfandl ⓝ ai·er·shpais·pfandl
  special Viennese omelette (Austria)
Eintopf ⓜ ain·topf stew
Eis ⓝ ais ice cream
Eisbein ⓝ ais·bain pickled pork knuckles
Emmentaler ⓜ e·men·tah·ler Swiss
  Emmental, whole-milk hard cheese
Ennstaler ⓜ ens·tah·ler blue cheese
  produced from mixed milk

Ente ① en·te duck
Erbse ① erp·se pea
Erbsensuppe ① erp·sen·zu·pe pea soup
Erdäpfel ⓜ pl ert·ep·fel potatoes
  —gulasch ⓜ ert·ep·fel·goo·lash
  spicy sausage & potato stew
  —knödel ⓜ pl ert·ep·fel·kner·del
  potato & semolina dumplings
  —nudeln ⓜ pl ert·ep·fel·noo·deln
  boiled potato balls fried & tossed in
  fried breadcrumbs
Erdbeere ① ert·bair·re strawberry
Erdbeermarmelade ①
  ert·bair·mar·me·lah·de strawberry jam
Erdnuss ① ert·nus peanut
Essig ⓜ e·sikh vinegar

F

Falscher Hase ⓜ fal·sher hah·ze
  'false hare' – baked mince meatloaf
Fasan ⓜ fa·zahn pheasant
Feige ① fai·ge fig
Filet ① fi·lay fillet
Fisch ⓜ fish fish
Fladen ⓜ flah·den
  round, flat dough cake
Flädle ⓜ pl flayt·le
  thin strips of pancake, added to soup
Fledermaus ① flay·der·mows
  'bat' – boiled beef in horseradish
  cream browned in the oven
Fleisch ⓝ flaish meat
  —brühe ① flaish·brü·e bouillon
  —pflanzerl ⓝ flaish·pflan·tserl
  meatballs, a Bavarian speciality
  —sülze ① flaish·zül·tse aspic
Fondue ⓝ fon·dü melted cheese with
  wine served with bread for dipping
Forelle ① fo·re·le trout
  — blau fo·re·le blow steamed trout
  with potatoes & vegetables
  — Müllerin fo·re·le mü·le·rin
  trout fried in batter with almonds
  geräucherte Forelle ① ge·roy·kher·te
  fo·re·le smoked trout

Frankfurter Kranz ⓝ *frank·fur·ter krants* sponge cake with rum, butter, cream & cherries (from Frankfurt)

Frikadelle ① *fri·ka·de·le* meatball

Frischling ⓜ *frish·ling* young wild boar

Frucht ① frukht fruit

Frühlingssuppe ① *frü·lingks·zu·pe* vegetable soup

Frühstücksspeck ⓜ *frü·shtüks·shpek* bacon

G

Gans ① gans goose

Garnele ① *gar·nay·le* shrimp • prawn

Gebäck ⓝ *ge·bek* pastries

Geflügel ⓝ *ge·flü·gel* poultry

gekocht *ge·kokht* boiled • cooked

Gemüse ⓝ *ge·mü·ze* vegetables
—**suppe** ① *ge·mü·ze·zu·pe* vegetable soup

geräuchert *ge·roy·khert* smoked

Geschnetzeltes ⓝ *ge·shne·tsel·tes* small slices of meat
Züricher Geschnetzeltes ⓝ *tsü·ri·kher ge·shne·tsel·tes* sliced veal with mushrooms & onions cooked in a white wine & cream sauce

Gitziprägel ⓝ *gi·tsi·pray·gel* baked rabbit in batter (Switzerland)

Graf Görz ⓜ grahf gerts Austrian soft cheese

Granat ⓜ *gra·naht* shrimp

Granatapfel ⓜ *gra·naht·ap·fel* pomegranate

Gratin ⓝ *gra·teng* a dish topped with cheese & baked in the oven

Graupensuppe ① *grow·pen·zu·pe* barley soup

Greyerzer ⓜ *grai·er·tser* Gruyère, a smooth, rich cheese

Grießklößchensuppe ① *grees·klers·khen·zu·pe* soup with semolina dumplings

Gröstl ⓝ grerstl grated fried potatoes with meat (Tyrol)

grüner Salat ⓜ *grü·ner za·laht* green salad

Grünkohl ⓜ **mit Pinkel** *grün·kawl mit ping·kel* cabbage with sausages (Bremen)

Güggeli ⓝ *gü·ge·lee* spring chicken (Switzerland)

Gurke ① *gur·ke* cucumber • gherkin

H

Hack
—**braten** ⓜ *hak·brah·ten* meatloaf
—**fleisch** ⓝ *hak·flaish* minced meat

Haferbrei ⓜ *hah·fer·brai* porridge

Hähnchen ⓝ *hayn·khen* chicken

Hämchen ⓝ *hem·khen* pork or hock shank, served with sauerkraut & potatoes (Cologne)

Handkäs ⓜ **mit Musik** *hant·kays mit mu·zeek* spicy cheese, marinated in vinegar & white wine

Hartkäse ⓜ *hart·kay·ze* hard cheese

Hase ⓜ *hah·ze* hare
—**nläufe** ⓜ pl in Jägerrahmsauce *hah·zen·loy·fe in yay·ger·rahm·zaw·se* hare thigh in dark cream sauce of mushroom, shallots, white wine & parsley
—**npfeffer** ⓜ *hah·zen·pfe·fer* hare stew with mushrooms & onions

Haselnuß ① *hah·zel·nus* hazelnut

Haxe ① *hak·se* knuckle

Hecht ⓜ hekht pike

Heidelbeere ① *hai·del·bair·re* bilberry • blueberry

Heidelbeermarmelade ① *hai·del·bair·mar·me·lah·de* blueberry/bilberry jam

Heilbutt ⓜ *hail·but* halibut

Hering ⓜ *hay·ring* herring
—**sschmaus** ⓜ *hay·rings·shmows* herring in creamy sauce
—**ssalat** ⓜ *hay·rings·za·laht* salad with herring & beetroot

Himbeere ① *him·bair·re* raspberry

Himmel und Erde *hi·mel unt er·de* 'Heaven & Earth' – mashed potatoes & apple sauce, sometimes served with slices of black pudding

Hirsch ⓜ hirsh male deer

Holsteiner Schnitzel ⓝ *hol*·shtai·ner *shni*·tsel *veal schnitzel with fried egg, accompanied by seafood*

Honig ⓜ *haw*·nikh *honey*

Hörnchen ⓝ *hern*·khen *croissant*

Hühnerbrust ① *hü*·ner·brust *chicken breast*

Hühnersuppe ① *hü*·ner·zu·pe *chicken soup*

Hummer ⓜ *hu*·mer *lobster*

Husarenfleisch ⓝ *hu*·zah·ren·flaish *braised beef, veal & pork fillets with sweet peppers, onions & sour cream*

Hutzelbrot ⓝ *hu*·tsel·brawt *bread made of prunes & other dried fruit*

I

Ingwer ⓜ *ing*·ver *ginger*

italienischer Salat ⓜ i·tal·yay·ni·sher za·laht *finely sliced veal, salami, anchovies, tomatoes, cucumber & celery in mayonnaise*

J

Joghurt ⓜ *yaw*·gurt *yogurt*

K

Kabeljau ⓜ *kah*·bel·yow *cod*

Kaiserschmarren ⓜ *kai*·zer·shmar·ren *'emperor's pancakes' – fluffy pancakes with raisins, served with fruit compote or chocolate sauce*

Kaisersemmeln ① pl *kai*·zer·ze·meln *'emperor's rolls' – Austrian bread rolls*

Kalbfleisch ⓝ *kalp*·flaish *veal*

Kalbsnierenbraten ⓜ *kalps*·nee·ren·brah·ten *roast veal stuffed with kidneys*

Kaninchen ⓝ ka·*neen*·khen *rabbit*

Kapern ① pl *kah*·pern *capers*

Karotte ① ka·ro·te *carrot*

Karpfen ⓜ *karp*·fen *carp*

Kartoffel ① kar·to·fel *potato*

—auflauf ⓜ kar·to·fel·owf·lowf *potato casserole*

—brei ⓜ kar·to·fel·brai *mashed potatoes*

—püree ⓝ kar·to·fel·pü·ray *mashed potatoes*

—salat ⓜ kar·to·fel·za·laht *potato salad*

Käse ⓜ *kay*·ze *cheese*

—fondue ⓝ *kay*·ze·fon·dü *melted cheese flavoured with wine & kirsch, into which bread is dipped*

Kasseler ⓜ *kas*·ler *smoked pork*

— Rippe ① **mit Sauerkraut** *kas*·ler *ri*·pe mit zow·er·krowt *smoked pork rib with sauerkraut*

Katenwurst ① *kah*·ten·vurst *country-style smoked sausage*

Katzenjammer ⓜ *ka*·tsen·ya·mer *cold slices of beef in mayonnaise with cucumbers or gherkin*

Keule ① *koy*·le *leg • haunch*

Kieler Sprotten ① pl *kee*·ler *shpro*·ten *small smoked herring*

Kirsche ① *kir*·she *cherry*

Kirtagssuppe ① *kir*·tahks·zu·pe *soup with caraway seed, thickened with potato*

Klöße ⓜ pl *kler*·se *dumplings*

Knackwurst ① *knak*·vurst *sausage lightly flavoured with garlic*

Knoblauch ⓜ *knawp*·lowkh *garlic*

Knödel ⓜ *kner*·del *dumpling*

—beignets ⓜ pl *kner*·del·ben·yays *fruit dumplings*

Kohl ⓜ *kawl* *cabbage*

—rabi ⓜ *kawl*·rah·bi *kohlrabi*

—roulade ① *kawl*·ru·lah·de *cabbage leaves stuffed with minced meat*

Kompott ⓝ kom·*pot* *stewed fruit*

Königinsuppe ① *ker*·ni·gin·zu·pe *creamy chicken soup with pieces of chicken breast*

Königsberger Klopse ⓜ pl *ker*·niks·ber·ger *klop*·se *meatballs in a sour cream & caper sauce*

Königstorte ① *ker*·niks·tor·te *rum-flavoured fruit cake*

Kopfsalat ⓜ *kopf·za·laht lettuce*

Kotelett ⓝ *kot·let chop*

Krabbe ⓕ *kra·be crab*

Krakauer ⓕ *krah·kow·er thick, paprika-spiced sausage of Polish origin*

Kraut ⓝ *krowt cabbage*
—salat ⓜ *krowt·za·laht coleslaw*

Kräuter ⓝ pl *kroy·ter herbs*

Krebs ⓜ *krayps crab • crayfish*

Kren ⓜ *krayn*
horseradish (Bavaria & Austria)

Krokette ⓕ *kro·ke·te croquette*

Kuchen ⓜ *koo·khen cake*

Kümmel ⓜ *kü·mel caraway (seeds)*

Kürbis ⓜ *kür·bis pumpkin*

Kutteln ⓕ pl *ku·teln tripe*

L

Labskaus ⓜ *laps·kows*
thick meat & potato stew

Lachs ⓜ *laks salmon*
geräucherter Lachs ⓜ *ge·roy·kher·ter laks smoked salmon*

Lamm
—fleisch ⓝ *lam·flaish lamb*
—keule ⓕ *lam·koy·le leg of lamb*

Landjäger ⓜ *lant·yay·ger*
thin, long, hard, spicy sausage

Languste ⓕ *lan·gus·te crayfish*

Lappenpickert ⓜ *la·pen·pi·kert pan-sized potato pancake usually served with jam or salted fish (Westphalia)*

Lauch ⓜ *lowkh leek*

Leber ⓕ *lay·ber liver*
—käse ⓜ *lay·ber·kay·ze*
seasoned meatloaf made of minced liver, pork & bacon
—knödel ⓜ *lay·ber·kner·del*
liver dumpling
—knödelsuppe ⓕ *lay·ber·kner·del·zu·pe hot broth with liver dumplings*
—wurst ⓕ *lay·ber·vurst liver sausage*

Lebkuchen ⓜ *layp·koo·khen*
gingerbread

Leckerli ⓝ *le·ker·lee*
honey-flavoured ginger biscuit

Leipziger Allerlei ⓝ *laip·tsi·ger a·ler·lai mixed vegetable stew (Leipzig)*

Lende ⓕ *len·de loin*

Limburger ⓜ *lim·bur·ger*
strong cheese flavoured with herbs

Linsen ⓕ pl *lin·zen lentils*
— mit Spätzle mit *shpets·le*
lentil stew with noodles & sausages
—suppe ⓕ *lin·zen·zu·pe lentil soup*

Linzer Torte ⓕ *lin·tser tor·te*
latticed tart with jam topping

Lorbeerblätter ⓝ pl *lor·bair·ble·ter bay leaves*

Lübecker Marzipan ⓝ *lü·be·ker mar·tsi·pahn marzipan (Lübeck)*

Lucullus-Eier ⓝ pl *lu·ku·lus·ai·er poached, boiled or scrambled eggs with goose liver, truffle & other garnishes, served with a sauce*

M

Mais ⓜ *mais sweet corn*

Majonnaise ⓕ *ma·yo·nay·ze mayonnaise*

Makrele ⓕ *ma·kray·le mackerel*

Mandarine ⓕ *man·da·ree·ne mandarine • tangerine*

Mandel ⓕ *man·del almond*

Marmelade ⓕ *mar·me·lah·de jam*

Matjes ⓜ *mat·yes young herring*

Maultasche ⓕ *mowl·ta·she filled pasta (Swabia)*

Meeresfrüchte ⓕ pl *mair·res·frükh·te seafood*

Meerrettich ⓜ *mair·re·tikh horseradish*

Mehl ⓝ *mayl flour*

Mett ⓝ *met lean minced pork*

Mettentchen ⓝ *met·ent·khen beer stick*

Milch ⓕ *milkh milk*
—rahmstrudel ⓜ
milkh·rahm·shtroo·del strudel filled with egg custard & soft cheese

Mohnbrötchen ⓝ *mawn·brert·khen bread roll with poppy seeds*

Möhre ⓕ *mer·re carrot*

Muschel ① *mu-*shel *clam • mussel*
Muskat ⓜ mus-*kaht nutmeg*
Müesli ⓝ *mü-*es-li *muesli*
Müsli ⓝ *müs-*li *muesli*

N

Nelken ① pl *nel-*ken *cloves*
Niere ① *nee-*re *kidney*
Nockerl ⓝ *no-*kerl
  small dumpling (Austria)
Nudeln ① pl *noo-*deln *noodles*
Nudelauflauf ⓜ *noo-*del-owf-lowf
  pasta casserole
Nürnberger Lebkuchen ⓜ nürn-ber-ger
  *layp-*koo-khen *cakes with chocolate,
  nuts, fruit peel, honey & spices*

O

Obatzter ⓜ *aw-*bats-ter
  Bavarian soft cheese mousse
Obst ⓝ *awpst fruit*
  —salat ⓜ *awpst-*za-laht *fruit salad*
Ochsenschwanz ⓜ *ok-*sen-shvants
  oxtail
  —suppe ① *ok-*sen-shvants-zu-pe
  oxtail soup
Öl ⓝ *erl oil*
Orangenmarmelade ① o-*rahng-*zhen-
  mar-me-lah-de *marmelade*

P

Palatschinken ⓜ pa-*lat-*shing-ken
  *pancake, usually filled with jam or
  cheese, sometimes served with a hot
  chocolate & nut topping*
Pampelmuse ① pam-pel-*moo-*ze
  grapefruit
Paprika ① *pap-*ri-kah *sweet pepper*
Pastetchen ⓝ pas-*tayt-*khen
  filled puff-pastry case
Pastete ① pas-*tay-*te *pastry • pie*
Pellkartoffeln ① pl *pel-*kar-to-feln
  *small jacket potatoes served in their
  skins, often served with quark*
Petersilie ① pay-ter-*zee-*li-e *parsley*
Pfälzer Saumagen ⓜ *pfel-*tser
  zow-*mah-*gen *stuffed stomach of pork*

Pfannkuchen ⓜ *pfan-*koo-khen
  pancake
Pfeffer ⓜ *pfe-*fer *pepper*
Pfifferling ⓜ *pfi-*fer-ling
  chanterelle mushroom
Pfirsich ⓜ *pfir-*zikh *peach*
Pflaume ① *pflow-*me *plum*
Pilz ⓜ *pilts mushroom*
Pichelsteiner ⓜ *pi-*khel-shtai-ner
  meat & vegetable stew
Pökelfleisch ⓝ *per-*kel-flaish
  marinated meat
Pomeranzensoße ① po-me-*ran-*tsen-
  zaw-se *sauce made of bitter oranges,
  wine & brandy, usually served with
  duck*
Pommes Frites pl pom frit *French fries*
Porree ⓜ *por-*ray *leek*
Preiselbeere ① *prai-*zel-bair-re *cran-
  berry*
Printe ① *prin-*te
  honey-flavoured biscuit
Pumpernickel ⓜ *pum-*per-ni-kel *very
  dark bread made with coarse wholemeal rye flour*
Putenbrust ① *poo-*ten-brust
  turkey breast
Puter ⓜ *poo-*ter *turkey*

Q

Quargel ⓜ *kvar-*gel *small, round, salty
  & slightly acidic cheese*
Quark ⓜ *kvark quark (curd cheese)*
Quitte ① *kvi-*te *quince*

R

Radieschen ⓝ ra-*dees-*khen *radish*
Ragout ⓝ ra-*goo stew*
Rahm ⓜ *rahm cream*
Rebhuhn ⓝ *rayp-*hoon *partridge*
Regensburger ⓜ *ray-*gens-bur-ger
  highly spiced smoked sausage
Reh ⓝ *ray venison*
  —pfeffer ⓜ *ray-*pfe-fer *jugged
  venison, fried & braised in its
  marinade, served with sour cream*
  —rücken ⓜ *ray-*rü-ken
  saddle of venison

Reibekuchen ⓝ *rai·be·koo·khen* potato cake

Reis ⓜ rais rice

Remouladensauce ① *re·mu·lah·den·zaw·se* mayonnaise sauce with mustard, anchovies, capers, gherkins, tarragon & chervil

Rettich ⓜ *re·tikh* radish

Rhabarber ⓜ *ra·bar·ber* rhubarb

Rheinischer Sauerbraten ⓜ **mit Kartoffelklößen** *rai·ni·sher zow·er·brah·ten mit kar·to·fel·kler·sen* roasted marinated meat, slightly sour, often served with potato dumpling

Rindfleisch ⓝ *rint·flaish* beef

Rippenspeer ⓜ *ri·pen·shpair* spare ribs

Rogen ⓜ *raw·gen* roe

Roggenbrot ⓝ *ro·gen·brawt* rye bread

Rohkost ① *raw·kost* uncooked vegetables • vegetarian food

Rollmops ⓜ *rol·mops* pickled herring fillet rolled around chopped onions or gherkins

Rosenkohl ⓜ *raw·zen·kawl* Brussels sprouts

Rosinen ① pl *ro·zee·nen* raisins

Rosmarin ⓜ *raws·ma·reen* rosemary

Rost
  —braten ⓜ *rost·brah·ten* roast
  —brätl ① *rost·braytl* grilled meat
  —hähnchen ⓝ *rost·hayn·khen* roast chicken

Rösti pl *rers·tee* grated, fried potatoes (Switzerland)

rot rawt red
  —e Beete ① *raw·te bay·te* beetroot
  —e Grütze ① *raw·te grü·tse* fruit pudding of cooked & sweetened berries, thickened & put in moulds
  —e Johannisbeere ① *raw·te yo·ha·nis·bair·e* redcurrant
  —kohl ⓜ *rawt·kawl* red cabbage
  —e Rüben ① pl *raw·te rü·ben* beetroot
  —wurst ① *rawt·vurst* black pudding

Roulade ① *ru·lah·de* collared beef – thin slices of beef stuffed with onion, bacon and dill pickles then rolled & braised

Rühreier ⓝ pl *rür·ai·er* scrambled eggs

Russische Eier ⓝ pl *ru·si·she ai·er* 'Russian eggs' – eggs with mayonnaise

S

Sahne ① *zah·ne* cream

Salat ⓜ *za·laht* salad
  grüner Salat ⓜ *grü·ner za·laht* green salad
  italienischer Salat ⓜ *i·tal·yay·ni·sher za·laht* finely sliced veal, salami, anchovies, tomatoes, cucumber & celery in mayonnaise

Salbei ⓜ *zal·bai* sage

Salz ⓝ *zalts* salt

Salzburger Nockerln ⓝ pl *zalts·bur·ger no·kerln* Austrian dessert of sweet dumplings poached in milk & served with warm vanilla sauce

Salzkartoffeln ① pl *zalts·kar·to·feln* boiled potatoes

Sauerbraten ⓜ *zow·er·brah·ten* marinated roasted beef served with a sour cream sauce

Sauerkraut ⓝ *zow·er·krowt* pickled cabbage

Schafskäse ⓜ *shahfs·kay·ze* sheep's milk feta

Schellfisch ⓜ *shel·fish* haddock

Schinken ⓜ *shing·ken* ham
  gekochter Schinken ⓜ *ge·kokh·ter shing·ken* cooked ham
  geräucherter Schinken ⓜ *ge·roy·kher·ter shing·ken* gammon

Schlachtplatte ① *shlakht·pla·te* selection of pork & sausage

Schmalzbrot ⓝ *shmalts·brawt* slice of bread with dripping

Schmorbraten ⓜ *shmawr·brah·ten* beef pot roast

Schnitte ① *shni·te* slice of bread • small square piece of cake

Schnittlauch ⓝ *shnit·lowkh* chives

Schnitzel ⓝ *shni·tsel* pork, veal or chicken breast pounded flat, covered in breadcrumbs & pan-fried

Holsteiner Schnitzel ⓝ *hol·shtai·ner shni·tsel* veal schnitzel with fried egg, accompanied by seafood

Wiener Schnitzel ⓝ *vee·ner shni·tsel* crumbed veal

Scholle ⓕ *sho·le* plaice

schwarze Johannisbeere ⓕ *shvar·tse yo·ha·nis·bair·re* blackcurrant

Schwarzwälder Kirschtorte ⓕ *shvarts·vel·der kirsh·tor·te* Black Forest cake (chocolate layer cake filled with cream & cherries)

Schwein ⓝ *shvain* pork

—ebraten ⓜ *shvai·ne·brah·ten* roast pork

—efleisch ⓝ *shvai·ne·flaish* pork

—shaxe ⓕ *shvains·hak·se* crispy leg of pork served with dumplings

Seezunge ⓕ *zay·tsung·e* sole

Seidfleisch ⓝ *zait·flaish* boiled meat

Sekt ⓜ *zekt* German champagne

Selchfleisch ⓝ *zelkh·flaish* smoked pork

Sellerie ⓜ *ze·le·ree* celery

Semmel ⓕ *ze·mel* bread roll (Austria & Bavaria)

—knödel ⓜ pl *ze·mel·kner·del* dumplings made of dry rolls dunked in milk (Bavaria)

Senf ⓜ *zenf* mustard

Sonnenblumenkerne ⓜ pl *zo·nen·bloo·men·ker·ne* sunflower seeds

Soße ⓕ *zaw·se* sauce • gravy

spanische Soße ⓕ *shpah·ni·she zaw·se* brown sauce with herbs

Spanferkel ⓝ *shpahn·fer·kel* suckling pig

Spargel ⓜ *shpar·gel* asparagus

Spätzle pl *shpets·le* thick noodles

Speck ⓜ *shpek* bacon

Spekulatius ⓜ *shpe·ku·lah·tsi·us* almond biscuits

Spiegelei ⓝ *shpee·gel·ai* fried egg

Spinat ⓜ *shpi·naht* spinach

Sprossenkohl ⓜ *shpro·sen·kawl* Brussels sprouts

Sprotten ⓕ pl *shpro·ten* sprats (small herring-like fish)

Steckrübe ⓕ *shtek·rü·be* turnip

Steinbuscher ⓜ *shtain·bu·sher* semi-hard, creamy cheese with a strong, slightly bitter flavour

Steinbutt ⓜ *shtain·but* turbot (flatfish)

Stelze ⓕ *shtel·tse* knuckle of pork

Sterz ⓜ *shterts* Austrian polenta

Stollen ⓜ *shto·len* spiced loaf with candied peel, traditionally eaten at Christmas

Strammer Max ⓜ *shtra·mer maks* sandwich with ham (or sausage or spiced minced pork), served with fried eggs & sometimes onions

Streichkäse ⓜ *shtraikh·kay·ze* any kind of soft cheese spread

Streuselkuchen ⓜ *shtroy·zel·koo·khen* coffee cake topped with a mixture of butter, sugar, flour & cinnamon

Strudel ⓜ *shtroo·del* loaf-shaped pastry filled with something sweet or savoury

Suppe ⓕ *zu·pe* soup

T

Tascherl ⓝ *ta·sherl* pastry turnover with meat, cheese or jam filling

Tatarenbrot ⓝ *ta·tah·ren·brawt* open sandwich topped with raw spiced minced beef

Teigwaren pl *taik·vah·ren* pasta

Thunfisch ⓜ *toon·fish* tuna

Thüringer ⓕ *tü·ring·er* long, thin, spiced sausage

Thymian ⓜ *tü·mi·ahn* thyme

Toast ⓜ *tawst* toast

Tomate ⓕ *to·mah·te* tomato

—nketchup ⓜ *to·mah·ten·ket·chap* tomato sauce

—nsuppe ⓕ *to·mah·ten·zu·pe* tomato soup

Topfen ⓜ *top·fen* curd cheese (Austria)
Törtchen ⓝ *tert·khen* small tart or cake
Torte ⓕ *tor·te* layer cake
Truthahn ⓜ *troot·hahn* turkey
Tunke ⓕ *tung·ke* sauce • gravy

V

Vollkornbrot ⓝ *fol·korn·brawt*
wholemeal bread
Voressen ⓝ *fawr·e·sen* meat stew

W

Wachtel ⓕ *vakh·tel* quail
Walnuss ⓕ *val·nus* walnut
Wecke ⓕ *ve·ke* bread roll (Austria &
southern Germany)
Weichkäse ⓜ *vaikh·kay·ze* soft cheese
Weinbergschnecken ⓕ pl
vain·berk·shne·ken snails
Weinkraut ⓝ *vain·krowt*
white cabbage, braised with apples &
simmered in wine
Weintraube ⓕ *vain·trow·be* grape
Weißbrot ⓝ *vais·brawt* white bread
Weißwurst ⓕ *vais·vurst* veal sausage,
found mainly in southern Germany
Westfälischer Schinken ⓜ
vest·fay·li·sher shing·ken
variety of cured & smoked ham
Wiener *vee·ner* in the Viennese style
— **Würstchen** ⓝ *vee·ner vürst·khen*
frankfurter (sausage)
— **Schnitzel** ⓝ *vee·ner shni·tsel*
crumbed veal

Wiezenbrot ⓝ *vai·tsen·brawt*
wheat bread
Wild ⓝ *vilt* game
— **braten** ⓜ *vilt·brah·ten*
roast venison
— **ente** ⓕ *vilt·en·te* wild duck
— **schwein** ⓝ *vilt·shvain* wild boar
Wilstermarschkäse ⓜ
vils·ter·marsh·kay·ze semi-hard cheese
Wurst ⓕ *vurst* sausage
Würstchen ⓝ *vürst·khen* small sausage
Wurstplatte ⓕ *vurst·pla·te* cold cuts

Z

Ziege ⓕ *tsee·ge* goat
Zimt ⓜ *tsimt* cinnamon
Zitrone ⓕ *tsi·traw·ne* lemon
Zucker ⓜ *tsu·ker* sugar
Zunge ⓕ *tsung·e* tongue
Zwetschge ⓕ *tsvetsh·ge* plum
— **ndatschi** ⓜ *tsvetsh·gen·dat·shi*
damson plum tart
Zwieback ⓜ *tsvee·bak* rusk
Zwiebel ⓕ *tsvee·bel* onion
— **fleisch** ⓝ *tsvee·bel·flaish*
beef sauteed with onion
— **kuchen** ⓜ *tsvee·bel·koo·khen*
onion quiche, often served with
Federweißer (new wine)
— **suppe** ⓕ *tsvee·bel·zu·pe*
onion soup
— **wurst** ⓕ *tsvee·bel·vurst*
liver & onion sausage
Zwischenrippenstück ⓝ
tsvi·shen·ri·pen·shtük rib eye steak

culinary reader

emergencies

notfälle

Help!	*Hilfe!*	hil·fe
Stop!	*Halt!*	halt
Go away!	*Gehen Sie weg!*	gay·en zee vek
Thief!	*Dieb!*	deeb
Fire!	*Feuer!*	foy·er
Watch out!	*Vorsicht!*	for·zikht

signs

Unfallstation	un·fal·sta·tsyawn	**Casualty**
Polizei	po·li·tsai	**Police**
Polizeirevier	po·li·tsai·re·veer	**Police Station**

It's an emergency!
Es ist ein Notfall! — es ist ain *nawt*·fal

There's been an accident.
Es gab einen Unfall. — es gahp *ai*·nen *un*·fal

Do you have a first-aid kit?
Haben Sie einen Erste-Hilfe-Kasten? — *hah*·ben zee *ai*·nen ayr·ste·*hil*·fe·ka·sten

Call the police!
Rufen Sie die Polizei! — *roo*·fen zee dee po·li·*tsai*

Call a doctor!
Rufen Sie einen Arzt! — *roo*·fen zee *ai*·nen artst

Call an ambulance!
Rufen Sie einen Krankenwagen! — *roo*·fen zee *ai*·nen *krang*·ken·vah·gen

Could you please help me/us?
Könnten Sie mir/ uns bitte helfen? — *kern*·ten zee meer/ uns *bi*·te *hel*·fen

Where are the toilets?
Wo ist die Toilette? — vo ist dee to·a·*le*·te

I have to use the telephone.
   Ich muss das Telefon   ikh mus das te·le·*fawn*
   benutzen.   be·*nu*·tsen

I'm lost.
   Ich habe mich verirrt.   ikh *hah*·be mikh fer·*irt*

police

polizei

Where's the police station?
   Wo ist das Polizeirevier?   vaw ist das po·li·*tsai*·re·veer

I want to report an offence.
   Ich möchte eine   ikh *merkh*·te *ai*·ne
   Straftat melden.   *shtrahf*·taht *mel*·den

It was him/her.
   Es war er/sie.   es vahr air/zee

My ... was/	*Man hat mir ...*	man hat meer ...
were stolen.	*gestohlen.*	ge·*shtaw*·len
I've lost my...	*Ich habe ... verloren.*	ikh *hah*·be ... fer·*law*·ren
backpack	*meinen Rucksack*	*mai*·nen *ruk*·zak
bags	*meine Reisetaschen*	*mai*·ne *rai*·ze·ta·shen
credit card	*meine Kreditkarte*	*mai*·ne kre·*deet*·karte
handbag	*meine Handtasche*	*mai*·ne *hant*·ta·she
jewellery	*meinen Schmuck*	*mai*·nen shmuk
money	*mein Geld*	main gelt
papers	*meine Papiere*	*mai*·ne pa·*pee*·re
passport	*meinen Pass*	*mai*·nen pas
purse	*mein Portemonnaie*	main port·mo·*nay*
wallet	*meine Brieftasche*	*mai*·ne *breef*·ta·she
He/She tried	*Er/Sie hat versucht,*	air/zee hat fer·*zookht*
to ... me.	*mich zu ...*	mikh tsoo ...
assault	*überfallen*	an·ge·*gri*·fen
rape	*vergewaltigen*	fer·ge·*val*·ti·gen
rob	*bestehlen*	be·*shtay*·len

I've been ...	*Ich bin ... worden.*	ikh bin ... *vor*·den
He/She	*Er/Sie ist ...*	air/zee ist ...
has been ...	*worden.*	*vor*·den
assaulted	*angegriffen*	*an*·ge·gri·fen
raped	*vergewaltigt*	fer·ge·*val*·tikht
robbed	*bestohlen*	be·*shtaw*·len

I have insurance.
Ich bin versichert. ikh bin fer·*zi*·khert

I apologise.
Entschuldigen Sie bitte. ent·*shul*·di·gen zee *bi*·te

I didn't realise I was doing anything wrong.
Ich war mir nicht bewusst, ikh vahr meer nikht be·*vust*
etwas Unrechtes getan et·vas *un*·rekh·tes ge·*tahn*
zu haben. tsoo *hah*·ben

I didn't do it.
Das habe ich nicht getan. das *hah*·be ikh nikht ge·*tahn*

I'm innocent.
Ich bin unschuldig. ikh bin *un*·shul·dikh

Can I call someone?
Kann ich jemanden kan ikh *yay*·man·den
anrufen? *an*·roo·fen

Can I call a lawyer?
Kann ich einen kan ikh *ai*·nen
Rechtsanwalt anrufen? *rekhts*·an·valt *an*·roo·fen

Can I have a lawyer who speaks English?
Kann ich einen Rechtsanwalt kan ikh *ai*·nen *rekhts*·an·valt
haben, der Englisch spricht? *hah*·ben dair *eng*·lish shprikht

Is there a fine we can pay to clear this?
Können wir eine Geldbuße *ker*·nen veer *ai*·ne *gelt*·boo·se
dafür bezahlen? da·*für* be·*tsah*·len

I want to	*Ich möchte*	ikh *merkh*·te
contact my ...	*mich mit ... in*	mikh mit ... in
	Verbindung setzen.	fer·*bin*·dung ze·tsen
consulate	*meinem Konsulat*	*mai*·nem kon·zu·*laht*
embassy	*meiner Botschaft*	*mai*·ner *bawt*·shaft

This drug is for personal use.
Diese Droge ist für meinen persönlichen Gebrauch.
dee·ze draw·ge ist für mai·nen per·zern·li·khen ge·browkh

I have a prescription for this drug.
Ich habe ein Rezept für dieses Medikament.
ikh hah·be ain re·tsept für dee·zes me·di·ka·ment

Can I have a copy, please?
Kann ich davon bitte eine Kopie bekommen?
kan ikh da·fon bi·te ai·ne kaw·pee be·ko·men

I (don't) understand.
Ich verstehe (nicht).
ikh fer·shtay·e (nikht)

I know my rights.
Ich kenne meine Rechte.
ikh ke·ne mai·ne rekh·te

What am I accused of?
Wessen werde ich beschuldigt?
ve·sen ver·de ikh be·shul·dikht

Where's the	*Wo ist der/die/das*	vaw ist dair/dee/das
nearest ...?	*nächste ...?* m/f/n	*naykhs*·te ...
chemist	*Apotheke* f	a·po·*tay*·ke
dentist	*Zahnarzt* m	*tsahn*·artst
doctor	*Arzt* m	artst
hospital	*Krankenhaus* n	*krang*·ken·hows
optometrist	*Augenoptiker* m	*ow*·gen·op·ti·ker

I need a doctor (who speaks English).
Ich brauche einen Arzt   ikh *brow*·khe *ai*·nen artst
(der Englisch spricht).   (dair *eng*·lish shprikht)

Could I see a female doctor?
Könnte ich von einer   *kern*·te ikh fon *ai*·ner
Ärztin behandelt werden?   *erts*·tin be·*han*·delt *ver*·den

Could the doctor come here?
Könnte der Arzt hierher   *kern*·te dair artst heer·*hair*
kommen?   *ko*·men

Is there a (night) chemist nearby?
Gibt es in der Nähe eine   gipt es in dair *nay*·e *ai*·ne
(Nacht)Apotheke?   (*nakht*·)a·po·*tay*·ke

I don't want a blood transfusion.
Ich möchte keine   ikh *merkh*·te *kai*·ne
Bluttransfusion.   *bloot*·trans·fu·zyawn

Please use a new syringe.
Bitte benutzen   *bi*·te be·*nu*·tsen
Sie eine neue Spritze.   zee *ai*·ne *noy*·e *shpri*·tse

I have my own syringe.
Ich habe meine   ikh *hah*·be *mai*·ne
eigene Spritze.   *ai*·ge·ne *shpri*·tse

I've been vaccinated for ...	*Ich bin gegen ... geimpft worden.*	ikh bin *gay*·gen ... ge·*impft* vor·den
He/She has been vaccinated for ...	*Er/Sie ist gegen ... geimpft worden.*	air/zee ist *gay*·gen ... ge·*impft* vor·den
... fever	*...Fieber*	...*fee*·ber
hepatitis A/B/C	*Hepatitis A/B/C*	he·pa·*tee*·tis ah/bay/tsay
tetanus	*Tätanus*	*tay*·ta·nus
typhoid	*Typhus*	*tü*·fus
I need new ...	*Ich brauche ...*	ikh *brow*·khe ...
contact lenses	*neue Kontaktlinsen*	*noy*·e kon·*takt*·lin·zen
glasses	*eine neue Brille*	*ai*·ne *noy*·e *bri*·le

I've run out of my medication.
Ich habe keine Medikamente mehr. — ikh *hah*·be *kai*·ne me·di·ka·*men*·te mair

My prescription is ...
Mein Rezept ist ... — main re·*tsept* ist ...

Can I have a receipt for my insurance?
Kann ich eine Quittung für meine Versicherung bekommen? — kan ikh *ai*·ne *kvi*·tung für *mai*·ne fer·*zi*·khe·rung be·*ko*·men

---

the doctor may say ...

What's the problem?
Was fehlt Ihnen? — vas faylt *ee*·nen

Where does it hurt?
Wo tut es weh? — vaw toot es vay

Do you have a temperature?
Haben Sie Fieber? — *hah*·ben zee *fee*·ber

How long have you been like this?
Seit wann haben Sie diese Beschwerden? — zait van *hah*·ben zee *dee*·ze be·*shver*·den

the doctor may say ...

Have you had this before?

Hatten Sie das	ha·ten zee das
schon einmal?	shawn ain·mahl

How long are you travelling for?

Wie lange dauert	vee lang·e dow·ert
Ihre Reise?	ee·re rai·ze

Are you on medication?

Nehmen Sie irgendwelche	nay·men zee ir·gent·vel·khe
Medikamente?	me·di·ka·men·te

Are you allergic to anything?

Sind Sie gegen bestimmte	zint zee gay·gen be·shtim·te
Stoffe allergisch?	shto·fe a·lair·gish

Do you ...?

drink	Trinken Sie?	tring·ken zee
smoke	Rauchen Sie?	row·khen zee
take drugs	Nehmen	nay·men
	Sie Drogen?	zee draw·gen

Are you sexually active?

Sind Sie sexuell aktiv?	zint zee zek·su·el ak·teef

Have you had unprotected sex?

Hatten Sie ungeschützten	ha·ten zee un·ge·shüts·ten
Geschlechtsverkehr?	ge·shlekhts·fer·kair

You need to be admitted to hospital.

Sie müssen in ein	zee mü·sen in ain
Krankenhaus	krang·ken·hows
eingewiesen werden.	ain·ge·vee·zen ver·den

You should have it checked when you go home.

Sie sollten es zu Hause	zee zol·ten es tsoo how·ze
untersuchen lassen.	un·ter·zoo·khen la·sen

You should return home for treatment.

Sie sollten nach Hause	zee zol·ten nahkh how·ze
fahren, um sich	fah·ren um zikh
behandeln zu lassen.	be·han·deln tsoo la·sen

symptoms & conditions

I'm sick.
Ich bin krank.   ikh bin krangk

My friend is sick.
Mein Freund/Meine   main froynt/*mai*·ne
Freundin ist krank. m/f   froyn·din ist krangk

It hurts here.
Es tut hier weh.   es toot heer vay

I've been vomiting.
Ich habe mich übergeben.   ikh *hah*·be mikh *ü*·ber·*gay*·ben

I can't sleep.
Ich kann nicht schlafen.   ikh kan nikht *shlah*·fen

I feel ...		
anxious	*Ich habe Ängste.*	ikh *hah*·be *engs*·te
better	*Ich fühle*	ikh *fü*·le
	mich besser.	mikh *be*·ser
depressed	*Ich bin deprimiert.*	ikh bin de·pri·*meert*
dizzy	*Mir ist*	meer ist
	schwindelig.	*shvin*·de·likh
hot and cold	*Mir ist*	meer ist
	abwechselnd	*ap*·vek·selnt
	heiß und kalt.	hais unt kalt
nauseous	*Mir ist übel.*	meer ist *ü*·bel
shivery	*Mich fröstelt.*	mikh *frers*·telt
strange	*Mir ist komisch.*	meer ist *kaw*·mish
weak	*Ich fühle mich*	ikh *fü*·le mikh
	schwach.	shvakh
worse	*Ich fühle mich*	ikh *fü*·le mikh
	schlechter.	*shlekh*·ter

I have (a) ...	*Ich habe ...*	ikh *hah*·be ...
diarrhoea	*Durchfall*	*durkh*·fal
fever	*Fieber*	*fee*·ber
headache	*Kopfschmerzen*	*kopf*·shmer·tsen
pain	*Schmerzen*	*shmer*·tsen

I've noticed a lump here.
Ich habe hier einen   ikh *hah*·be heer *ai*·nen
Knoten bemerkt.   *knaw*·ten be·*merkt*

I have an infection.
Ich habe eine Infektion.   ikh *hah*·be *ai*·ne in·fek·*tsyawn*

I have a rash.
Ich habe einen Ausschlag.   ikh *hah*·be *ai*·nen *ows*·shlahk

I've recently had ...
Ich hatte vor kurzem ...   ikh *ha*·te fawr *kur*·tsem ...

I'm on medication for ...
Ich nehme   ikh *nay*·me
Medikamente gegen ...   me·di·ka·*men*·te *gay*·gen ...

asthma	*Asthma* n	*ast*·ma
heart condition	*Herzbeschwerden* f	*herts*·be·shver·den
venereal disease	*Geschlechts-*	ge·*shlekhts*·
	krankheit f	krangk·hait

For more symptoms and conditions, see the **dictionary**.

women's health

gesundheit bei frauen

(I think) I'm pregnant.
(Ich glaube,) Ich bin   (ikh *glow*·be) ikh bin
schwanger.   *shvang*·er

I'm on the Pill.
Ich nehme die Pille.   ikh *nay*·me dee *pi*·le

I haven't had my period for ... weeks.
Ich habe seit ... Wochen   ikh *hah*·be zait ... *vo*·khen
meine Periode nicht gehabt.   *mai*·ne pe·ri·*aw*·de nikht ge·*hahpt*

I have period pain.
Ich habe Regelschmerzen.   ikh *hah*·be *ray*·gel·shmer·tsen

contraception	*Verhütungsmittel* n	fer·*hü*·tungks·mi·tel
pregnancy test	*Schwangerschafts-*	*shvang*·er·shafts·
	test m	test
the morning- after pill	*die Pille danach* f	dee *pi*·le da·*nahkh*

the doctor may say ...

Are you using contraception?
Benutzen Sie — be·*nu*·tsen zee
Verhütungsmittel? — fer·*hü*·tungks·mi·tel

Are you menstruating?
Haben Sie Ihre — hah·ben zee ee·re
Periode? — pe·ri·aw·de

Are you pregnant?
Sind Sie schwanger? — zint zee shvang·er

When did you last have your period?
Wann hatten Sie — van ha·ten zee
Ihre letzte Periode? — ee·re lets·te pe·ri·aw·de

You're pregnant.
Sie sind schwanger. — zee zint shvang·er

allergies

allergien

I have a skin allergy.
Ich habe eine Hautallergie. — ikh hah·be ai·ne howt·a·ler·gee

I'm allergic to ...	*Ich bin allergisch gegen ...*	ikh bin a·*lair*·gish gay·gen ...
antibiotics	*Antibiotika*	an·ti·bi·*aw*·ti·ka
anti-inflammatories	*entzündungs-hemmende Mittel*	en·*tsün*·dungks·he·men·de *mi*·tel
aspirin	*Aspirin*	as·pi·*reen*
bees	*Bienen*	*bee*·nen
codeine	*Kodein*	ko·de·*een*
penicillin	*Penizillin*	pe·ni·tsi·*leen*
pollen	*Pollen*	*po*·len

antihistamines	*Antihistamine* n pl	an·ti·his·ta·*mee*·ne
inhaler	*Inhalator* m	in·ha·*lah*·tor
injection	*Injektion* f	in·yek·*tsyawn*
sulphur-based drugs	*schwefel-basierte Arzneimittel* n pl	*shvay*·fel·ba·zeer·te arts·*nai*·mi·tel

For food-related allergies, see **special diets & allergies**, page 161.

parts of the body

My ... hurts.
*Mir tut der/die/
das ... weh.* m/f/n

meer toot dair/dee/
das ... vay

I can't move my ...
*Ich kann meinen/meine/
mein ... nicht bewegen.* m/f/n

ikh kan *mai*·nen/*mai*·ne/
main ... nikht be·*vay*·gen

I have a cramp in my ...
*Ich habe einen Krampf in
meinem/meiner/
meinem ...* m/f/n

ikh *hah*·be *ai*·nen krampf in
mai·nem/*mai*·ner/
mai·nem ...

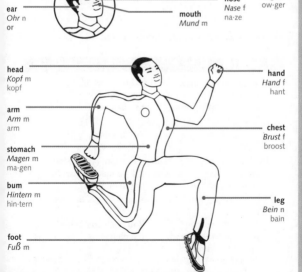

eye
Auge n
ow·ger

nose
Nase f
na·ze

ear
Ohr n
or

mouth
Mund m

head
Kopf m
kopf

hand
Hand f
hant

arm
Arm m
arm

chest
Brust f
broost

stomach
Magen m
ma·gen

bum
Hintern m
hin·tern

leg
Bein n
bain

foot
Fuß m

My ... is swollen.
Mein/Meine/Mein ... ist   main/*mai*·ne/main ... ist
geschwollen. m/f/n   ge·*shvo*·len

For other parts of the body, see the **dictionary**.

chemist

die apotheke

I need something for ...
Ich brauche etwas gegen ...   ikh *brow*·khe *et*·vas *gay*·gen ...

Do I need a prescription for ...?
Brauche ich für ... ein Rezept?   *brow*·khe ikh für ... ain re·*tsept*

How many times a day?
Wie oft am Tag?   vee oft am tahk

Will it make me drowsy?
Macht es müde?   makht es *mü*·de

For pharmaceutical items, see the **dictionary**.

---

listen for ...

hah·ben zee das shawn *ain*·mahl *ain*·ge·no·men
  Haben Sie das schon   **Have you taken**
  einmal eingenommen?   **this before?**

tsvai·mahl am tahk (tsum *e*·sen)
  Zweimal am Tag   **Twice a day**
  (zum Essen).   **(with food).**

zee *ker*·nen es in (*tsvan*·tsikh mi·*noo*·ten) *ap*·haw·len
  Sie können es in (zwanzig   **It'll be ready to pick up**
  Minuten) abholen.   **in (20 minutes).**

zee *mü*·sen dee me·di·ka·*men*·te bis tsum *en*·de
ain·nay·men
  Sie müssen die   **You must complete**
  Medikamente bis zum   **the course.**
  Ende einnehmen.

dentist

der zahnartz

I have a ...	Ich habe...	ikh hah·be ...
broken tooth	einen abgebrochenen Zahn	ai·nen ap·ge· bro·khe·nen tsahn
cavity	ein Loch	ain lokh
toothache	Zahnschmerzen	tsahn·shmer·tsen

I need ...	Ich brauche ...	ikh brow·khe ...
an anaesthetic	eine Betäubung	ai·ne be·toy·bung
a filling	eine Füllung	ai·ne fü·lung

listen for ...

bai·sen zee heer drowf
Beißen Sie hier drauf. — Bite down on this.

be·vay·gen zee zikh nikht
Bewegen Sie sich nicht. — Don't move.

bi·te dayn munt vait erf·nen
Bitte den Mund weit öffnen. — Open wide.

das toot fi·laikht ain bis·khen vay
Das tut vielleicht — This might hurt a little.
ein bisschen weh.

das toot gar nikht vay
Das tut gar nicht weh. — This won't hurt a bit.

ko·men zee tsu·rük ikh bin nokh nikht fer·tikh
Kommen Sie zurück, — Come back,
ich bin noch nicht fertig! — I haven't finished!

shpü·len
Spülen. — Rinse.

I've lost a filling.
Ich habe eine   ikh *hah*·be ai·ne
Füllung verloren.   *fü*·lung fer·*law*·ren

My dentures are broken.
Mein Gebiss ist zerbrochen.   main ge·*bis* ist tser·*bro*·khen

My orthodontic braces broke.
Meine Zahnspange ist   *mai*·ne *tsahn*·shpang·e ist
kaputt.   ka·*put*

My orthodontic braces fell off.
Meine Zahnspange   *mai*·ne *tsahn*·shpang·e
hat sich gelöst.   haht zikh ge·*lerst*

My gums hurt.
Das Zahnfleisch   das *tsahn*·flaish
tut mir weh.   toot meer vay

I don't want it extracted.
Ich will ihn nicht   ikh vil een nikht
ziehen lassen.   *tsee*·en *la*·sen

Ouch!
Au!   ow

As the climate change debate heats up, the matter of sustainability becomes an important part of the travel vernacular. In practical terms, this means assessing our impact on the environment and local cultures and economies – and acting to make that impact as positive as possible. Here are some basic phrases to get you on your way …

communication & cultural differences

I'd like to learn some words and phrases from the local dialect.
Ich möchte ein paar Wörter und Ausdrücke aus dem lokalen Dialekt lernen.
ikh *merkh*·te ain pahr *ver*·ter
unt *ows*·drü·ke ows daym
law·*kah*·len dee·a·*lekt lair*·nen

Would you like me to teach you some English?
Möchten Sie, dass ich Ihnen ein bisschen Englisch beibringe?
merkh·ten zee das ikh *ee*·nen
ain *bis*·khen *eng*·lish
bai·bring·e

Is this a local or national custom?
Ist dies ein lokaler oder landesweiter Brauch?
ist dees ain lo·*kah*·ler *aw*·der
lan·des·vai·ter browkh

I respect your customs.
Ich respektiere Ihre Bräuche.
ikh res·pek·*tee*·re ee·re *broy*·khe

community benefit & involvement

What sorts of issues is this community facing?
Welche Probleme gibt es hier?
vel·khe pro·*blay*·me
gipt es heer

aging population	*Überalterung* f	ü·ber·*al*·te·rung
climate change	*Klimawandel* m	*klee*·ma·van·del

globalisation	*Globalisierung* f	glaw·bah·li·*zee*·rung
integration of immigrants	*Integration* f *von Einwanderern*	in·tay·gra·*tsyawn* fon *ain*·van·de·rern
racism	*Rassismus* m	ra·*sis*·mus
unemployment	*Arbeitslosigkeit* f	ar·baits·law·zikh·kait

I'd like to volunteer my skills.
Ich möchte meine Mitarbeit   ikh *merkh*·te *mai*·ne *mit*·ar·bait
als Freiwilliger anbieten.   als *frai*·vi·li·ger *an*·bee·ten

Are there any volunteer programs available in the area?
Gibt es hier in der Region   gipt es heer in dair re·*gyawn*
irgendwelche   *ir*·gent·vel·khe
Freiwilligenprogramme?   *frai*·vi·li·gen·pro·gra·me

environment

Where can I recycle this?
Wo kann ich das recyceln?   vaw kan ikh das ri·*sai*·keln

transport

Can we get there by public transport?
Können wir mit öffentlichen   *ker*·nen veer mit *er*·fent·li·khen
Verkehrsmitteln dahin   fair·*kairs*·mi·teln dah·*hin*
kommen?   *ko*·men

Can we get there by bike?
Können wir mit dem   *ker*·nen veer mit daym
Fahrrad dahin kommen?   *fah*·raht dah·*hin ko*·men

I'd prefer to walk there.
Ich gehe lieber zu Fuß   ikh *gay*·e *lee*·ber tsoo foos
dahin.   dah·*hin*

accommodation

Are there any eco-hotels here?
Gibt es hier irgendwelche   gipt es heer *ir*·gent·vel·khe
Öko-Hotels?   *er*·kaw·ho·tels

I'd like to stay at a locally run hotel.

Ich möchte in einem Hotel   ikh *merkh*·te in *ai*·nem ho·*tel*
übernachten, das   ü·ber·*nakh*·ten das
Einheimischen gehört.   *ain*·hai·mi·shen ge·*hert*

Can I turn the air conditioning off and open the window?

Kann ich die Klimaanlage   kan ikh dee *klee*·ma·an·lah·ge
ausschalten und das   *ows*·shal·ten unt das
Fenster öffnen?   *fens*·ter *erf*·nen

There's no need to change my sheets/towels.

Sie brauchen meine   zee *brow*·khen *mai*·ne
Bettwäsche/Handtücher   *bet*·ve·she/*han*·tü·kher
nicht zu wechseln.   nikht tsoo *ve*·kseln

shopping

Where can I buy locally produced goods/souvenirs?

Wo kann ich örtlich   vaw kan ikh *ert*·likh
produzierte Waren/   pro·du·*tseer*·te *vah*·ren/
Andenken kaufen?   *an*·deng·ken *kow*·fen

Do you sell Fair Trade products?

Verkaufen Sie Produkte   fer·*kow*·fen zee pro·*duk*·te
aus fairem Handel?   ows *fair*·rem *han*·del

food

Can you tell me which traditional foods I should try?

Können Sie mir sagen,   *ker*·nen zee meer *zah*·gen
welche traditionellen   *vel*·khe tra·di·tsyo·*ne*·len
Speisen ich probieren sollte?   *shpai*·zen ikh pro·*bee*·ren *zol*·te

Do you sell ...?	*Verkaufen Sie ...?*	fer·*kow*·fen zee ...
locally produced	*örtlich*	*ert*·likh
food	*produzierte*	pro·du·*tseer*·te
	Lebensmittel	*lay*·bens·mi·tel
organic produce	*Bioprodukte*	*bee*·o·pro·duk·te

sightseeing

Does your company hire local guides?

Beschäftigt Ihre Firma   be·*shef*·tikht ee·re *fir*·ma
Führer von hier?   *fü*·rer fon heer

Does your company donate money to charity?

Spendet Ihre Firma Geld   *shpen*·det ee·re *fir*·ma gelt
für wohltätige Zwecke?   für *vawl*·tay·ti·ge *tsve*·ke

Does your company visit local businesses?

Besucht Ihre Firma   be·*zookht* ee·re *fir*·ma
örtliche Betriebe?   *ert*·li·khe be·*tree*·be

Are cultural tours available?

Gibt es Kulturtouren?   gipt es kul·*toor*·too·ren

Does the guide speak the local dialect?

Spricht der Führer den   shprikht dair *fü*·rer dayn
örtlichen Dialekt?   *ert*·li·khen dee·a·*lekt*

Bavarian	*Bairisch* n	*bai*·rish
Low German	*Plattdeutsch* n	*plat*·doytsh
Saxonian	*Sächsisch* n	*ze*·ksish
Swabian	*Schwäbisch* n	*shvay*·bish
Swiss German	*Schwyzerdütsch* n	*shvee*·tser·dütsh

Nouns in the dictionary, and adjectives affected by gender, have their gender indicated by ⓕ, ⓜ or ⓝ. If it's a plural noun, you'll also see pl. Where a word that could be either a noun or a verb has no gender indicated, it's a verb.

A

(to be) able können *ker*·nen
aboard *an Bord* an bort
abortion *Abtreibung* ⓕ ap·trai·bung
about *über* ü·ber
above *über* ü·ber
abroad *im Ausland* im ows·lant
accident *Unfall* ⓜ un·fal
accommodation *Unterkunft* ⓕ
  un·ter·kunft
accountant *Buchhalter(in)* ⓜ/ⓕ
  bookh·hal·ter/bookh·hal·te·rin
across (from) *gegenüber* gay·gen·ü·ber
across (to) *hinüber* hi·nü·ber
activist *Aktivist(in)* ⓜ/ⓕ
  ak·ti·vist/ak·ti·vis·tin
actor *Schauspieler(in)* ⓜ/ⓕ
  show·shpee·ler/show·shpee·le·rin
acupuncture *Akupunktur* ⓕ
  a·ku·pungk·toor
adaptor *Adapter* ⓜ a·dap·ter
addicted *abhängig* ap·heng·ikh
address *Adresse* ⓕ a·dre·se
administration *Verwaltung* ⓕ
  fer·val·tung
admire *bewundern* be·vun·dern
admission price *Eintrittspreis* ⓜ
  ain·trits·prais
admit (allow to enter) *einlassen*
  ain·la·sen
admit (accept as true) *zugeben*
  tsoo·gay·ben
adult *Erwachsene* ⓜ&ⓕ er·vak·se·ne
advertisement *Anzeige* ⓕ an·tsai·ge
advice *Rat* ⓜ raht
advise *raten* rah·ten
aerobics *Aerobics* pl e·ro·biks
aerogram *Aerogramm* ⓝ air·ro·gram
aeroplane *Flugzeug* ⓝ flook·tsoyk
(to be) afraid *Angst (haben)*
  angkst (hah·ben)
Africa *Afrika* ⓝ a·fri·kah

after *nach* nahk
(this) afternoon *(heute) Nachmittag* ⓜ
  (hoy·te) nahkh·mi·tahk
aftershave *Aftershave* ⓝ ahf·ter·shayf
again *wieder* vee·der
against *gegen* gay·gen
age *Alter* ⓝ al·ter
(three days) ago *vor (drei Tagen)*
  fawr (drai tah·gen)
agree *zustimmen* tsoo·shti·men
agriculture *Landwirtschaft* ⓕ
  lant·virt·shaft
ahead *vor uns* fawr uns
AIDS *AIDS* ⓝ aydz
air *Luft* ⓕ luft
airmail *Luftpost* ⓕ luft·post
air pollution *Luftverschmutzung* ⓕ
  luft·fer·shmu·tsung
air-conditioned *mit Klimaanlage* ⓕ
  mit klee·ma·an·lah·ge
airline *Fluglinie* ⓕ flook·lee·ni·e
airplane *Flugzeug* ⓝ flook·tsoyk
airport *Flughafen* ⓜ flook·hah·fen
airport tax *Flughafengebühr* ⓕ
  flook·hah·fen·ge·bür
airsickness *Luftkrankheit* ⓕ
  luft·krangk·hait
aisle *Gang* ⓜ gang
aisle seat *Platz* ⓜ *am Gang*
  plats am gang
alarm clock *Wecker* ⓜ ve·ker
alcohol *Alkohol* ⓜ al·ko·hawl
alcoholic *Alkoholiker(in)* ⓜ/ⓕ
  al·ko·haw·li·ker/al·ko·haw·li·ke·rin
alcoholic *alkoholisch* al·ko·haw·lish
all *alle* a·le
allergy *Allergie* ⓕ a·lair·gee
allow *erlauben* er·low·ben
almond *Mandel* ⓕ man·del
almost *fast* fast
alone *allein* a·lain
already *schon* shawn
also *auch* owkh

altar *Altar* ⓜ al·*tahr*
altitude *Höhe* ⓕ *her*·e
always *immer* i·mer
amateur *Amateur(in)* ⓜ/ⓕ
a·ma·*ter*/a·ma·*ter*·rin
amazing *erstaunlich* er·*shtown*·likh
ambassador *Botschafter(in)* ⓜ/ⓕ
bawt·shaf·ter/*bawt*·shaf·te·rin
ambulance *Krankenwagen* ⓜ
krang·ken·vah·gen
among *unter* un·ter
amount *Betrag* ⓜ be·*trahk*
anaesthetic *Betäubung* ⓕ be·*toy*·bung
anarchist *Anarchist(in)* ⓜ/ⓕ
a·nar·*khist*/a·nar·*khis*·tin
ancient *alt* alt
and *und* unt
angry *wütend* vü·tent
animal *Tier* ⓝ teer
ankle *Knöchel* ⓜ *kner*·khel
answer *Antwort* ⓕ *ant*·vort
answer *antworten* *ant*·vor·ten
ant *Ameise* ⓕ ah·mai·ze
antibiotics *Antibiotika* ⓝ pl
an·ti·bi·*aw*·ti·ka
antinuclear *Anti-Atom-* an·ti·a·*tawm*·
antique *Antiquität* ⓕ an·ti·kvi·*tayt*
antiseptic *Antiseptikum* ⓝ
an·ti·*zep*·ti·kum
any *irgendein* ir·gent·*ain*
anything *(irgend)etwas* (ir·gent·)et·vas
anywhere *irgendwo* ir·gent·*vaw*
apart from *(besides)* *außer* ow·ser
apartment *Wohnung* ⓕ *vaw*·nung
appendix *Blinddarm* ⓜ *blint*·darm
apple *Apfel* ⓜ ap·fel
appointment *Termin* ⓜ ter·*meen*
apprentice *Auszubildende* ⓜ&ⓕ
ows·tsu·bil·den·de
approximately *ungefähr* un·ge·*fair*
apricot *Aprikose* ⓕ a·pri·*kaw*·ze
archaeological *archäologisch*
ar·khe·o·*law*·gish
architecture *Architektur* ⓕ ar·khi·tek·*toor*
area code *Vorwahl* ⓕ *fawr*·vahl
argue *streiten* *shtrai*·ten
arm *Arm* ⓜ arm
aromatherapy *Aromatheraphie* ⓕ
a·*raw*·ma·tay·ra·pee

arrest *Verhaftung* ⓕ fer·*haf*·tung
arrivals *Ankunft* ⓕ *an*·kunft
arrive *ankommen* *an*·ko·men
art *Kunst* ⓕ kunst
art collection *Kunstsammlung* ⓕ
kunst·zam·lung
art gallery *Kunstgalerie* ⓕ
kunst·ga·le·ree
artist *Künstler(in)* ⓜ/ⓕ
künst·ler/*künst*·le·rin
arts & crafts *Kunstgewerbe* ⓝ
kunst·ge·ver·be
as far as *bis zu* bis tsoo
ashtray *Aschenbecher* ⓜ
a·shen·be·kher
Asia *Asien* ⓝ ah·zi·en
ask a question *eine Frage stellen*
ai·ne frah·ge shte·len
ask (for something) *um etwas bitten*
um et·vas bi·ten
asleep *schlafen* *shlah*·fen
asparagus *Spargel* ⓜ *shpar*·gel
aspirin *Kopfschmerztablette* ⓕ
kopf·shmerts·ta·ble·te
asthma *Asthma* ⓝ ast·ma
asylum seeker *Asylant(in)* ⓜ/ⓕ
a·zü·*lant*/a·zü·*lan*·tin
at *in* • *an* • *auf* • *bei* • *zu*
in • an • owf • bai • tsoo
athletics *Leichtathletik* ⓕ
laikht·at·lay·tik
atmosphere *Atmosphäre* ⓕ
at·mos·*fair*·re
attic *Dachboden* ⓜ *dakh*·baw·den
aubergine *Aubergine* ⓕ aw·ber·*zhee*·ne
aunt *Tante* ⓕ tan·te
Australia *Australien* ⓝ ows·*trah*·li·en
Austria *Österreich* ⓝ *ers*·ter·raikh
author *Autor(in)* ⓜ/ⓕ
ow·tor/ow·taw·rin
automatic *automatisch* ow·to·*mah*·tish
automatic teller machine (ATM)
Geldautomat ⓜ *gelt*·ow·to·maht
autumn *Herbst* ⓜ herpst
avalanche *Lawine* ⓕ la·vee·ne
avenue *Allee* ⓕ a·lay
avocado *Avokado* ⓕ a·vo·kah·do
axe *Axt* ⓕ akst

B

baby *Baby* ⓝ bay·bi
baby food *Babynahrung* ⓕ
　bay·bi·nah·rung
baby powder *Babypuder* ⓜ
　bay·bi·poo·der
babysitter *Babysitter* ⓜ bay·bi·si·ter
back (body) *Rücken* ⓜ rü·ken
back (return) *zurück* tsu·rük
backpack *Rucksack* ⓜ ruk·zak
bacon *Frühstücksspeck* ⓜ
　frü·shtüks·shpek
bad *schlecht* shlekht
badger *Dachs* ⓜ daks
bag *Tasche* ⓕ ta·she
baggage *Gepäck* ⓝ ge·pek
baggage allowance *Freigepäck* ⓝ
　frai·ge·pek
baggage claim *Gepäckausgabe* ⓕ
　ge·pek·ows·gah·be
bait *Köder* ⓜ ker·der
bakery *Bäckerei* ⓕ be·ke·rai
balance (account) *Kontostand* ⓜ
　kon·to·shtant
balcony *Balkon* ⓜ bal·kawn
ball *Ball* ⓜ bal
ballet *Ballett* ⓝ ba·let
banana *Banane* ⓕ ba·nah·ne
band (music) *Band* ⓕ bent
bandage *Verband* ⓜ fer·bant
Band-aids *Pflaster* ⓝ pflas·ter
bank *Bank* ⓕ bangk
bank account *Bankkonto* ⓝ
　bangk·kon·to
bankdraft *Bankauszug* ⓜ
　bangk·ows·tsook
banknote *Geldschein* ⓜ gelt·shain
baptism *Taufe* ⓕ tow·fe
bar *Lokal* ⓝ lo·kahl
baseball *Baseball* ⓜ bays·bawl
basket *Korb* ⓜ korp
bath *Bad* ⓝ baht
bath towel *Badetuch* ⓝ bah·de·tookh
bathing suit *Badeanzug* ⓜ
　bah·de·an·tsook
bathroom *Badezimmer* ⓝ
　bah·de·tsi·mer

battery *Batterie* ⓕ ba·te·ree
bay *Bucht* ⓕ bukht
be *sein* zain
beach *Strand* ⓜ shtrant
bean *Bohne* ⓕ baw·ne
bear *Bär* ⓜ bair
beautiful *schön* shern
beauty salon *Schönheitssalon* ⓜ
　shern·haits·za·long
because *weil* vail
because of *wegen* vay·gen
bed *Bett* ⓝ bet
bed & breakfast *Pension* ⓕ
　pahng·zyawn
bedding *Bettzeug* ⓝ bet·tsoyk
bedroom *Schlafzimmer* ⓝ
　shlahf·tsi·mer
bee *Biene* ⓕ bee·ne
beef *Rindfleisch* ⓝ rint·flaish
beer *Bier* ⓝ beer
beetroot *rote Beete* ⓕ raw·te bay·te
before *vor* fawr
beggar *Bettler(in)* ⓜ/ⓕ bet·ler/bet·le·rin
begin *beginnen* be·gi·nen
behind *hinter* hin·ter
Belgium *Belgien* ⓝ bel·gi·en
below *unter* un·ter
belt *Gürtel* ⓜ gür·tel
beside *neben* nay·ben
best *beste* bes·te
bet *Wette* ⓕ ve·te
better *besser* be·ser
between *zwischen* tsvi·shen
bible *Bibel* ⓕ bee·bel
bicycle *Fahrrad* ⓝ fahr·raht
big *groß* graws
bike *Fahrrad* ⓕ fahr·raht
bike chain *Fahrradkette* ⓕ fahr·raht·ke·te
bike path *Radweg* ⓜ raht·vayk
bill (account) *Rechnung* ⓕ rekh·nung
bin (rubbish) *Mülleimer* ⓜ mül·ai·mer
binoculars *Fernglas* ⓝ fern·glahs
bird *Vogel* ⓜ faw·gel
birth certificate *Geburtsurkunde* ⓕ
　ge·burts·oor·kun·de
birthday *Geburtstag* ⓜ ge·burts·tahk
biscuit *Keks* ⓜ kayks
bite (dog) *Biss* ⓜ bis
bite (insect) *Stich* ⓜ shtikh

bitter *bitter* bi·ter
black *schwarz* shvarts
B&W (film) *schwarzweiß* shvarts·vais
blanket *Decke* ① de·ke
bless *segnen* zayg·nen
blind *blind* blint
blister *Blase* ① blah·ze
blocked *blockiert* blo·keert
blood *Blut* ⓝ bloot
blood group *Blutgruppe* ① bloot·gru·pe
blood pressure *Blutdruck* ⓜ bloot·druk
blood test *Bluttest* ⓜ bloot·test
blue *blau* blow
boar *Wildschwein* ⓝ vilt·shvain
board *Brett* ⓝ bret
board (plane, ship) *besteigen*
　be·shtai·gen
boarding house *Pension* ①
　pahng·zyawn
boarding pass *Bordkarte* ① bort·kar·te
boat *Boot* ⓝ bawt
body *Körper* ⓜ ker·per
bone *Knochen* ⓜ kno·khen
book *Buch* ⓝ bookh
book (reserve) *buchen* boo·khen
booked out *ausgebucht* ows·ge·bookht
bookshop *Buchhandlung* ①
　bookh·hand·lung
boot (trunk) *Kofferraum* ⓜ ko·fer·rowm
boot (footwear) *Stiefel* ⓜ shtee·fel
border *Grenze* ① gren·tse
bored *gelangweilt* ge·lang·vailt
boring *langweilig* lang·vai·likh
borrow *(aus)leihen* (ows)·lai·en
boss *Chef(in)* ⓜ/① shef/she·fin
botanic garden *Botanischer Garten* ⓜ
　bo·tah·ni·sher gar·ten
both *beide* bai·de
bottle *Flasche* ① fla·she
bottle opener *Flaschenöffner* ⓜ
　fla·shen·erf·ner
at the bottom *unten* un·ten
bouncer (doorman) *Türsteher* ⓜ
　tür·shtay·er
bowl *Schüssel* ① shü·sel
box *Karton* ⓜ kar·tong
boxer shorts *Shorts* pl shorts
boxing *Boxen* ⓝ bok·sen
boy *Junge* ⓜ yung·e

boyfriend *Freund* ⓜ froynt
bra *BH* ⓜ bay·hah
Braille *Blindenschrift* ① blin·den·shrift
brake fluid *Bremsflüssigkeit* ①
　brems·flü·sikh·kait
brakes *Bremsen* ① pl brem·zen
brandy *Weinbrand* ⓜ vain·brant
brave *mutig* moo·tikh
bread *Brot* ⓝ brawt
bread roll *Brötchen* ⓝ brert·khen
break (zer)brechen (tser·)bre·khen
break down *eine Panne haben*
　ai·ne pa·ne hah·ben
breakdown service *Abschleppdienst* ⓜ
　ap·shlep·deenst
breakfast *Frühstück* ⓝ frü·shtük
breast *Brust* ① brust
breathe *atmen* aht·men
brewery *Brauerei* ① brow·e·rai
bribe *bestechen* be·shte·khen
bricklayer *Maurer(in)* ⓜ/①
　mow·rer/mow·re·rin
bridge *Brücke* ① brü·ke
bridle path *Reitweg* ⓜ rait·vayk
briefcase *Aktentasche* ① ak·ten·ta·she
brilliant *brillant* bril·yant
bring *bringen* bring·en
broccoli *Brokkoli* ⓜ pl bro·ko·li
brochure *Broschüre* ① bro·shü·re
broken *kaputt* ka·put
bronchitis *Bronchitis* ① bron·khee·tis
brother *Bruder* ⓜ broo·der
brown *braun* brown
bruise *Schramme* ① shra·me
Brussels sprouts *Rosenkohl* ⓜ
　raw·zen·kawl
bucket *Eimer* ⓜ ai·mer
Buddhist *Buddhist(in)* ⓜ/①
　bu·dist/bu·dis·tin
buffet *Buffet* ⓝ bü·fay
bug (animal) *Insekt* ⓝ in·zekt
build *bauen* bow·en
building *Gebäude* ⓝ ge·boy·de
bumbag *Hüfttasche* ① hüft·ta·she
burn *(ver)brennen* (fer·)bre·nen
bus (city) *Bus* ⓜ bus
bus (intercity) *Fernbus* ⓜ fern·bus
bus station *Busbahnhof* ⓜ
　bus·bahn·hawf
bus stop *Bushaltestelle* ①
　bus·hal·te·shte·le

business Geschäft ⓝ ge·sheft
business class Business Class ⓕ
bi·zi·nes klahs
business person
Geschäftsmann/Geschäftsfrau ⓜ/ⓕ
ge·shefts·man/ge·shefts·frow
business trip Geschäftsreise ⓕ
ge·shefts·rai·ze
busker Straßenmusiker(in) ⓜ/ⓕ
shtrah·sen·moo·zi·ker/
shtrah·sen·moo·zi·ke·rin
busy (person) beschäftigt be·shef·tikht
busy (phone) besetzt be·zetst
but aber ah·ber
butcher's shop Metzgerei ⓕ
mets·ge·rai
butter Butter ⓕ bu·ter
butterfly Schmetterling ⓜ shme·ter·ling
button Knopf ⓝ knopf
buy kaufen kow·fen

C

cabbage Kohl ⓜ kawl
cable Kabel ⓝ kah·bel
cable car Seilbahn ⓕ zail·bahn
cafe Café ⓝ ka·fay
cake Kuchen ⓜ koo·khen
cake shop Konditorei ⓕ kon·dee·to·rai
calculator Taschenrechner ⓜ
ta·shen·rekh·ner
calendar Kalender ⓜ ka·len·der
camera Kamera ⓕ ka·me·ra
camp zelten tsel·ten
camping ground Campingplatz ⓜ
kem·ping·plats
camping stove Kocher ⓜ ko·kher
camp site Zeltplatz ⓜ tselt·plats
can (be able) können ker·nen
can (have permission) können ker·nen
can (tin) Dose ⓕ daw·ze
can opener Dosenöffner ⓜ
daw·zen·erf·ner
Canada Kanada ⓝ ka·na·dah
canary Kanarienvogel ⓜ
ka·nah·ri·en·faw·gel
cancel stornieren shtor·nee·ren
cancer Krebs ⓜ krayps
candle Kerze ⓕ ker·tse

candy Bonbon ⓜ bong·bong
cantaloupe Beutelmelone ⓕ
boy·tel·me·law·ne
canteen Kantine ⓕ kan·tee·ne
cape (offshore) Kap ⓝ kap
capitalism Kapitalismus ⓜ
ka·pi·ta·lis·mus
capsicum Paprika ⓕ pap·ri·kah
car Auto ⓝ ow·to
car hire Autoverleih ⓜ ow·to·fer·lai
car owner's title (document)
Fahrzeugpapiere ⓝ pl
fahr·tsoyk·pa·pee·re
car registration (PKW-)Zulassung ⓕ
(pay·kah·vay·)tsoo·la·sung
caravan Wohnwagen ⓜ vawn·vah·gen
carburettor Vergaser ⓜ fer·gah·zer
cards Karten ⓕ pl kar·ten
care (for someone) sich kümmern um
zikh kü·mern um
careful vorsichtig fawr·zikh·tikh
caring liebevoll lee·be·fol
carpark Parkplatz ⓜ park·plats
carpenter Schreiner(in) ⓜ/ⓕ
shrai·ner/shrai·ne·rin
carriage (train) Wagen ⓜ vah·gen
carrot Mohrrübe ⓕ mawr·rü·be
carry tragen trah·gen
carton Karton ⓜ kar·tong
carton (milk) Tüte ⓕ tü·te
cash Bargeld ⓝ bahr·gelt
cash (a cheque) (einen Scheck)
einlösen (ai·nen shek) ain·ler·zen
cash register Kasse ⓕ ka·se
cashew Cashewnuss ⓕ kesh·yoo·nus
cashier Kassierer(in) ⓜ/ⓕ
ka·see·rer/ka·see·re·rin
casino Kasino ⓝ ka·zee·no
cassette Kassette ⓕ ka·se·te
castle Burg ⓕ burk
casual work Gelegenheitsarbeit ⓕ
ge·lay·gen·haits·ar·bait
cat Katze ⓕ ka·tse
cathedral Dom ⓜ dawm
Catholic Katholik(in) ⓜ/ⓕ
ka·to·leek/ka·to·lee·kin
cauliflower Blumenkohl ⓜ
bloo·men·kawl
cave Höhle ⓕ her·le

caviar *Kaviar* ⓜ *kah·vi·ahr*
CD *CD* ① *tsay·day*
celebration *Feier* ① *fai·er*
cellar *Keller* ⓜ *ke·ler*
cemetery *Friedhof* ⓜ *freet·hawf*
centigrade *Celsius* ⓜ *tsel·zi·us*
centimetre *Zentimeter* ⓜ
  tsen·ti·may·ter
central heating *Zentralheizung* ①
  tsen·*trahl*·hai·tsung
centre *Zentrum* ⓝ *tsen·trum*
ceramic *Keramik* ① *ke·rah·mik*
cereal *Frühstücksflocke* ①
  frü·shtüks·flo·ke
certificate *Zertifikat* ⓝ *tser·ti·fi·kaht*
chain *Kette* ① *ke·te*
chair *Stuhl* ⓜ *shtool*
chairlift (skiing) *Sessellift* ⓜ *ze·se·lift*
championships *Meisterschaften* ① pl
  mais·ter·shaf·ten
chance *Zufall* ⓜ *tsoo·fal*
change (coins) *Wechselgeld* ⓝ
  vek·sel·gelt
change (money) *wechseln* vek·seln
change (trains) *umsteigen* um·shtai·gen
changing room *Umkleideraum* ⓜ
  um·klai·de·rowm
chapel *Kapelle* ① ka·pe·le
charming *charmant* shar·mant
chat up *anbaggern* an·ba·gern
cheap *billig* bi·likh
cheat *Betrüger(in)* ⓜ/①
  be·trü·ger/be·trü·ge·rin
check (banking) *Scheck* ⓜ shek
check (bill) *Rechnung* ① rekh·nung
check *prüfen* prü·fen
check-in (desk) *Abfertigungsschalter* ⓜ
  ap·fer·ti·gungks·shal·ter
checkpoint *Kontrollstelle* ①
  kon·*trol*·shte·le
cheese *Käse* ⓜ kay·ze
chef *Koch/Köchin* ⓜ/① kokh/ker·khin
chemist *Apotheke* ① a·po·tay·ke
cheque (banking) *Scheck* ⓜ shek
chess *Schach* ⓝ shakh
chest *Brustkorb* ⓜ brust·korp
chewing gum *Kaugummi* ⓝ kow·gu·mi
chicken *Huhn* ⓝ hoon
chicken breast *Hühnerbrust* ①
  hü·ner·brust

chicken drumstick *Hähnchenschenkel* ⓜ
  hayn·khen·sheng·kel
chickpea *Kichererbse* ① ki·kher·erp·se
child *Kind* ⓝ kint
child seat *Kindersitz* ⓜ kin·der·zits
childminding *Kinderbetreuung* ①
  kin·der·be·troy·ung
children *Kinder* ⓝ pl kin·der
chiropractor *Chiropraktiker* ⓜ
  khee·ro·prak·ti·ker
chocolate *Schokolade* ① sho·ko·lah·de
choose *(aus)wählen* (ows·)vay·len
christening *Taufe* ① tow·fe
Christian *Christ(in)* ⓜ/① krist/kris·tin
Christian name *Vorname* ⓜ
  fawr·nah·me
Christmas *Weihnachten* ⓝ vai·nakh·ten
Christmas Day (erster)
  Weihnachtsfeiertag ⓜ (ers·ter)
  vai·nakhts·fai·er·tahk
Christmas Eve *Heiligabend* ⓜ
  hai·likh·ah·bent
Christmas tree *Weihnachtsbaum* ⓜ
  vai·nakhts·bowm
church *Kirche* ① kir·khe
cider *Apfelmost* ⓜ ap·fel·most
cigar *Zigarre* ① tsi·ga·re
cigarette *Zigarette* ① tsi·ga·re·te
cigarette lighter *Feuerzeug* ⓝ
  foy·er·tsoyk
cinema *Kino* ⓝ kee·no
circus *Zirkus* ⓜ tsir·kus
citizenship *Staatsbürgerschaft* ①
  shtahts·bür·ger·shaft
city *Stadt* ① shtat
city centre *Innenstadt* ① i·nen·shtat
civil rights *Bürgerrechte* ⓝ pl
  bür·ger·rekh·te
civil servant *Beamte/Beamtin* ⓜ/①
  be·am·te/be·am·tin
class *Klasse* ① kla·se
classical *klassisch* kla·sish
cleaning *Reinigung* ① rai·ni·gung
client *Kunde/Kundin* ⓜ/①
  kun·de/kun·din
cliff *Klippe* ① kli·pe
climate *Klima* ⓝ klee·ma
climb *klettern* kle·tern

cloak *Mantel* ⓜ man·tel
cloakroom *Garderobe* ① gar·draw·be
clock *Uhr* ① oor
close (shut) *schließen* shlee·sen
close (nearby) *nahe* nah·e
closed *geschlossen* ge·shlo·sen
clothesline *Wäscheleine* ①
ve·she·lai·ne
clothing *Kleidung* ① klai·dung
clothing store *Bekleidungsgeschäft* ⓝ
be·klai·dungks·ge·sheft
cloud *Wolke* ① vol·ke
cloudy *wolkig* vol·kikh
clove (spice) *Gewürznelke* ①
ge·vürts·nel·ke
clove (of garlic) *Zehe* ① tsay·e
clutch (car) *Kupplung* ① kup·lung
coach (bus) *Bus* ⓜ bus
coach (sport) *Trainer(in)* ⓜ/①
tray·ner/tray·ne·rin
coast *Küste* ① küs·te
coat *Mantel* ⓜ man·tel
cocaine *Kokain* ⓝ ko·ka·een
cockroach *Kakerlake* ① kah·ker·lah·ke
cocoa *Kakao* ⓝ ka·kow
coffee *Kaffee* ⓜ ka·fay
coins *Münzen* ① pl mün·tsen
cold *kalt* kalt
have a cold *erkältet sein* er·kel·tet zain
colleague *Kollege/Kollegin* ⓜ/①
ko·lay·ge/ko·lay·gin
collect call *R-Gespräch* ⓝ
air·ge·shpraykh
college *College* ⓝ ko·lidzh
colour *Farbe* ① far·be
comb *Kamm* ⓜ kam
come *kommen* ko·men
comedy *Komödie* ① ko·mer·di·e
comfortable *bequem* be·kvaym
communion *Kommunion* ①
ko·mun·yawn
companion *Begleiter(in)* ⓜ/①
be·glai·ter/be·glai·te·rin
company *Firma* ① fir·ma
compass *Kompass* ⓜ kom·pas
complain *sich beschweren*
zikh be·shvair·ren
computer *Computer* ⓜ kom·pyoo·ter
computer game *Computerspiel* ⓝ
kom·pyoo·ter·shpeel

concert *Konzert* ⓝ kon·tsert
concert hall *Konzerthalle* ①
kon·tsert·ha·le
conditioner *Spülung* ① shpü·lung
condom *Kondom* ⓝ kon·dawm
conductor *Schaffner(in)* ⓜ/①
shaf·ner/shaf·ne·rin
confession (religious) *Beichte* ①
baikh·te
confirm (a booking) *bestätigen*
be·shtay·ti·gen
connection *Verbindung* ① fer·bin·dung
conservative *konservativ*
kon·zer·va·teef
constipation *Verstopfung* ①
fer·shtop·fung
consulate *Konsulat* ⓝ kon·zu·laht
contact lenses *Kontaktlinsen* ① pl
kon·takt·lin·zen
contraceptives *Verhütungsmittel* ⓝ
fer·hü·tungks·mi·tel
contract *Vertrag* ⓜ fer·trahk
convenience store *Kiosk* ⓜ kee·osk
convent *Kloster* ⓝ klaws·ter
cook *Koch/Köchin* ⓜ/① kokh/ker·khin
cook *kochen* ko·khen
cookie *Keks* ⓜ kayks
corner *Ecke* ① e·ke
cornflakes *Cornflakes* pl korn·flayks
corrupt *korrupt* ko·rupt
cost *kosten* kos·ten
cottage cheese *Hüttenkäse* ⓜ
hü·ten·kay·ze
cotton *Baumwolle* ① bowm·vo·le
cotton balls *Watte-Pads* pl va·te·pedz
cough *husten* hoos·ten
cough medicine *Hustensaft* ⓜ
hoos·ten·zaft
count *zählen* tsay·len
counter (at bar) *Theke* ① tay·ke
country *Land* ⓝ lant
countryside *Land* ⓝ lant
coupon *Coupon* ⓜ ku·pong
courgette *Zucchini* ① tsu·kee·ni
court (legal) *Gericht* ⓝ ge·rikht
court (tennis) *Platz* ⓜ plats
couscous *Couscous* ⓝ kus·kus
cousin *Cousin(e)* ⓜ/① ku·zen/ku·zee·ne

cover charge *Eintrittsgeld* ⑩
ain·trits·gelt

cow *Kuh* ① koo

cracker *Cracker* ⑩ kre·ker

crafts *Handwerk* ⑩ hant·verk

cramp *Krampf* ⑩ krampf

crash *Zusammenstoß* ⑩
tsu·za·men·staws

crazy *verrückt* fe·rükt

cream *Sahne* ① zah·ne

cream cheese *Frischkäse* ⑩ frish·kay·ze

creche *Kinderkrippe* ① kin·der·kri·pe

credit card *Kreditkarte* ①
kre·deet·kar·te

cricket *Cricket* ⑩ kri·ket

crop *Feldfrucht* ① felt·frukht

cross (religious) *Kreuz* ⑩ kroyts

cross (angry) *wütend* vü·tent

crowded *überfüllt* ü·ber·fült

cuckoo clock *Kuckucksuhr* ①
ku·kuks·oor

cucumber *Gurke* ① gur·ke

cup *Tasse* ① ta·se

cupboard *Schrank* ⑩ shrangk

currency *Währung* ① vair·rung

currency exchange *Geldwechsel* ⑩
gelt·vek·sel

current (electricity) *Strom* ⑩ shtrawm

current affairs *Aktuelles* ⑩ ak·tu·e·les

curry (powder) *Curry(pulver)* ⑩
ker·ri(·pul·ver)

customs *Zoll* ⑩ tsol

cut *schneiden* shnai·den

cutlery *Besteck* ⑩ be·shtek

CV *Lebenslauf* ⑩ lay·bens·lowf

cycle *radfahren* raht·fah·ren

cycling *Radsport* ⑩ raht·shport

cyclist *Radfahrer(in)* ⑩/①
raht·fah·rer/raht·fah·re·rin

cystitis *Blasenentzündung* ①
blah·zen·en·tsün·dung

D

dad *Papa* ⑩ pa·pa

daily *täglich* tayk·likh

dairy products *Milchprodukte* ⑩ pl
milkh·pro·duk·te

damp *feucht* foykht

dance *tanzen* tan·tsen

dangerous *gefährlich* ge·fair·likh

dark *dunkel* dung·kel

date (a person)
mit jemandem ausgehen
mit yay·man·dem ows·gay·en

date (appointment) *Verabredung* ①
fer·ap·ray·dung

date (day) *Datum* ⑩ dah·tum

date of birth *Geburtsdatum* ⑩
ge·burts·dah·tum

daughter *Tochter* ① tokh·ter

daughter-in-law *Schwiegertochter* ①
shvee·ger·tokh·ter

dawn *Dämmerung* ① de·me·rung

day *Tag* ⑩ tahk

day after tomorrow *übermorgen*
ü·ber·mor·gen

day before yesterday *vorgestern*
fawr·ges·tern

dead *tot* tawt

deaf *taub* towp

deal (cards) *austeilen* ows·tai·len

decide *entscheiden* ent·shai·den

deep *tief* teef

deforestation *Abholzung* ① ap·hol·tsung

degree *Grad* ⑩ graht

delay *Verspätung* ① fer·shpay·tung

delicatessen *Feinkostgeschäft* ⑩
fain·kost·ge·sheft

delicious *köstlich* kerst·likh

deliver (aus)liefern (ows·)lee·fern

demand *Forderung* ① for·de·rung

democracy *Demokratie* ①
de·mo·kra·tee

demonstration *Demonstration* ①
de·mons·tra·tsyawn

Denmark *Dänemark* ⑩ dair·ne·mark

dental floss *Zahnseide* ① tsahn·zai·de

dentist *Zahnarzt/Zahnärztin* ⑩/①
tsahn·artst/tsahn·erts·tin

deodorant *Deo* ⑩ day·o

depart (leave) *abfahren* ap·fah·ren

department store *Warenhaus* ⑩
vah·ren·hows

departure *Abfahrt* ① ap·fahrt

deposit *Anzahlung* ① an·tsah·lung

descendant *Nachkomme* ⑩
nahkh·ko·me

desert *Wüste* ① vüs·te
design *entwerfen* ent·ver·fen
destination *(Reise)Ziel* ① (rai·ze·)tseel
detail *Detail* ① de·tai
diabetes *Diabetis* ① di·a·bay·tis
dial tone *Wählton* ⑩ vayl·tawn
diaper *Windel* ① vin·del
diaphragm (body) *Zwerchfell* ①
   tsverkh·fel
diarrhoea *Durchfall* ⑩ durkh·fal
diary (for appointments)
   Terminkalender ⑩
   ter·meen·ka·len·der
diary (record of events) *Tagebuch* ①
   tah·ge·bookh
dice (die) *Würfel* ⑩ vür·fel
dictionary *Wörterbuch* ① ver·ter·bookh
die *sterben* shter·ben
diet *Diät* ① di·ayt
different *andere* an·de·re
difficult *schwierig* shvee·rikh
dining car *Speisewagen* ⑩
   shpai·ze·vah·gen
dinner *Abendessen* ① ah·bent·e·sen
direct *direkt* di·rekt
direct-dial *Durchwahl* ① durkh·vahl
director *Regisseur(in)* ⑩/①
   re·zhi·ser/re·zhi·ser·rin
directory enquiries *Telefonauskunft* ①
   te·le·fawn·ows·kunft
dirty *schmutzig* shmu·tsikh
disabled *behindert* be·hin·dert
disco *Disko(thek)* ① dis·ko(·tayk)
discount *Rabatt* ⑩ ra·bat
discrimination *Diskriminierung* ①
   dis·kri·mi·nee·rung
disease *Krankheit* ① krangk·hait
disk (computer) *Diskette* ① dis·ke·te
diving *Tauchen* ⑩ tow·khen
dizzy *schwindelig* shvin·de·likh
do *tun* toon
doctor (medical) *Arzt/Ärztin* ⑩/①
   artst/erts·tin
doctor (title) *Doktor(in)* ⑩/①
   dok·tor/dok·taw·rin
documentary *Dokumentation* ①
   do·ku·men·ta·tsyawn
dog *Hund* ⑩ hunt

dole (unemployment benefit)
   Arbeitslosengeld ①
   ar·baits·law·zen·gelt
doll *Puppe* ① pu·pe
dollar *Dollar* ⑩ do·lahr
door *Tür* ① tür
dope (drugs) *Dope* ⑩ dawp/dohp
double *doppelt* do·pelt
double bed *Doppelbett* ① do·pel·bet
down (nach) unten (nahkh) un·ten
downhill *abwärts* ap·verts
dozen *Dutzend* ① du·tsent
drama *Schauspiel* ⑩ show·shpeel
dream *träumen* troy·men
dress *Kleid* ① klait
dried fruit *Trockenobst* ⑩
   tro·ken·awpst
drink *Getränk* ⑩ ge·trengk
drink *trinken* tring·ken
drive *fahren* fah·ren
driving licence *Führerschein* ⑩
   fü·rer·shain
drug *Droge* ① draw·ge
drug addiction *Drogenabhängigkeit* ①
   draw·gen·ap·heng·ikh·kait
drug dealer *Drogenhändler* ⑩
   draw·gen·hen·dler
drunk *betrunken* be·trung·ken
dry (clothes) *trocknen* trok·nen
dry (wine) *trocken* tro·ken
dry-cleaner *chemische Reinigung* ①
   khay·mi·she rai·ni·gung
duck *Ente* ① en·te
dummy (pacifier) *Schnuller* ⑩ shnu·ler
during *während* vair·rent
dusk *Dämmerung* ① de·me·rung

E

each *jeder/jede/jedes* ⑩/①/⑩
   yay·der/yay·de/yay·des
ear *Ohr* ⑩ awr
early *früh* frü
earn *verdienen* fer·dee·nen
earplugs *Ohrenstöpsel* ⑩
   aw·ren·shterp·sel
earrings *Ohrringe* ⑩ pl awr·ring·e
Earth *Erde* ① er·de

earthquake *Erdbeben* ⑩ ert·bay·ben

east *Osten* ⑩ os·ten

Easter *Ostern* ⓝ aws·tern

easy *leicht* laikht

eat *essen* e·sen

economy class *Touristenklasse* ⓕ tu·*ris*·ten·kla·se

eczema *Ekzem* ⓝ ek·*tsaym*

editor *Herausgeber(in)* ⑩/ⓕ he·*rows*·gay·ber/he·*rows*·gay·be·rin

education *Erziehung* ⓕ er·*tsee*·ung

egg *Ei* ⓝ ai

eggplant *Aubergine* ⓕ aw·ber·*zhee*·ne

elections *Wahlen* ⓕ pl *vah*·len

electrical store *Elektrogeschäft* ⓝ e·*lek*·tro·ge·sheft

electrician *Elektriker(in)* ⑩/ⓕ e·*lek*·tri·ker/e·*lek*·tri·ke·rin

electricity *Elektrizität* ⓕ e·lek·tri·tsi·*tayt*

elevator *Lift* ⑩ lift

embarrassed *verlegen* fer·*lay*·gen

embassy *Botschaft* ⓕ *bawt*·shaft

embroidery *Stickerei* ⓕ shti·ke·*rai*

emergency *Notfall* ⑩ *nawt*·fal

emotional *emotional* e·mo·tsyo·*nahl*

employee *Angestellte* ⑩&ⓕ *an*·ge·shtel·te

employer *Arbeitgeber* ⑩ *ar*·bait·gay·ber

empty *leer* lair

end *Ende* ⓝ *en*·de

end *beenden* be·*en*·den

endangered (species) *bedrohte (Art)* ⓕ be·*draw*·te art

energy *Energie* ⓕ e·ner·*gee*

engagement (marriage) *Verlobung* ⓕ fer·*law*·bung

engine *Motor* ⑩ *maw*·tor/mo·*tawr*

engineer *Ingenieuer(in)* ⑩/ⓕ in·zhe·*nyer*/in·zhe·*nyer*·rin

engineering *Ingenieurwesen* ⓝ in·zhe·*nyer*·vay·zen

England *England* ⓝ *eng*·lant

English *Englisch* ⓝ *eng*·lish

enjoy (oneself) *sich amüsieren* zikh a·mü·*zee*·ren

enough *genug* ge·*nook*

enter *eintreten* *ain*·tray·ten

entertainment guide *Veranstaltungskalender* ⑩ fer·*an*·shtal·tungks·ka·len·der

envelope *Briefumschlag* ⑩ *breef*·um·shlahk

environment *Umwelt* ⓕ *um*·velt

epilepsy *Epilepsie* ⓕ e·pi·lep·*see*

equal opportunity *Chancengleichheit* ⓕ *shahng*·sen·glaikh·hait

equality *Gleichheit* ⓕ *glaikh*·hait

equipment *Ausrüstung* ⓕ *ows*·rüs·tung

escalator *Rolltreppe* ⓕ *rol*·tre·pe

euro *Euro* ⑩ *oy*·ro

Europe *Europa* ⓝ oy·*raw*·pa

euthanasia *Euthanasie* ⓕ oy·ta·na·*zee*

evening *Abend* ⑩ *ah*·bent

every *jeder/jede/jedes* ⑩/ⓕ/ⓝ *yay*·der/yay·de/yay·des

every day *alltäglich* al·*tayk*·likh

everyone *jeder* yay·der

everything *alles* a·les

example *Beispiel* ⓝ *bai*·shpeel

for example *zum Beispiel* tsum *bai*·shpeel

excellent *ausgezeichnet* *ows*·ge·tsaikh·net

excess baggage *Übergepäck* ⓝ *ü*·ber·ge·pek

exchange *Umtausch* ⑩ *um*·towsh

exchange *wechseln* *vek*·seln

exchange rate *Wechselkurs* ⑩ *vek*·sel·kurs

excluded *ausgeschlossen* *ows*·ge·shlo·sen

exhaust (car) *Auspuff* ⑩ *ows*·puf

exhibition *Ausstellung* ⓕ *ows*·shte·lung

exit *Ausgang* ⑩ *ows*·gang

expensive *teuer* *toy*·er

experience *Erfahrung* ⓕ er·*fah*·rung

exploitation *Ausbeutung* ⓕ *ows*·boy·tung

express *Express* eks·*pres*·

express mail *Expresspost* ⓕ eks·*pres*·post

extension (visa) *Verlängerung* ⓕ fer·*leng*·e·rung

eye *Auge* ⓝ *ow*·ge

eye drops *Augentropfen* ⑩ pl *ow*·gen·trop·fen

F

fabric *Gewebe* ⓝ ge·vay·be
face *Gesicht* ⓝ ge·zikht
face cloth *Waschlappen* ⓜ vash·la·pen
factory *Fabrik* ⓕ fa·breek
factory worker *Fabrik-arbeiter(in)* ⓜ/ⓕ
fa·breek·ar·bai·ter/fa·breek·ar·bai·te·rin
fair (trade) *Messe* ⓕ me·se
fall (autumn) *Herbst* ⓜ herpst
false *falsch* falsh
family *Familie* ⓕ fa·mee·li·e
family name *Familienname* ⓜ
fa·mee·li·en·nah·me
famous *berühmt* be·rümt
fan (sports) *Fan* ⓜ fen
fan (machine) *Ventilator* ⓜ
ven·ti·lah·tor
fanbelt *Keilriemen* ⓜ kail·ree·men
far *weit* vait
farm *Bauernhof* ⓜ bow·ern·hawf
farmer *Bauer/Bäuerin* ⓜ/ⓕ
bow·er/boy·e·rin
fast *schnell* shnel
fat *dick* dik
father *Vater* ⓜ fah·ter
father-in-law *Schwiegervater* ⓜ
shvee·ger·fah·ter
faucet *Wasserhahn* ⓜ va·ser·hahn
fault (someone's) *Schuld* ⓕ shult
faulty *fehlerhaft* fay·ler·haft
fax *Fax* ⓝ faks
feed *füttern* fü·tern
feel *fühlen* fü·len
feelings *Gefühle* ⓝ pl ge·fü·le
fence *Zaun* ⓜ tsown
fencing (sport) *Fechten* ⓝ fekh·ten
ferry *Fähre* ⓕ fair·re
festival *Fest* ⓝ fest
fever *Fieber* ⓝ fee·ber
few *wenige* vay·ni·ge
a few *ein paar* ain pahr
fiance/fiancee *Verlobte* ⓜ&ⓕ
fer·lawp·te
fiction *Prosa* ⓕ praw·za
field *Feld* ⓝ felt
fig *Feige* ⓕ fai·ge
fight *Kampf* ⓜ kampf
fill *füllen* fü·len

fillet *Filet* ⓝ fi·lay
film (cinema & camera) *Film* ⓜ film
film (for camera) *Film* ⓜ film
film speed *Empfindlichkeit* ⓕ
emp·fint·likh·kait
filtered *gefiltert* ge·fil·tert
find *finden* fin·den
fine (payment) *Geldbuße* ⓕ gelt·boo·se
finger *Finger* ⓜ fing·er
finish *beenden* be·en·den
fire *Feuer* ⓝ foy·er
firewood *Brennholz* ⓝ bren·holts
first *erste* ers·te
first class *erste Klasse* ⓕ ers·te kla·se
first-aid kit *Verbandskasten* ⓜ
fer·bants·kas·ten
fish *Fisch* ⓜ fish
fish shop *Fischgeschäft* ⓝ fish·ge·sheft
fishing *Fischen* ⓝ fi·shen
fishing rod *Angel* ⓕ ang·el
flag *Flagge* ⓕ fla·ge
flash *Blitz* ⓜ blits
flashlight *Taschenlampe* ⓕ
ta·shen·lam·pe
flat *flach* flakh
flea *Floh* ⓜ flaw
flea-market *Flohmarkt* ⓜ flaw·markt
flight *Flug* ⓜ flook
flooding *Überschwemmung* ⓕ
ü·ber·shve·mung
floor *Boden* ⓜ baw·den
floor (storey) *Stock* ⓜ shtok
florist *Blumenhändler* ⓜ
bloo·men·hen·dler
flour *Mehl* ⓝ mayl
flower *Blume* ⓕ bloo·me
fly *Fliege* ⓕ flee·ge
fly *fliegen* flee·gen
foggy *neblig* nay·blikh
follow *folgen* fol·gen
food *Essen* ⓝ e·sen
food poisoning
Lebensmittelvergiftung ⓕ
lay·bens·mi·tel·fer·gif·tung
foot *Fuß* ⓜ foos
football (soccer) *Fußball* ⓜ foos·bal
American football *American Football* ⓜ
e·me·ri·ken fut·bawl
Australian Rules Football
Australian Rules Football ⓜ
aws·tray·li·en roolz fut·bawl

footpath *Gehweg* ⓜ *gay*·vayk
for *für* für
foreign *ausländisch* ows·len·dish
forest *Wald* ⓜ valt
forever *immer* i·mer
forget *vergessen* fer·ge·sen
forgive *verzeihen* fer·tsai·en
fork *Gabel* ① *gah*·bel
formal *formell* for·mel
fortnight *vierzehn Tage* ⓜ pl
  feer·tsayn tah·ge
foul *Foul* ⓝ fowl
fountain *Brunnen* ⓜ bru·nen
foyer *Foyer* ① fo·a·yay
fragile *zerbrechlich* tser·brekh·likh
frame *Rahmen* ⓜ rah·men
France *Frankreich* ⓝ frangk·raikh
free (gratis) *gratis* grah·tis
free (not bound) *frei* frai
freeze *gefrieren* ge·free·ren
fresh (not stale) *frisch* frish
Friday *Freitag* ⓜ frai·tahk
friend *Freund(in)* ⓜ/① froynt/froyn·din
friendly *freundlich* froynt·likh
frog *Frosch* ⓜ frosh
from *aus* • *von* ows • fon
in front of *vor* fawr
frost *Frost* ⓜ frost
fruit *Frucht* ① frukht
fruit picking *Obsternte* ① *awpst*·ern·te
fry *braten* brah·ten
frying pan *Bratpfanne* ① *braht*·pfa·ne
fuel *Brennstoff* ⓜ *bren*·shtof
full *voll* fol
full-time *Vollzeit* ① *fol*·tsait
fun *Spaß* ⓜ shpahs
funeral *Begräbnis* ⓝ be·*grayp*·nis
funny *lustig* lus·tikh
furniture *Möbel* ⓜ pl mer·bel
fuse *Sicherung* ① *zi*·khe·rung
future *Zukunft* ① *tsoo*·kunft

G

game (sport) *Spiel* ⓝ shpeel
garage (car repair) *Werkstatt* ①
  verk·shtat
garage (car shelter) *Garage* ①
  ga·rah·zhe

garbage *Abfall* ⓜ *ap*·fal
garden *Garten* ⓜ gar·ten
garlic *Knoblauch* ⓜ *knawp*·lowkh
gas (for cooking) *Gas* ⓝ gahs
gas (petrol) *Benzin* ⓝ ben·tseen
gas cartridge *Gaskartusche* ①
  gahs·kar·tu·she
gas cylinder *Gasflasche* ① gahs·fla·she
gastroenteritis *Magen-Darm-Katarrh* ⓜ
  mah·gen·darm·ka·tar
gate *Tor* ⓝ tawr
gay *schwul* shvool
gears *Gänge* ⓜ pl geng·e
general *allgemein* al·ge·main
German *Deutsch* ⓝ doytsh
Germany *Deutschland* ⓝ doytsh·lant
gift *Geschenk* ⓝ ge·shengk
gig *Auftritt* ⓜ *owf*·trit
gin *Gin* ⓝ dzhin
ginger *Ingwer* ⓜ *ing*·ver
girl *Mädchen* ⓝ mayt·khen
girlfriend *Freundin* ① froyn·din
give *geben* gay·ben
glacier *Gletscher* ⓜ *glet*·sher
glandular fever *Drüsenfieber* ⓝ
  drü·zen·fee·ber
glass *Glas* ⓝ glahs
glasses (spectacles) *Brille* ① bri·le
glove *Handschuh* ⓜ *hant*·shoo
go (on foot) *gehen* gay·en
go (by vehicle) *fahren* fah·ren
go out with *ausgehen mit*
  ows·gay·en mit
go shopping *einkaufen gehen*
  ain·kow·fen gay·en
goal *Tor* ⓝ tawr
goalkeeper *Torwart/Torhüterin* ⓜ/①
  tawr·vart/tawr·hü·te·rin
goat *Ziege* ① tsee·ge
god *Gott* ⓜ got
goggles (skiing) *Skibrille* ① shee·bri·le
gold *Gold* ⓝ golt
golf ball *Golfball* ⓜ golf·bal
golf course *Golfplatz* ⓜ golf·plats
good *gut* goot
gorge *Schlucht* ① shlukht
government *Regierung* ① re·gee·rung
gram *Gramm* ⓝ gram
grandchild *Enkelkind* ⓝ eng·kel·kint

grandfather *Großvater • Opa* ⑩
  graws·fah·ter • aw·pa
grandmother *Großmutter • Oma* ①
  graws·mu·ter • aw·ma
grandparents *Großeltern* ⑩ pl
  graws·el·tern
grapefruit *Pampelmuse* ①
  pam·pel·moo·ze
grapes *Weintrauben* ① pl *vain·trow·ben*
graphic art *grafische Kunst* ①
  grah·fi·she kunst
grass *Gras* ⑩ *grahs*
grave *Grab* ⑩ *grahp*
gray *grau* grow
great *groß* graws
green *grün* grün
greengrocer *Lebensmittelhändler* ⑩
  lay·bens·mi·tel·hen·dler
grey *grau* grow
grocery store *Lebensmittelladen* ⑩
  lay·bens·mi·tel·lah·den
groundnut *Erdnuss* ① *ert·nus*
grow *wachsen* *vak·sen*
guess *raten* *rah·ten*
guide (audio) *Führer* ① *fü·rer*
guide (person) *Führer* ⑩ *fü·rer*
guide dog *Blindenhund* ⑩
  blin·den·hunt
guidebook *Reiseführer* ⑩ *rai·ze·fü·rer*
guided tour *Führung* ① *fü·rung*
guilty *schuldig* *shul·dikh*
guitar *Gitarre* ① *gi·ta·re*
gum (mouth) *Zahnfleisch* ⑩
  tsahn·flaish
gym *Fitness-Studio* ⑩ *fit·nes·shtoo·di·o*
gymnastics *Gymnastik* ① *güm·nas·tik*
gynaecologist
  Gynäkologe/Gynäkologin ⑩/①
  gü·ne·ko·law·ge/gü·ne·ko·law·gin

H

hair *Haar* ⑩ *hahr*
hairbrush *Haarbürste* ① *hahr·bürs·te*
hairdresser *Friseur(in)* ⑩/①
  fri·zer/fri·zer·rin
Halal *Halal-* *ha·lal·*
half *Hälfte* ① *helf·te*
half a litre *ein halber Liter* ⑩ *ain*
  hal·ber lee·ter

hallucinate *halluzinieren*
  ha·lu·tsi·nee·ren
ham *Schinken* ⑩ *shing·ken*
hammer *Hammer* ⑩ *ha·mer*
hammock *Hängematte* ① *heng·e·ma·te*
hamster *Hamster* ⑩ *hams·ter*
hand *Hand* ① *hant*
handbag *Handtasche* ① *hant·ta·she*
handicrafts *Kunsthandwerk* ⑩
  kunst·hant·verk
handlebar *Lenker* ⑩ *leng·ker*
handmade *handgemacht*
  hant·ge·makht
handsome *gutaussehend*
  goot·ows·zay·ent
hang-gliding *Drachenfliegen* ⑩
  dra·khen·flee·gen
happy *glücklich* *glük·likh*
harassment *Belästigung* ①
  be·les·ti·gung
harbour *Hafen* ⑩ *hah·fen*
hard (difficult) *schwer* shvair
hard (not soft) *hart* hart
hardware store *Eisenwarengeschäft* ⑩
  ai·zen·vah·ren·ge·sheft
hash *Haschee* ⑩ *ha·shay*
hat *Hut* ⑩ hoot
hate *hassen* *ha·sen*
have *haben* *hah·ben*
hay fever *Heuschnupfen* ⑩
  hoy·shnup·fen
he *er* air
head *Kopf* ⑩ kopf
headache *Kopfschmerzen* ⑩ pl
  kopf·shmer·tsen
headlights *Scheinwerfer* ⑩ pl
  shain·ver·fer
health *Gesundheit* ① *ge·zunt·hait*
hear *hören* *her·ren*
hearing aid *Hörgerät* ⑩ *her·ge·rayt*
heart *Herz* ⑩ *herts*
heart condition *Herzleiden* ⑩
  herts·lai·den
heat *Hitze* ① *hi·tse*
heater *Heizgerät* ⑩ *haits·ge·rayt*
heavy *schwer* shvair
hello *hallo* *ha·lo*
helmet *Helm* ⑩ helm

help *helfen* hel·fen
hepatitis *Hepatitis* ① he·pa·*tee*·tis
her *ihr* eer
herbalist *Naturheilkundige* ⑩&① na·*toor*·hail·kun·di·ge
herbs *Kräuter* ⑩ pl kroy·ter
here *hier* heer
heroin *Heroin* ① he·ro·*een*
herring *Hering* ⑩ *hay*·ring
high *hoch* hawkh
high school *Sekundarschule* ① ze·kun·*dahr*·shoo·le
hike *wandern* van·dern
hiking *Wandern* ⑩ van·dern
hiking boots *Wanderstiefel* ⑩ pl van·der·shtee·fel
hiking route *Wanderweg* ⑩ van·der·vayk
hill *Hügel* ⑩ *hü*·gel
Hindu *Hindu* ⑩&① hin·du
hire *mieten* mee·ten
his *sein* zain
historical *historisch* his·*taw*·rish
hitchhike *trampen* trem·pen
HIV positive *HIV-positiv* hah·ee·fow·*paw*·zi·teef
hockey *Hockey* ⑩ ho·ki
holiday *Urlaub* ⑩ oor·lowp
holidays *Ferien* pl *fair*·ri·en
holy *heilig* hai·likh
Holy Week *Karwoche* ① kahr·vo·khe
home *Heim* ⑩ haim
(at) home *zu Hause* tsoo *how*·ze
(go) home *nach Hause* nahkh *how*·ze
homeless *obdachlos* op·dakh·laws
homemaker *Hausmann/Hausfrau* ⑩/① hows·man/hows·frow
to be homesick *Heimweh haben* haim·vay *hah*·ben
homeopathic medicine *homöopathisches Mittel* ⑩ haw·mer·o·*pah*·ti·shes *mi*·tel
homosexual *homosexuell* haw·mo·zek·su·*el*
honest *ehrlich* air·likh
honey *Honig* ⑩ *haw*·nikh
honeymoon *Flitterwochen* ① pl *fli*·ter·vo·khen

horoscope *Horoskop* ⑩ ho·ros·*kawp*
horse *Pferd* ⑩ pfert
horse riding *Reiten* ⑩ *rai*·ten
horseradish *Meerrettich* ⑩ *mair*·re·tikh
hospital *Krankenhaus* ⑩ *krang*·ken·hows
hospitality *Gastfreundschaft* ① gast·froynt·shaft
hot *heiß* hais
hot water *warmes Wasser* ⑩ var·mes va·ser
hotel *Hotel* ⑩ ho·*tel*
house *Haus* ⑩ hows
housework *Hausarbeit* ① hows·ar·bait
how *wie* vee
hug *umarmen* um·ar·men
huge *riesig* ree·zikh
human *menschlich* mensh·likh
human rights *Menschenrechte* ⑩ pl men·shen·rekh·te
humanities *Geisteswissenschaften* ① pl gais·tes·vi·sen·shaf·ten
hundred *hundert* hun·dert
hungry *hungrig* hung·rikh
hunting *Jagd* ① yahkt
in a hurry *in Eile* in *ai*·le
hurt *verletzen* fer·le·tsen
hurt (yourself) *sich weh tun* zikh vay toon
husband *Ehemann* ⑩ *ay*·e·man
hut *Hütte* ① *hü*·te

I

I *ich* ikh
ice *Eis* ⑩ ais
ice axe *Eispickel* ⑩ *ais*·pi·kel
ice cream *Eiscreme* ① *ais*·kraym
ice cream parlour *Eisdiele* ① *ais*·dee·le
ice hockey *Eishockey* ⑩ *ais*·ho·ki
ice skating *Eislaufen* ⑩ *ais*·low·fen
idea *Idee* ① i·*day*
identification *Ausweis* ⑩ *ows*·vais
identification card *Personalausweis* ⑩ per·zo·*nahl*·ows·vais
idiot *Idiot* ⑩ i·di·*awt*
if *wenn* ven
ignition *Zündung* ① tsün·dung

ill *krank* krangk
illegal *illegal* i·le·gahl
imagination *Phantasie* ① fan·ta·zee
immediately *sofort* zo·fort
immigration *Immigration* ①
i·mi·gra·tsyawn
important *wichtig* vikh·tikh
impossible *unmöglich* un·merk·likh
in *in* in
in front of *vor* fawr
included *inbegriffen* in·be·gri·fen
income tax *Einkommensteuer* ①
ain·ko·men·shtoy·er
India *Indien* ⑩ in·di·en
indicator *Blinker* ⑩ bling·ker
indigestion *Magenverstimmung* ①
mah·gen·fer·shti·mung
industry *Industrie* ① in·dus·tree
inequality *Ungleichheit* ①
un·glaikh·hait
infection *Entzündung* ① en·tsün·dung
inflammation *Entzündung* ①
en·tsün·dung
influenza *Grippe* ① gri·pe
information *Auskunft* ① ows·kunft
ingredient *Zutat* ① tsoo·taht
inject *injizieren* in·yi·tsee·ren
injection (car) *Einspritzung* ①
ain·shpri·tsung
injection (medical) *Injektion* ①
in·yek·tsyawn
injury *Verletzung* ① fer·le·tsung
in-line skating *Rollschuhfahren* ⑩
rol·shoo·fah·ren
innocent *unschuldig* un·shul·dikh
insect repellent *Insektenschutzmittel* ⑩
in·zek·ten·shuts·mi·tel
inside *innen* i·nen
instead of *(an)statt* (an·)shtat
instructor *Lehrer(in)* ⑩/①
lair·rer/lair·re·rin
insurance *Versicherung* ①
fer·zi·khe·rung
interesting *interessant* in·tre·sant
intermission *Pause* ① pow·ze
international *international*
in·ter·na·tsyo·nahl
Internet *Internet* ⑩ in·ter·net

Internet cafe *Internetcafé* ⑩
in·ter·net·ka·fay
interpreter *Dolmetscher(in)* ⑩/①
dol·met·sher/dol·met·she·rin
interview *Interview* ⑩ in·ter·vyoo
invite *einladen* ain·lah·den
Ireland *Irland* ⑩ ir·lant
iron (clothes) *bügeln* bü·geln
island *Insel* ① in·zel
IT *Informationstechnologie* ①
in·for·ma·tsyawns·tekh·no·lo·gee
Italy *Italien* ⑩ ee·tah·li·en
itch *Juckreiz* ⑩ yuk·raits
itemised *einzeln aufgeführt*
ain·tseln owf·ge·fürt
itinerary *Reiseroute* ① rai·ze·roo·te
IUD *Intrauterinpessar* ⑩
in·tra·u·te·reen·pe·sahr

J

jacket *Jacke* ① ya·ke
jail *Gefängnis* ⑩ ge·feng·nis
jam *Marmelade* ① mar·me·lah·de
Japan *Japan* ⑩ yah·pahn
jar *Glas* ⑩ glahs
jaw *Kiefer* ⑩ kee·fer
jealous *eifersüchtig* ai·fer·zükh·tikh
jeans *Jeans* ① pl dzheens
jeep *Jeep* ⑩ dzheep
jet lag *Jetlag* ⑩ dzhet·leg
jewellery *Schmuck* ⑩ shmuk
Jewish *jüdisch* yü·dish
job *Arbeitsstelle* ① ar·baits·shte·le
jockey *Jockey* ⑩ dzho·ki
jogging *Joggen* ⑩ dzho·gen
joke *Witz* ⑩ vits
journalist *Journalist(in)* ⑩/①
zhur·na·list/zhur·na·lis·tin
journey *Reise* ① rai·ze
judge *Richter(in)* ⑩/①
rikh·ter/rikh·te·rin
juice *Saft* ⑩ zaft
jump *springen* shpring·en
jumper (sweater) *Pullover* ⑩ pu·law·ver
jumper leads *Überbrückungskabel* ⑩
ü·ber·brü·kungks·kah·bel
justice *Gerechtigkeit* ①
ge·rekh·tikh·kait

K

ketchup Ketchup ⓜ *ket*·chap
kettle Kessel ⓜ *ke*·sel
key Schlüssel ⓜ *shlü*·sel
keyboard Tastatur ⓕ tas·ta·*toor*
kick treten *tray*·ten
kill töten *ter*·ten
kilogram Kilogramm ⓝ *kee*·lo·gram
kilometre Kilometer ⓜ ki·lo·*may*·ter
kind nett net
kindergarten Kindergarten ⓜ
  kin·der·gar·ten
king König ⓜ *ker*·nikh
kiss Kuss ⓜ kus
kiss küssen *kü*·sen
kitchen Küche ⓕ *kü*·khe
kitten Kätzchen ⓝ *kets*·khen
kiwifruit Kiwifrucht ⓕ *kee*·vi·frukht
knapsack Rucksack ⓜ *ruk*·zak
knee Knie ⓝ knee
knife Messer ⓝ *me*·ser
know (a person) kennen *ke*·nen
know (something) wissen vi·sen
kosher koscher *kaw*·sher

L

labourer Arbeiter(in) ⓜ/ⓕ
  ar·*bai*·ter/ar·*bai*·te·rin
lace Spitze ⓕ *shpi*·tse
lager Lager ⓝ *lah*·ger
lake See ⓜ zay
lamb Lamm ⓝ lam
land Land ⓝ lant
landlady Vermieterin ⓕ fer·*mee*·te·rin
landlord Vermieter ⓜ fer·*mee*·ter
language Sprache ⓕ *shprah*·khe
laptop Laptop ⓝ *lep*·top
lard Schmalz ⓝ shmalts
large groß graws
last (week) letzte (Woche)
  lets·te (vo·khe)
late spät shpayt
laugh lachen *la*·khen
laundrette Wäscherei ⓕ ve·she·*rai*
laundry (room) Waschküche ⓕ
  vash·kü·khe

law (subject) Jura ⓝ *yoo*·ra
law (rules) Gesetz ⓝ ge·*zets*
lawyer Rechtsanwalt/
  Rechtsanwältin ⓜ/ⓕ
  rekhts·an·valt/*rekhts*·an·vel·tin
laxatives Abführmittel ⓝ *ap*·für·mi·tel
lazy faul fowl
leader Anführer ⓜ *an*·fü·rer
leaf Blatt ⓝ blat
learn lernen *ler*·nen
lease Mietvertrag ⓝ *meet*·fer·trahk
leather Leder ⓝ *lay*·der
leave (depart) abfahren *ap*·fah·ren
lecturer Dozent(in) ⓜ/ⓕ
  do·*tsent*/do·*tsen*·tin
leek Lauch ⓜ lowkh
left (direction) links lingks
left luggage Gepäckaufbewahrung ⓕ
  ge·*pek*·owf·be·vah·rung
left-wing links(gerichtet)
  lingks(·ge·rikh·tet)
leg (body) Bein ⓝ bain
legal legal le·*gahl*
legislation Gesetzgebung ⓕ
  ge·*zets*·gay·bung
legume Hülsenfrucht ⓕ *hül*·zen·frukht
lemon Zitrone ⓕ tsi·*traw*·ne
lemonade Limonade ⓕ li·mo·*nah*·de
lens (camera) Objektiv ⓝ op·yek·*teef*
Lent Fastenzeit ⓕ *fas*·ten·tsait
lentil Linse ⓕ *lin*·ze
lesbian Lesbierin ⓕ *les*·bi·e·rin
less weniger *vay*·ni·ger
letter Brief ⓜ breef
lettuce Kopfsalat ⓜ *kopf*·za·laht
liar Lügner(in) ⓜ/ⓕ *lüg*·ner/*lüg*·ne·rin
library Bibliothek ⓕ bi·bli·o·*tayk*
lice Läuse ⓕ pl *loy*·ze
license plate number Autokennzeichen ⓝ *ow*·to·ken·tsai·khen
lie (not stand) liegen *lee*·gen
life Leben ⓝ *lay*·ben
lifejacket Schwimmweste ⓕ
  shvim·ves·te
lift (elevator) Lift ⓜ lift
light Licht ⓝ likht
light hell hel
light bulb Glühbirne ⓕ *glü*·bir·ne
light meter Belichtungsmesser ⓜ
  be·*likh*·tungks·me·ser

lighter (cigarette) *Feuerzeug* ⓝ
foy·er·tsoyk

lightning *Blitz* ⓜ blits

lights (on car) *Scheinwerfer* ⓜ pl
shain·ver·fer

like *mögen* mer·gen

lime *Limone* ⓕ li·maw·ne

line *Linie* ⓕ lee·ni·e

linen (bed) *Bettwäsche* ⓕ bet·ve·she

linen (fabric) *Leinen* ⓝ lai·nen

lip balm *Lippenbalsam* ⓜ
li·pen·bal·zahm

lips *Lippen* ⓕ pl li·pen

lipstick *Lippenstift* ⓜ li·pen·shtift

liquor store *Getränkehandel* ⓜ
ge·treng·ke·han·del

listen *hören* her·ren

little *klein* klain

little (not much) *wenig* vay·nikh

a little *ein bisschen* ain bis·khen

live *leben* lay·ben

live (reside) *wohnen* vaw·nen

liver *Leber* ⓕ lay·ber

lizard *Echse* ⓕ ek·se

local *örtlich* ert·likh

lock *Schloss* ⓝ shlos

locked *abgeschlossen* ap·ge·shlo·sen

lollies *Süßigkeiten* ⓕ pl zü·sikh·kai·ten

lonely *einsam* ain·zahm

long *lang* lang

long-sleeved *langärmelig*
lang·er·me·likh

look *(an)sehen (an·)zay·en

look after *sich kümmern um*
zikh kü·mern um

look for *suchen nach* zoo·khen nahkh

lookout *Aussichtspunkt* ⓜ
ows·zikhts·pungkt

loose change *Kleingeld* ⓝ klain·gelt

lose *verlieren* fer·lee·ren

lost *verloren* fer·law·ren

lost property office *Fundbüro* ⓝ
funt·bü·raw

a lot (of) *viel* feel

loud *laut* lowt

love *lieben* lee·ben

lover *Liebhaber(in)* ⓜ/ⓕ
leep·hah·ber/leep·hah·be·rin

low *niedrig* nee·drikh

lubricant *Schmiermittel* ⓝ
shmeer·mi·tel

luck *Glück* ⓝ glük

lucky *glücklich* glük·likh

luggage *Gepäck* ⓝ ge·pek

luggage lockers *Schließfächer* ⓝ pl
shlees·fe·kher

luggage tag *Adressanhänger* ⓜ
a·dres·an·heng·er

lump (health) *Knoten* ⓜ knaw·ten

lunch *Mittagessen* ⓝ mi·tahk·e·sen

lungs *Lungen* ⓕ pl lung·en

luxury *luxuriös* luk·su·ri·ers

M

machine *Maschine* ⓕ ma·shee·ne

made of (cotton) *aus (Baumwolle)*
ows (bowm·vo·le)

magazine *Zeitschrift* ⓕ tsait·shrift

magician *Zauberer(in)* ⓜ/ⓕ
tsow·be·rer/tsow·be·re·rin

mail *Post* ⓕ post

mailbox *Briefkasten* ⓜ breef·kas·ten

main *Haupt-* howpt

main square *Hauptplatz* ⓜ howpt·plats

make *machen* ma·khen

make-up *Schminke* ⓕ shming·ke

mammogram *Mammogramm* ⓝ
ma·mo·gram

man *Mann* ⓜ man

man (human being) *Mensch* ⓜ mensh

manager *Manager(in)* ⓜ/ⓕ
me·ne·dzher/me·ne·dzhe·rin

mandarin *Mandarine* ⓕ man·da·ree·ne

mango *Mango* ⓕ mang·go

manual worker *Arbeiter(in)* ⓜ/ⓕ
ar·bai·ter/ar·bai·te·rin

many *viele* fee·le

map *Karte* ⓕ kar·te

margarine *Margarine* ⓕ mar·ga·ree·ne

marijuana *Marihuana* ⓝ ma·ri·hu·ah·na

marital status *Familienstand* ⓜ
fa·mee·li·en·shtant

market *Markt* ⓜ markt

market square *Marktplatz* ⓜ
markt·plats

marmalade *Orangenmarmelade* ⓕ
o·rahng·zhen·mar·me·lah·de

marriage *Ehe* ⓕ ay·e

marry *heiraten* hai·rah·ten

martial arts *Kampfsport* ⑩
kampf·shport

mass (Catholic) *Messe* ① me·se

massage *Massage* ① ma·sah·zhe

masseur *Masseur* ⑩ ma·ser

masseuse *Masseurin* ① ma·ser·rin

mat *Matte* ① ma·te

match (sport) *Spiel* ⑩ shpeel

matches *Streichhölzer* ⑩ pl
shtraikh·herl·tser

material *Material* ⑩ ma·te·ri·ahl

mattress *Matratze* ① ma·tra·tse

maybe *vielleicht* fi·laikht

mayonnaise *Majonnaise* ①
ma·yo·nay·ze

mayor *Bürgermeister(in)* ⑩/①
bür·ger·mais·ter/bür·ger·mais·te·rin

measles *Masern* pl mah·zern

meat *Fleisch* ⑩ flaish

mechanic *Mechaniker(in)* ⑩/①
me·khah·ni·ker/me·khah·ni·ke·rin

media *Medien* pl may·di·en

medicine *Medizin* ① me·di·tseen

meditation *Meditation* ①
me·di·ta·tsyawn

meet *treffen* tre·fen

melon *Melone* ① me·law·ne

member *Mitglied* ⑩ mit·gleet

member of parliament
Abgeordnete ⑩&① ap·ge·ord·ne·te

menstruation *Menstruation* ①
mens·tru·a·tsyawn

menu *Speisekarte* ① shpai·ze·kar·te

message *Mitteilung* ① mi·tai·lung

metal *Metall* ⑩ me·tal

metre *Meter* ⑩ may·ter

metro station *U-Bahnhof* ⑩
oo·bahn·hawf

microwave *Mikrowelle* ① mee·kro·ve·le

Middle East *Nahe Osten* ⑩ nah·e os·ten

midnight *Mitternacht* ① mi·ter·nakht

migraine *Migräne* ① mi·gray·ne

military *Militär* ⑩ mi·li·tair

military service *Wehrdienst* ⑩
vair·deenst

milk *Milch* ① milkh

millimetre *Millimeter* ⑩ mi·li·may·ter

million *Million* ① mi·lyawn

mince *Gehacktes* ⑩ ge·hak·tes

mind (look after) *aufpassen* owf·pa·sen

mineral water *Mineralwasser* ⑩
mi·ne·rahl·va·ser

mints *Pfefferminzbonbons* ⑩ pl
pfe·fer·mints·bong·bongs

minute *Minute* ① mi·noo·te

mirror *Spiegel* ⑩ shpee·gel

miscarriage *Fehlgeburt* ① fayl·ge·burt

miss (feel absence of) *vermissen*
fer·mi·sen

miss (the bus) *verpassen* fer·pa·sen

mistake *Fehler* ⑩ fay·ler

mix *mischen* mi·shen

mobile phone *Handy* ⑩ hen·di

modem *Modem* ⑩ maw·dem

moisturiser *Feuchtigkeitscreme* ①
foykh·tikh·kaits·kraym

monastery *Kloster* ⑩ klaws·ter

Monday *Montag* ⑩ mawn·tahk

money *Geld* ⑩ gelt

month *Monat* ⑩ maw·nat

monument *Denkmal* ⑩ dengk·mahl

(full) moon *(Voll) Mond* ⑩
(fol·)mawnt

more *mehr* mair

morning (6am–10am) *Morgen* ⑩
mor·gen

morning (10am–12pm) *Vormittag* ⑩
fawr·mi·tahk

morning sickness
(Schwangerschafts-)Erbrechen ⑩
(shvang·er·shafts·)er·bre·khen

mosque *Moschee* ① mo·shay

mosquito *Stechmücke* ① shtekh·mü·ke

mosquito coil *Moskitospirale* ①
mos·kee·to·shpi·rah·le

mother *Mutter* ① mu·ter

mother-in-law *Schwiegermutter* ①
shvee·ger·mu·ter

motorboat *Motorboot* ⑩
maw·tor·bawt

motorcycle *Motorrad* ⑩ maw·tor·raht

motorway (tollway) *Autobahn* ①
ow·to·bahn

mountain *Berg* ⑩ berk

mountain bike *Mountainbike* ⑩
mown·ten·baik

mountain hut *Berghütte* ① berk·hü·te

mountain path *Bergweg* ⓜ *berk·vayk*
mountain range *Gebirgszug* ⓜ
  ge·birks·tsook
mountaineering *Bergsteigen* ⓝ
  berk·shtai·gen
mouse *Maus* ⓕ *mows*
mouth *Mund* ⓜ *munt*
movie *Film* ⓜ *film*
mud *Schlamm* ⓜ *shlam*
muesli *Müsli* ⓝ *müs·li*
muggy *schwül* *shvül*
mum *Mama* ⓕ *ma·ma*
muscle *Muskel* ⓜ *mus·kel*
museum *Museum* ⓜ *mu·zay·um*
mushroom *Pilz* ⓜ *pilts*
music *Musik* ⓕ *mu·zeek*
musician *Musiker(in)* ⓜ/ⓕ
  moo·zi·ker/moo·zi·ke·rin
Muslim *Moslem/Moslime* ⓜ/ⓕ
  mos·lem/mos·lee·me
mussel *Muschel* ⓕ *mu·shel*
mustard *Senf* ⓜ *zenf*
mute *stumm* *shtum*
my *mein/meine/mein* ⓜ/ⓕ/ⓝ
  main/mai·ne/main

N

nail clippers *Nagelknipser* ⓜ pl
  nah·gel·knip·ser
name *Name* ⓜ *nah·me*
napkin *Serviette* ⓕ *zer·vye·te*
nappy *Windel* ⓕ *vin·del*
nappy rash *Windeldermatitis* ⓕ
  vin·del·der·ma·tee·tis
national park *Nationalpark* ⓜ
  na·tsyo·nahl·park
nationality *Staatsangehörigkeit* ⓕ
  shtahts·an·ge·her·rikh·kait
nature *Natur* ⓕ *na·toor*
nature reserve *Naturreservat* ⓝ
  na·toor·re·zer·vaht
naturopathy *Naturheilkunde* ⓕ
  na·toor·hail·kun·de
nausea *Übelkeit* ⓕ *ü·bel·kait*
near *nahe* *nah·e*
nearby *in der Nähe* *in dair nay·e*
nearest *nächste* *naykhs·te*
necessary *notwendig* *nawt·ven·dikh*

necklace *Halskette* ⓕ *hals·ke·te*
need *brauchen* *brow·khen*
needle (sewing) *Nadel* ⓕ *nah·del*
needle (syringe) *Nadel* ⓕ *nah·del*
neither *auch nicht* *owkh nikht*
nephew *Neffe* ⓜ *ne·fe*
net *Netz* ⓝ *nets*
Netherlands *Niederlande* pl
  nee·der·lan·de
never *nie* *nee*
new *neu* *noy*
New Year's Day *Neujahrstag* ⓜ
  noy·yahrs·tahk
New Year's Eve *Silvester* ⓝ *zil·ves·ter*
New Zealand *Neuseeland* ⓝ
  noy·zay·lant
news *Nachrichten* ⓕ pl *nahkh·rikh·ten*
newsagency *Zeitungshändler* ⓜ
  tsai·tungks·hen·dler
newspaper *Zeitung* ⓕ *tsai·tung*
newsstand *Zeitungskiosk* ⓜ
  tsai·tungks·kee·osk
next *nächste* *naykhs·te*
next to *neben* *nay·ben*
nice *nett* *net*
nickname *Spitzname* ⓜ *shpits·nah·me*
niece *Nichte* ⓕ *nikh·te*
night *Nacht* ⓕ *nakht*
no *nein* *nain*
noisy *laut* *lowt*
none *keine* *kai·ne*
non-smoking *Nichtraucher-*
  nikht·row·kher·
noodles *Nudeln* ⓕ pl *noo·deln*
noon *Mittag* ⓜ *mi·tahk*
north *Norden* ⓜ *nor·den*
nose *Nase* ⓕ *nah·ze*
not *nicht* *nikht*
notebook *Notizbuch* ⓝ *no·teets·bookh*
nothing *nichts* *nikhts*
now *jetzt* *yetst*
nuclear energy *Atomenergie* ⓕ
  a·tawm·e·ner·gee
nuclear testing *Atomtest* ⓜ
  a·tawm·test
nuclear waste *Atommüll* ⓜ
  a·tawm·mül
number (numeral) *Zahl* ⓕ *tsahl*
number (telephone) *Nummer* ⓕ *nu·mer*

nun *Nonne* ① no·ne
nurse *Krankenpfleger/*
  Krankenschwester ⓜ/①
  krang·ken·pflay·ger/
  krang·ken·shves·ter
nut *Nuss* ① nus

O

oats *Hafer(flocken)* ⓜ pl
  hah·fer(·flo·ken)
obvious *offensichtlich* o·fen·zikht·likh
occupation *Beruf* ⓜ be·roof
ocean *Ozean* ⓜ aw·tse·ahn
off (food) *schlecht* shlekht
office *Büro* ⓝ bü·raw
office worker *Büroangestellte* ⓜ&①
  bü·raw·an·ge·shtel·te
offside *abseits* ap·zaits
often *oft* oft
oil *Öl* ⓝ erl
OK *okay* o·kay
old *alt* alt
olive *Olive* ① o·lee·ve
olive oil *Olivenöl* ⓝ o·lee·ven·erl
Olympic Games *Olympische*
  Spiele ⓝ pl o·lüm·pi·she shpee·le
on *auf* owf
once *einmal* ain·mahl
one *ein(s)* ain(s)
onion *Zwiebel* ① tsvee·bel
only *nur* noor
open *offen* o·fen
open (unlock) *öffnen* erf·nen
opening hours *Öffnungszeiten* ① pl
  erf·nungks·tsai·ten
opera *Oper* ① aw·per
opera house *Opernhaus* ⓝ
  aw·pern·hows
operation *Operation* ① o·pe·ra·tsyawn
operator *Vermittlung* ① fer·mit·lung
opinion *Meinung* ① mai·nung
opposite *gegenüber* gay·gen·ü·ber
optician *Optiker(in)* ⓜ/①
  op·ti·ker/op·ti·ke·rin
or *oder* aw·der
orange (fruit) *Orange* ① o·rahng·zhe
orange (colour) *orange* o·rahngzh
orange juice *Orangensaft* ⓜ
  o·rahng·zhen·zaft

orchestra *Orchester* ⓝ or·kes·ter
order (restaurant) *Bestellung* ①
  be·shte·lung
order *bestellen* be·shte·len
ordinary *normal* nor·mahl
organ (church) *Orgel* ① or·gel
organise *organisieren* or·ga·ni·zee·ren
orgasm *Orgasmus* ⓜ or·gas·mus
original (not copied) *Original-*
  o·ri·gi·nahl
other *andere* an·de·re
our *unser* un·zer
out *aus* ows
outside *draußen* drow·sen
ovarian cyst *Eierstockzyste* ①
  ai·er·shtok·tsüs·te
oven *Ofen* ⓜ aw·fen
over *über* ü·ber
overcoat *Mantel* ⓜ man·tel
overdose *Überdosis* ① ü·ber·daw·zis
overnight *über Nacht* ü·ber nakht
owe *schulden* shul·den
owner *Besitzer(in)* ⓜ/①
  be·zi·tser/be·zi·tse·rin
oxygen *Sauerstoff* ⓜ zow·er·shtof
oyster *Auster* ① ows·ter
ozone layer *Ozonschicht* ①
  o·tsawn·shikht

P

pacemaker (heart) *Herzschrittmacher* ⓜ
  herts·shrit·ma·kher
pacifier (dummy) *Schnuller* ⓜ shnu·ler
package *Paket* ⓝ pa·kayt
packet (general) *Packung* ① pa·kung
padlock *Vorhängeschloss* ⓝ
  fawr·heng·e·shlos
page *Seite* ① zai·te
pain *Schmerz* ⓜ shmerts
painful *schmerzhaft* shmerts·haft
painkillers *Schmerzmittel* ⓝ
  shmerts·mi·tel
painter *Maler(in)* ⓜ/①
  mah·ler/mah·le·rin
painting (the art) *Malerei* ① mah·le·rai
paints *Farben* ① pl far·ben
pair (couple) *Paar* ⓝ pahr
palace *Schloss* ⓝ shlos
pan *Pfanne* ① pfa·ne

pants (trousers) *Hose* ① *haw·ze*
panty liner *Slipeinlage* ①
  slip·ain·lah·ge
pantyhose *Strumpfhose* ①
  shtrumpf·haw·ze
pap smear *Abstrich* ⑩ *ap·shtrikh*
paper *Papier* ⑪ *pa·peer*
paperback *Taschenbuch* ⑪
  ta·shen·bookh
paperwork *Schreibarbeit* ①
  shraip·ar·bait
parachuting *Fallschirmspringen* ⑩
  fal·shirm·shpring·en
paragliding *Gleitschirmfliegen* ⑩
  glait·shirm·flee·gen
paraplegic *Querschnittsgelähmte* ⑩&①
  kvair·shnits·ge·laym·te
parcel *Paket* ⑩ *pa·kayt*
parents *Eltern* ① pl *el·tern*
park *Park* ⑩ *park*
park (car) *Parkplatz* ⑩ *park·plats*
parliament *Parlament* ⑪ *par·la·ment*
parrot *Papagei* ⑩ *pa·pa·gai*
parsley *Petersilie* ① *pay·ter·zee·li·e*
part *Teil* ⑪ *tail*
participate *sich beteiligen*
  zikh be·tai·li·gen
part-time *Teilzeit-* ① *tail·tsait·*
party (fiesta/ball) *Fest* ⑩ *fest*
party (politics) *Partei* ① *par·tai*
pass *Pass* ⑩ *pas*
passenger (bus/taxi) *Fahrgast* ⑩
  fahr·gast
passenger (plane) *Fluggast* ⑩
  flook·gast
passenger (train) *Reisende(r)* ⑩/①
  rai·zen·de
passport *(Reise)Pass* ⑩ *(rai·ze·)pas*
passport number *Passnummer* ①
  pas·nu·mer
past *Vergangenheit* ① *fer·gang·en·hait*
pasta *Nudeln* ① pl *noo·deln*
path *Pfad* ⑩ *pfaht*
patio *Terrasse* ① *ter·ra·se*
pay *bezahlen* *be·tsah·len*
pay phone *Münztelefon* ⑩
  münts·te·le·fawn
payment *Zahlung* ① *tsah·lung*
pea *Erbse* ① *erp·se*

peace *Frieden* ⑩ *free·den*
peach *Pfirsich* ⑩ *pfir·zikh*
peak *Gipfel* ⑩ *gip·fel*
peanuts *Erdnüsse* ① pl *ert·nü·se*
pear *Birne* ① *bir·ne*
pedal *Pedal* ⑪ *pe·dahl*
pedestrian *Fußgänger(in)* ⑩/①
  foos·geng·er/foos·geng·e·rin
pen (ballpoint) *Kugelschreiber* ⑩
  koo·gel·shrai·ber
pencil *Bleistift* ⑩ *blai·shtift*
penis *Penis* ⑩ *pay·nis*
penknife *Taschenmesser* ⑪
  ta·shen·me·ser
pensioner *Rentner(in)* ⑩/①
  rent·ner/rent·ne·rin
people *Menschen* ⑩ pl *men·shen*
pepper *Pfeffer* ⑩ *pfe·fer*
pepper (bell) *Paprika* ① *pap·ri·kah*
per *pro* *praw*
percent *Prozent* ⑪ *pro·tsent*
performance *Aufführung* ①
  owf·fü·rung
perfume *Parfüm* ⑪ *par·füm*
period pain
  Menstruationsbeschwerden ① pl
  mens·tru·a·tsyawns·be·shver·den
permission *Erlaubnis* ① *er·lowp·nis*
permit *Genehmigung* ①
  ge·nay·mi·gung
person *Person* ① *per·zawn*
personal *persönlich* *per·zern·likh*
petition *Petition* ① *pe·ti·tsyawn*
petrol *Benzin* ⑪ *ben·tseen*
petrol can *Benzinkanister* ⑩
  ben·tseen·ka·nis·ter
pharmacy *Apotheke* ① *a·po·tay·ke*
phone book *Telefonbuch* ⑪
  te·le·fawn·bookh
phone box *Telefonzelle* ①
  te·le·fawn·tse·le
phonecard *Telefonkarte* ①
  te·le·fawn·kar·te
photo *Foto* ⑪ *faw·to*
photograph *Fotografie* ① *fo·to·gra·fee*
photograph *fotografieren*
  fo·to·gra·fee·ren
photographer *Fotograf(in)* ⑩/①
  fo·to·grahf/fo·to·grah·fin

photography *Fotografie* ①
fo·to·gra·*fee*

phrasebook *Sprachführer* ⑩
shprahkh·fü·rer

physics *Physik* ① fü·*zeek*

piano *Klavier* ⑩ kla·*veer*

pick *pflücken* pflü·ken

pick up *aufheben* owf·hay·ben

pickaxe *Spitzhacke* ① shpits·ha·ke

picnic *Picknick* ⑩ pik·nik

pie *Pastete* ① pas·*tay*·te

piece *Stück* ⑩ shtük

pig *Schwein* ⑩ shvain

pilgrimage *Pilgerfahrt* ① pil·ger·fahrt

pill *Pille* ① pi·le

the Pill *die Pille* ① dee pi·le

pillow *Kissen* ⑩ ki·sen

pillowcase *Kissenbezug* ⑩
ki·sen·be·tsook

pineapple *Ananas* ① a·na·nas

pink *rosa* raw·za

pipe *Pfeife* ① pfai·fe

pistachio *Pistazie* ① pis·*tah*·tsi·e

place *Platz* ⑩ plats

place of birth *Geburtsort* ⑩
ge·*burts*·ort

plain *Ebene* ① ay·be·ne

plane *Flugzeug* ⑩ flook·tsoyk

planet *Planet* ⑩ pla·*nayt*

plant *Pflanze* ① pflan·tse

plastic *Plastik* ⑩ plas·tik

plate *Teller* ⑩ te·ler

plateau *Hochebene* ① hawkh·ay·be·ne

platform *Bahnsteig* ⑩ bahn·shtaik

play (theatre) *Schauspiel* ⑩
show·shpeel

play (game) *spielen* shpee·len

play (instrument) *spielen* shpee·len

please *bitte* bi·te

plenty *viel* feel

plug (bath) *Stöpsel* ⑩ shterp·sel

plug (electricity) *Stecker* ⑩ shte·ker

plum *Pflaume* ① pflow·me

plumber *Installateur(in)* ⑩/①
in·sta·la·*ter*/in·sta·la·*ter*(·rin)

pocket *Tasche* ① ta·she

poetry *Dichtung* ① dikh·tung

point *Punkt* ⑩ pungkt

point *zeigen* tsai·gen

poisonous *giftig* gif·tikh

poker (game) *Poker* ⑩ paw·ker

police *Polizei* ① po·li·*tsai*

police station *Polizeirevier* ⑩
po·li·*tsai*·re·veer

policy *Politik* ① po·li·*teek*

politician *Politiker(in)* ⑩/①
po·lee·ti·ker/po·lee·ti·ke·rin

politics *Politik* ① po·li·*teek*

pollen *Pollen* ⑩ po·len

polls *Umfrage* ① um·frah·ge

pollution *Umweltverschmutzung* ①
um·velt·fer·shmu·tsung

pony *Pony* ⑩ po·ni

pool (game) *Billard* ⑩ bil·yart

pool (swimming, indoors) *Hallenbad* ⑩
ha·len·baht

pool (swimming, outdoors) *Freibad* ⑩
frai·baht

poor *arm* arm

popular *beliebt* be·*leept*

pork *Schweinefleisch* ⑩ shvai·ne·flaish

port *Hafen* ⑩ hah·fen

possible *möglich* merk·likh

post office *Postamt* ⑩ post·amt

postage *Porto* ⑩ por·to

postcard *Postkarte* ① post·kar·te

postcode *Postleitzahl* ① post·lai·tsahl

poste restante *postlagernd*
post·lah·gernt

poster *Plakat* ⑩ pla·*kaht*

pot (ceramics) *Topf* ⑩ topf

pot (dope) *Gras* ⑩ grahs

potato *Kartoffel* ① kar·to·fel

pottery *Töpferwaren* ① pl
terp·fer·vah·ren

pound (money & weight) *Pfund* ⑩
pfunt

poverty *Armut* ① ar·moot

power *Kraft* ① kraft

practical *praktisch* prak·tish

prawn *Garnele* ① gar·nay·le

prayer *Gebet* ⑩ ge·*bayt*

prefer *vorziehen* fawr·tsee·en

pregnancy test kit
Schwangerschaftstest ⑩
shvang·er·shafts·test

pregnant *schwanger* shvang·er

premenstrual tension
prämenstruelle Störung ①
pray·mens·tru·e·le shter·rung

prepare *vorbereiten* fawr·be·rai·ten
present (gift) *Geschenk* ⑩ ge·shengk
present (time) *Gegenwart* ①
gay·gen·vart
president *Präsident(in)* ⑩/①
pre·zi·dent/pre·zi·den·tin
pressure *Druck* ⑩ druk
pretty *hübsch* hüpsh
prevent *verhindern* fer·hin·dern
price *Preis* ⑩ prais
priest *Priester* ⑩ prees·ter
prime minister
Premierminister(in) ⑩/①
prem·yay·mi·nis·ter/
prem·yay·mi·nis·te·rin
prime minister (in Germany &
Austria) *Bundeskanzler(in)* ⑩/①
bun·des·kants·ler/bun·des·kants·le·rin
print (artwork) *Druck* ⑩ druk
print (photography) *Abzug* ⑩ ap·tsook
prison *Gefängnis* ⑩ ge·feng·nis
prisoner *Gefangene* ⑩&① ge·fang·e·ne
private *privat* pri·vaht
produce *produzieren* pro·du·tsee·ren
profession *Beruf* ⑩ be·roof
profit *Gewinn* ⑩ ge·vin
program *Programm* ⑩ pro·gram
projector *Projektor* ⑩ pro·yek·tor
promise *versprechen* fer·shpre·khen
proposal *Vorschlag* ⑩ fawr·shlahk
prostitute *Prostituierte* ①
pros·ti·tu·eer·te
protect *beschützen* be·shü·tsen
protected *geschützte* ge·shüts·te
protest *Protest* ⑩ pro·test
protest *protestieren* pro·tes·tee·ren
provisions *Verpflegung* ①
fer·pflay·gung
prune *Backpflaume* ① bak·pflow·me
psychology *Psychologie* ①
psü·kho·lo·gee
pub *Kneipe* ① knai·pe
public telephone *öffentliches Telefon* ⑩
er·fent·li·khes te·le·fawn
public toilet *öffentliche Toilette* ①
er·fent·li·khe to·a·le·te
pull *ziehen* tsee·en
pump *(Luft)Pumpe* ① (luft·)pum·pe
pumpkin *Kürbis* ⑩ kür·bis
puncture *Reifenpanne* ① rai·fen·pa·ne

punish *bestrafen* be·shtrah·fen
pure *rein* rain
purple *lila* lee·la
push *schieben* shee·ben
put (horizontal) *legen* lay·gen
put (vertical) *stellen* shte·len

Q

qualifications *Qualifikationen* ① pl
kva·li·fi·ka·tsyaw·nen
quality *Qualität* ① kva·li·tayt
quarantine *Quarantäne* ①
ka·ran·tay·ne
quarrel *Streit* ⑩ shtrait
quarter *Viertel* ⑩ feer·tel
queen *Königin* ① ker·ni·gin
question *Frage* ① frah·ge
queue *Schlange* ① shlang·e
quick *schnell* shnel
quiet *ruhig* roo·ikh
quit (job) *kündigen* kün·di·gen

R

rabbit *Kaninchen* ⑩ ka·neen·khen
race (sport) *Rennen* ⑩ re·nen
racetrack *Rennbahn* ① ren·bahn
racing bike *Rennrad* ⑩ ren·raht
racism *Rassismus* ⑩ ra·sis·mus
racquet *Schläger* ⑩ shlay·ger
radiator *Kühler* ⑩ kü·ler
radio *Radio* ⑩ rah·di·o
radish *Rettich* ⑩ re·tikh
railway station *Bahnhof* ⑩ bahn·hawf
rain *Regen* ⑩ ray·gen
raincoat *Regenmantel* ⑩
ray·gen·man·tel
raisin *Rosine* ① ro·zee·ne
rally *Rallye* ① re·li
rape *vergewaltigen* fer·ge·val·ti·gen
rapids *Stromschnellen* ⑩ pl
shtrawm·shne·len
rare *selten* zel·ten
rash *Ausschlag* ⑩ ows·shlahk
raspberry *Himbeere* ① him·bair·re
rat *Ratte* ① ra·te
rate of pay *Lohn(satz)* ⑩ lawn(·zats)
raw *roh* raw

razor *Rasierer* ⓜ ra·zee·rer
razor blades *Rasierklingen* ⓕ pl
ra·zeer·kling·en
read *lesen* lay·zen
reading *Lesung* ⓕ lay·zung
ready *fertig* fer·tikh
real estate agent *Makler(in)* ⓜ/ⓕ
mahk·ler/mahk·le·rin
realistic *realistisch* re·a·lis·tish
reason *Grund* ⓜ grunt
receipt *Quittung* ⓕ kvi·tung
receive *erhalten* er·hal·ten
recently *vor kurzem* fawr kur·tsem
recharge *aufladen* owf·lah·den
recommend *empfehlen* emp·fay·len
recording *Aufnahme* ⓕ owf·nah·me
recyclable *wiederverwertbar*
vee·der·fer·vert·bahr
recycle *recyceln* ri·sai·keln
red *rot* rawt
referee *Schiedsrichter(in)* ⓜ/ⓕ
sheets·rikh·ter/sheets·rikh·te·rin
reference (work) *Zeugnis* ⓝ tsoyk·nis
referendum *Volksentscheid* ⓜ
folks·ent·shait
reflexology *Fußreflexzonenmassage* ⓕ
foos·ray·fleks·tsaw·nen·ma·sah·zhe
refrigerator *Kühlschrank* ⓜ kül·shrangk
refugee *Flüchtling* ⓜ flükht·ling
refund *Rückzahlung* ⓕ rük·tsah·lung
refuse *ablehnen* ap·lay·nen
region *Region* ⓕ re·gyawn
registered mail *Einschreiben* ⓝ
ain·shrai·ben
regulation *Vorschrift* ⓕ fawr·shrift
relation (family) *Verwandte* ⓜ&ⓕ
fer·van·te
relationship *Beziehung* ⓕ be·tsee·ung
relax *sich entspannen* zikh ent·shpa·nen
relic (religious) *Reliquie* ⓕ re·lee·kvi·e
religion *Religion* ⓕ re·li·gyawn
religious *religiös* re·li·gyers
remote *abgelegen* ap·ge·lay·gen
remote control *Fernbedienung* ⓕ
fern·be·dee·nung
rent *mieten* mee·ten
repair *reparieren* re·pa·ree·ren
repeat *wiederholen* vee·der·haw·len
republic *Republik* ⓕ re·pu·bleek

reservation *Reservierung* ⓕ
re·zer·vee·rung
reserve *reservieren* re·zer·vee·ren
rest *eine Pause machen*
ai·ne pow·ze ma·khen
restaurant *Restaurant* ⓝ res·to·rahng
resume (CV) *Lebenslauf* ⓜ
lay·bens·lowf
retired *pensioniert* pahng·zyo·neert
return *zurückkommen* tsu·rük·ko·men
return (ticket) *Rückfahrkarte* ⓕ
rük·fahr·kar·te
review (arts) *Kritik* ⓕ kri·teek
rhythm *Rhythmus* ⓜ rüt·mus
rice *Reis* ⓜ rais
rich (wealthy) *reich* raikh
ride *Ritt* ⓜ rit
ride (horse) *reiten* rai·ten
riding school *Reitschule* ⓕ rait·shoo·le
right (correct) *richtig* rikh·tikh
right (direction) *rechts* rekhts
right there *gleich dort* glaikh dort
right-wing *rechts(gerichtet)*
rekhts(·ge·rikh·tet)
ring (on finger) *Ring* ⓜ ring
ring (of phone) *klingeln* kling·eln
rip-off *Abzockerei* ⓕ ap·tso·ke·rai
risk *Risiko* ⓝ ree·zi·ko
river *Fluss* ⓜ flus
road *Straße* ⓕ shtrah·se
road map *Straßenkarte* ⓕ
shtrah·sen·kar·te
rob *berauben* be·row·ben
robbery *Raub* ⓜ rowp
rock *Fels* ⓜ fels
rock (music) *Rockmusik* ⓕ rok·mu·zeek
rock climbing *Klettern* ⓝ kle·tern
rock group *Rockgruppe* ⓕ rok·gru·pe
roll (bread) *Brötchen* ⓝ brert·khen
romantic *romantisch* ro·man·tish
roof *Dach* ⓝ dakh
room *Zimmer* ⓝ tsi·mer
rope *Seil* ⓝ zail
round *rund* runt
roundabout *Kreisverkehr* ⓜ krais·fer·kair
route *Route* ⓕ roo·te
rowing *Rudern* ⓝ roo·dern
rubbish *Müll* ⓜ mül
rug *Teppich* ⓜ te·pikh

rugby *Rugby* ⓝ *rag*·bi
ruins *Ruinen* ① pl *ru*·ee·nen
rules *Regeln* ① pl *ray*·geln
rum *Rum* ⓜ rum
run *laufen low*·fen
run out of *ausgehen ows*·gay·en

S

Sabbath *Sabbat* ⓜ *za*·bat
sad *traurig trow*·rikh
saddle *Sattel* ⓜ *za*·tel
safe *Safe* ⓝ sayf
safe *sicher zi*·kher
safe sex *Safe Sex* ⓜ sayf seks
safety *Sicherheit* ① *zi*·kher·hait
sailing *Segeln* ⓝ *zay*·geln
saint *Heilige* ⓜ&① *hai*·li·ge
salad *Salat* ⓜ za·*laht*
salami *Salami* ① za·*lah*·mi
salary *Gehalt* ⓝ ge·*halt*
sale *(Sonder)Angebot* ⓝ
  (zon·der·)*an*·ge·bawt
sales tax *Umsatzsteuer* ①
  um·zats·shtoy·er
salmon *Lachs* ⓜ laks
salt *Salz* ⓝ zalts
same *gleiche glai*·khe
sand *Sand* ⓜ zant
sandals *Sandalen* ① pl zan·*dah*·len
sanitary napkins *Damenbinden* ① pl
  dah·men·bin·den
sardine *Sardine* ① zar·*dee*·ne
Saturday *Samstag* ⓜ *zams*·tahk
sauce *Sauce/Soße* ① *zaw*·se
sauna *Sauna* ① *zow*·na
sausage *Wurst* ① vurst
save (money) *sparen shpah*·ren
save (someone) *retten re*·ten
say *sagen zah*·gen
scarf *Schal* ⓜ shahl
scenery *Landschaft* ① *lant*·shaft
school *Schule* ① *shoo*·le
science *Wissenschaft* ① *vi*·sen·shaft
scientist *Wissenschaftler(in)* ⓜ/①
  vi·sen·shaft·ler/*vi*·sen·shaft·le·rin
scissors *Schere* ① *shair*·re
score *ein Tor schießen* ain tawr *shee*·sen
scoreboard *Anzeigetafel* ①
  an·tsai·ge·tah·fel

Scotland *Schottland* ⓝ *shot*·lant
screen (TV/computer) *Bildschirm* ⓜ
  bilt·shirm
screwdriver *Schraubenzieher* ⓜ
  shrow·ben·tsee·er
script *Drehbuch* ⓝ *dray*·bookh
sculpture *Skulptur* ① skulp·*toor*
sea *Meer* ⓝ mair
seagull *Möwe* ① *mer*·ve
seasick *seekrank zay*·krangk
seaside *Meeresküste* ① *mair*·es·küs·te
season *Jahreszeit* ① *yah*·res·tsait
seat (car) *Sitz* ⓜ zits
seat (train/cinema) *Platz* ⓜ plats
seatbelt *Sicherheitsgurt* ⓜ
  zi·kher·haits·gurt
second *Sekunde* ① ze·*kun*·de
second *zweite tsvai*·te
second-hand *gebraucht* ge·*browkht*
second-hand shop
  Secondhandgeschäft ⓝ
  se·kend·*hend*·ge·sheft
secret *Geheimnis* ⓝ ge·*haim*·nis
secretary *Sekretär(in)* ⓜ/①
  ze·kre·*tair*(·rin)
see *sehen zay*·en
self-employed *selbstständig*
  zelpst·shten·dikh
selfish *egoistisch* e·go·*is*·tish
self-service *Selbstbedienung* ①
  zelpst·be·dee·nung
sell *verkaufen* fer·*kow*·fen
send *senden zen*·den
sensible *vernünftig* fer·*nünf*·tikh
sensual *sinnlich zin*·likh
separate *getrennt* ge·*trent*
serial *Serien- zair*·ri·en·
series *Serie* ① *zair*·ri·e
serious *ernst* ernst
service charge *Bedienungszuschlag* ⓜ
  be·*dee*·nungks·tsoo·shlahk
service station *Tankstelle* ①
  tangk·shte·le
several *einige ai*·ni·ge
sew *nähen nay*·en
sex *Sex* ⓜ seks
sexism *Sexismus* ⓜ sek·*sis*·mus
sexy *sexy sek*·si
shade *Schatten* ⓜ *sha*·ten

shadow *Schatten* ⓝ *sha*·ten
shampoo *Shampoo* ⓝ *sham*·poo
shape *Form* ⓕ form
share (with) *teilen (mit)* tai·len (mit)
shave *rasieren* ra·zee·ren
shaving cream *Rasiercreme* ⓕ
  ra·zeer·kraym
she *sie* zee
sheep *Schaf* ⓝ shahf
sheet (bed) *Bettlaken* ⓝ *bet*·lah·ken
shelf *Regal* ⓝ re·*gahl*
ship *Schiff* ⓝ shif
shirt *Hemd* ⓝ hemt
shoe shop *Schuhgeschäft* ⓝ
  shoo·ge·sheft
shoes *Schuhe* ⓝ pl *shoo*·e
shoot (gun) *schießen* *shee*·sen
shop *Geschäft* ⓝ ge·*sheft*
shopping centre *Einkaufszentrum* ⓝ
  ain·kowfs·tsen·trum
short *kurz* kurts
short (height) *klein* klain
shortage *Knappheit* ⓕ *knap*·hait
shortcut *Abkürzung* ⓕ *ap*·kür·tsung
shorts *Shorts* pl shorts
short-sleeved *kurzärmelig*
  kurts·er·me·likh
shoulder *Schulter* ⓕ *shul*·ter
shout *schreien* *shrai*·en
show *Show* ⓕ shoh
show *zeigen* *tsai*·gen
shower *Dusche* ⓕ *doo*·she
shrine *Schrein* ⓝ shrain
shut (closed) *geschlossen* ge·*shlo*·sen
shut (close) *schließen* *shlee*·sen
shy *schüchtern* *shükh*·tern
sick *krank* krangk
side *Seite* ⓕ *zai*·te
sign *Schild* ⓝ shilt
signature *Unterschrift* ⓕ *un*·ter·shrift
signpost *Wegweiser* ⓜ *vayk*·vai·zer
silk *Seide* ⓕ *zai*·de
silver *silbern* *zil*·bern
similar *ähnlich* *ayn*·likh
simple *einfach* *ain*·fakh
since (May) *seit (Mai)* zait (mai)
sing *singen* *zing*·en
Singapore *Singapur* ⓝ *zing*·a·poor
singer *Sänger(in)* ⓜ/ⓕ
  zeng·er/*zeng*·e·rin

single (person) *Single* ⓜ singl
single (unmarried) *ledig* lay·dikh
single room *Einzelzimmer* ⓝ
  ain·tsel·tsi·mer
singlet *Unterhemd* ⓝ *un*·ter·hemt
sister *Schwester* ⓕ *shves*·ter
sit *sitzen* *zi*·tsen
situation *Lage* ⓕ *lah*·ge
size *Größe* ⓕ *grer*·se
skate *eislaufen* *ais*·low·fen
skateboarding *Skateboarden* ⓝ
  skayt·bor·den
ski *skifahren* *shee*·fah·ren
skiing *Skifahren* ⓝ *shee*·fah·ren
skimmed milk *fettarme Milch* ⓕ
  fet·ar·me milkh
skin *Haut* ⓕ howt
skirt *Rock* ⓜ rok
sky *Himmel* ⓜ *hi*·mel
sleep *schlafen* *shlah*·fen
sleeping bag *Schlafsack* ⓜ *shlahf*·zak
sleeping car *Schlafwagen* ⓜ
  shlahf·vah·gen
sleeping pills *Schlaftabletten* ⓕ pl
  shlahf·ta·ble·ten
sleepy *schläfrig* *shlayf*·rikh
slide (film) *Dia* ⓝ *dee*·a
slippery *glatt* glat
slope *Hang* ⓜ hang
slow *langsam* *lang*·zahm
slowly *langsam* *lang*·zahm
small *klein* klain
smell *Geruch* ⓜ ge·*rookh*
smile *lächeln* *le*·kheln
smoke *rauchen* *row*·khen
snack *Snack* ⓜ snek
snail *Schnecke* ⓕ *shne*·ke
snake *Schlange* ⓕ *shlang*·e
snorkelling *Schnorcheln* ⓝ *shnor*·kheln
snow *Schnee* ⓜ shnay
snow pea *Zuckererbse* ⓕ *tsu*·ker·erp·se
snowboarding *Snowboarden* ⓝ
  snoh·bor·den
snowfield *Schneefeld* ⓝ *shnay*·felt
soap *Seife* ⓕ *zai*·fe
soap opera *Seifenoper* ⓕ
  zai·fen·aw·per
soccer *Fußball* ⓜ *foos*·bal
social welfare *Wohlfahrt* ⓕ *vawl*·fahrt

socialist *sozialistisch* zo·tsya·*lis*·tish
socks *Socken* ① pl zo·ken
soft drink *alkoholfreies Getränk* ⑥
al·ko·*hawl*·frai·es ge·*trengk*
sold out *ausverkauft* ows·fer·kowft
solid *fest* fest
some *einige* *ai*·ni·ge
someone *jemand* *yay*·mant
something *etwas* et·vas
sometimes *manchmal* *mankh*·mahl
son *Sohn* ⑥ zawn
song *Lied* ⑥ leet
son-in-law *Schwiegersohn* ⑥
shvee·ger·zawn
soon *bald* balt
sore *schmerzhaft* *shmerts*·haft
sore throat *Halsschmerzen* ⑥ pl
hals·shmer·tsen
soup *Suppe* ① *zu*·pe
sour cream *Schmand* ⑥ shmant
south *Süden* ⑥ *zü*·den
souvenir *Souvenir* ⑥ zu·ve·*neer*
souvenir shop *Souvenirladen* ⑥
zu·ve·*neer*·lah·den
soy milk *Sojamilch* ① *zaw*·ya·milkh
soy sauce *Sojasauce* ① *zaw*·ya·zaw·se
space *Raum* ⑥ rowm
spade *Spaten* ⑥ *shpah*·ten
Spain *Spanien* ⑥ *shpah*·ni·en
spare tyre *Reservereifen* ⑥
re·*zer*·ve·rai·fen
speak *sprechen* *shpre*·khen
special *speziell* shpe·*tsyel*
specialist *Spezialist(in)* ⑥/①
shpe·tsya·*list*/shpe·tsya·*lis*·tin
speed *Geschwindigkeit* ①
ge·*shvin*·dikh·kait
speed limit
Geschwindigkeits-begrenzung ①
ge·*shvin*·dikh·kaits·be·gren·tsung
spicy *würzig* *vür*·tsikh
spider *Spinne* ① *shpi*·ne
spinach *Spinat* ⑥ shpi·*naht*
spokes *Speichen* ① pl *shpai*·khen
spoon *Löffel* ⑥ *ler*·fel
sport *Sport* ⑥ shport
sportsperson *Sportler(in)* ⑥/①
shport·ler/*shport*·le·rin
sprain *Muskelzerrung* ①
mus·kel·tser·rung

spring (coil) *Feder* ① *fay*·der
spring (season) *Frühling* ⑥ *frü*·ling
square (town) *Platz* ⑥ plats
stadium *Stadion* ⑥ *shtah*·di·on
stage *Stadium* ⑥ *shtah*·di·um
stage (theatre) *Bühne* ① *bü*·ne
stairway *Treppe* ① *tre*·pe
stamp *Briefmarke* ① *breef*·mar·ke
standby ticket *Standby-Ticket* ⑥
stend·*bai*·ti·ket
standing room *Stehplatz* ⑥ *shtay*·plats
star sign *Sternzeichen* ⑥
shtern·tsai·khen
star *Stern* ⑥ shtern
(four-)star *(Vier-)Sterne-* (feer·)*shter*·ne·
start *Beginn* ⑥ be·*gin*
start (sport) *Start* ⑥ shtart
start *anfangen* *an*·fang·en
state *Staat* ⑥ shtaht
station *Bahnhof* ⑥ *bahn*·hawf
stationer *Schreibwarenhandlung* ①
shraip·vah·ren·han·dlung
statue *Statue* ① *shtah*·tu·e
stay (at a hotel) *übernachten*
ü·ber·*nakh*·ten
stay (not leave) *bleiben* *blai*·ben
steak (beef) *Steak* ⑥ stayk
steal *stehlen* *shtay*·len
steep *steil* shtail
step (stairs) *Stufe* ① *shtoo*·fe
stereo *Stereoanlage* ①
shtair·re·o·an·lah·ge
stingy *geizig* *gai*·tsikh
stock *Vorrat* ⑥ *fawr*·raht
stockings *Strümpfe* ⑥ pl *shtrümp*·fe
stomach *Magen* ⑥ *mah*·gen
stomachache *Magenschmerzen* ⑥ pl
mah·gen·shmer·tsen
stone *Stein* ⑥ shtain
stoned (drugged) *stoned* shtohnd
stop *Halt* ⑥ halt
stop *anhalten* *an*·hal·ten
storm *Sturm* ⑥ shturm
story *Geschichte* ① ge·*shikh*·te
stove *Herd* ⑥ hert
straight *gerade* ge·*rah*·de
strange *fremd* fremt
stranger *Fremde* ⑥&① *frem*·de
strawberry *Erdbeere* ① *ert*·bair·re

stream *Bach* ⓜ bakh
street *Straße* ⓕ shtrah·se
street kids *Straßenkinder* ⓜ pl
  shtrah·sen·kin·der
on strike *streiken* shtrai·ken
string *Schnur* ⓕ shnoor
strong *stark* shtark
stubborn *stur* shtoor
student *Student(in)* ⓜ/ⓕ
  shtu·dent/shtu·den·tin
student card *Studentenausweis* ⓜ
  shtu·den·ten·ows·vais
studio *Studio* ⓝ shtoo·di·o
studio (art) *Atelier* ⓝ a·tel·yay
study *studieren* shtu·dee·ren
stupid *dumm* dum
style *Stil* ⓜ shteel
subtitles *Untertitel* ⓜ pl un·ter·tee·tel
suburb *Vorort* ⓜ fawr·ort
subway *U-Bahn* ⓕ oo·bahn
sugar *Zucker* ⓜ tsu·ker
suitcase *Koffer* ⓜ ko·fer
summer *Sommer* ⓜ zo·mer
sun *Sonne* ⓕ zo·ne
sunblock *Sonnencreme* ⓕ
  zo·nen·kraym
sunburn *Sonnenbrand* ⓜ zo·nen·brant
Sunday *Sonntag* ⓜ zon·tahk
sunglasses *Sonnenbrille* ⓕ
  zo·nen·bri·le
sunny *sonnig* zo·nikh
sunrise *Sonnenaufgang* ⓜ
  zo·nen·owf·gang
sunset *Sonnenuntergang* ⓜ
  zo·nen·un·ter·gang
supermarket *Supermarkt* ⓜ
  zoo·per·markt
superstition *Aberglaube* ⓜ
  ah·ber·glow·be
supporters *Anhänger* ⓜ pl an·heng·er
surf *surfen* ser·fen
surface mail *normale Post* ⓕ
  nor·mah·le post
surfboard *Surfbrett* ⓝ serf·bret
surname *Nachname* ⓜ nahkh·nah·me
surprise *Überraschung* ⓕ ü·ber·ra·shung
sweater *Pullover* ⓜ pu·law·ver
Sweden *Schweden* ⓝ shvay·den
sweet *süß* züs

swim *schwimmen* shvi·men
swimming pool *Schwimmbad* ⓝ
  shvim·baht
swimsuit *Badeanzug* ⓜ
  bah·de·an·tsook
Switzerland *Schweiz* ⓕ shvaits
synagogue *Synagoge* ⓕ zü·na·gaw·ge
synthetic *synthetisch* zün·tay·tish
syringe *Spritze* ⓕ shpri·tse

table *Tisch* ⓜ tish
table tennis *Tischtennis* ⓝ tish·te·nis
tablecloth *Tischdecke* ⓕ tish·de·ke
tail *Schwanz* ⓜ shvants
tailor *Schneider(in)* ⓜ/ⓕ
  shnai·der/shnai·de·rin
take *nehmen* nay·men
take (to) *bringen* bring·en
take off *Abflug* ⓜ ap·flook
talk *sprechen* shpre·khen
tall *groß* graws
tampons *Tampons* ⓜ pl tam·pons
tanning lotion *Bräunungsmilch* ⓕ
  broy·nungks·milkh
tap *Wasserhahn* ⓜ va·ser·hahn
target *Ziel* ⓝ tseel
tasty *schmackhaft* shmak·haft
tax *Steuer* ⓕ shtoy·er
taxi *Taxi* ⓝ tak·si
taxi stand *Taxistand* ⓜ tak·si·shtant
tea *Tee* ⓜ tay
teacher *Lehrer(in)* ⓜ/ⓕ
  lair·rer/lair·re·rin
team *Mannschaft* ⓕ man·shaft
teaspoon *Teelöffel* ⓜ tay·ler·fel
technique *Technik* ⓕ tekh·nik
teeth *Zähne* ⓜ pl tsay·ne
telegram *Telegramm* ⓝ te·le·gram
telephone *Telefon* ⓝ te·le·fawn
telephone *telefonieren* te·le·fo·nee·ren
telephone book *Telefonbuch* ⓝ
  te·le·fawn·bookh
telephone centre *Telefonzentrale* ⓕ
  te·le·fawn·tsen·trah·le
telescope *Teleskop* ⓝ te·les·kawp
television *Fernseher* ⓜ fern·zay·er
tell *erzählen* er·tsay·len
temperature (fever) *Fieber* ⓝ fee·ber

temperature (weather) *Temperatur* ①
tem·pe·ra·toor

temple *Tempel* ⑩ tem·pel

ten *zehn* tsayn

tennis *Tennis* ① te·nis

tennis court *Tennisplatz* ⑩ te·nis·plats

tent *Zelt* ⑪ tselt

tent pegs *Heringe* ⑪ pl hay·ring·e

terminal (transport) *Endstation* ①
ent·shta·tsyawn

terrible *schrecklich* shrek·likh

test *Test* ⑩ test

thank *danken* dang·ken

theatre *Theater* ⑪ te·ah·ter

their *ihr* eer

there *dort* dort

thermos *Thermosflasche* ①
ter·mos·fla·she

they *sie* zee

thick *dick* dik

thief *Dieb* ⑩ deep

thin *dünn* dün

think *denken* deng·ken

third *dritte* dri·te

thirsty *durstig* durs·tikh

this (month) *diesen (Monat)*
dee·zen (maw·nat)

this (one) *dieser/diese/dieses* ⑩/①/⑪
dee·zer/dee·ze/dee·zes

thousand *tausend* tow·zent

throat *Hals* ⑩ hals

through *durch* durkh

thrush (condition) *Mundfäule* ①
munt·foy·le

thunder *Donner* ⑩ do·ner

Thursday *Donnerstag* ⑩ do·ners·tahk

ticket (bus/metro/train) *Fahrkarte* ①
fahr·kar·te

ticket (cinema/museum)
Eintrittskarte ① ain·trits·kar·te

ticket (plane) *Flugticket* ⑪ flook·ti·ket

ticket collector
Fahrkartenkontrolleur/in ⑩/①
fahr·kar·ten·kon·tro·ler/
fahr·kar·ten·kon·tro·ler·rin

ticket machine *Fahrkartenautomat* ⑩
fahr·kar·ten·ow·to·maht

ticket office *Fahrkartenverkauf* ⑩
fahr·kar·ten·fer·kowf

ticket office (theatre) *Theaterkasse* ①
te·ah·ter·ka·se

tides *Gezeiten* pl ge·tsai·ten

tight *eng* eng

time *Zeit* ① tsait

time difference *Zeitunterschied* ⑩
tsait·un·ter·sheet

timetable *Fahrplan* ⑩ fahr·plahn

tin (can) *Dose* ① daw·ze

tin opener *Dosenöffner* ⑩
daw·zen·erf·ner

tiny *winzig* vin·tsikh

tip (gratuity) *Trinkgeld* ⑪ tringk·gelt

tire *ermüden* er·mü·den

tired *müde* mü·de

tissues *Papiertaschentücher* ⑪ pl
pa·peer·ta·shen·tü·kher

toast *Toast* ⑩ tawst

toaster *Toaster* ⑩ taws·ter

tobacco *Tabak* ⑩ ta·bak

tobacconist *Tabakladen* ⑩
ta·bak·lah·den

tobogganing *Rodeln* ⑪ raw·deln

today *heute* hoy·te

toe *Zehe* ① tsay·e

tofu *Tofu* ⑪ taw·fu

together *zusammen* tsu·za·men

toilet *Toilette* ① to·a·le·te

toilet paper *Toilettenpapier* ⑪
to·a·le·ten·pa·peer

tomato *Tomate* ① to·mah·te

tomato sauce *Tomatensauce* ①
to·mah·ten·zaw·se

tomb *Grab* ⑩ grahp

tomorrow *morgen* mor·gen

tomorrow morning *morgen früh*
mor·gen frü

tonight *heute Abend* hoy·te ah·bent

too (also) *auch* owkh

too (many) *zu (viele)* tsoo (fee·le)

tools *Werkzeug* ⑪ verk·tsoyk

tooth *Zahn* ⑩ tsahn

toothache *Zahnschmerzen* ⑩ pl
tsahn·shmer·tsen

toothbrush *Zahnbürste* ① tsahn·bürs·te

toothpaste *Zahnpasta* ① tsahn·pas·ta

toothpick *Zahnstocher* ⑩
tsahn·shto·kher

torch (flashlight) *Taschenlampe* ①
ta·shen·lam·pe

touch *berühren* be·rü·ren
tour *Tour* ① toor
tourist *Tourist/in* ⑩/① tu·rist/tu·ris·tin
tourist office *Fremdenverkehrsbüro* ⑩
  frem·den·fer·kairs·bü·raw
towards *auf ... zu* owf ... tsoo
towel *Handtuch* ⑩ hant·tookh
tower *Turm* ⑩ turm
town *Stadt* ① shtat
toxic waste *Giftmüll* ⑩ gift·mül
toy *Spielzeug* ⑩ shpeel·tsoyk
track (path) *Weg* ⑩ vayk
track (sports) *Bahn* ① bahn
trade *Handel* ⑩ han·del
traffic *Verkehr* ⑩ fer·kair
traffic lights *Ampel* ① am·pel
trail *Pfad* ⑩ pfaht
train *Zug* ⑩ tsook
train station *Bahnhof* ⑩ bahn·hawf
tram *Straßenbahn* ① shtrah·sen·bahn
transit lounge *Transitraum* ⑩
  tran·zeet·rowm
translate *übersetzen* ü·ber·ze·tsen
transport *Transport* ⑩ trans·port
travel *reisen* rai·zen
travel agency *Reisebüro* ⑩
  rai·ze·bü·raw
travel sickness *Reisekrankheit* ①
  rai·ze·krangk·hait
travellers cheque *Reisescheck* ⑩
  rai·ze·shek
tree *Baum* ⑩ bowm
trip *Reise* ① rai·ze
trousers *Hose* ① haw·ze
truck *Lastwagen* ⑩ last·vah·gen
true *wahr* vahr
trust *trauen* trow·en
try (attempt) *versuchen* fer·zoo·khen
T-shirt *T-Shirt* ⑩ tee·shert
tube (tyre) *Schlauch* ⑩ shlowkh
Tuesday *Dienstag* ⑩ deens·tahk
tuna *Thunfisch* ⑩ toon·fish
tune *Melodie* ① me·lo·dee
turkey *Truthahn* ⑩ troot·hahn
turn *abbiegen* ap·bee·gen
TV (set) *Fernseher* ⑩ fern·zay·er
TV series *Fernsehserie* ①
  fern·zay·zair·ri·e
tweezers *Pinzette* ① pin·tse·te

twice *zweimal* tsvai·mahl
twin beds *zwei Einzelbetten* ⑩ pl
  tsvai ain·tsel·be·ten
twins *Zwillinge* ⑩ pl tsvi·ling·e
type *Typ* ⑩ tüp
typical *typisch* tü·pish
tyre *Reifen* ⑩ rai·fen

U

ultrasound *Ultraschall* ⑩ ul·tra·shal
umbrella *Regenschirm* ⑩ ray·gen·shirm
uncle *Onkel* ⑩ ong·kel
uncomfortable *unbequem* un·be·kvaym
under *unter* un·ter
underground *U-Bahn* ① oo·bahn
understand *verstehen* fer·shtay·en
underwear *Unterwäsche* ①
  un·ter·ve·she
unemployed *arbeitslos* ar·baits·laws
unemployment *Arbeitslosigkeit* ①
  ar·baits·law·zikh·kait
unfair *unfair* un·fair
uniform *Uniform* ① u·ni·form
universe *Universum* ⑩ u·ni·vair·zum
university *Universität* ① u·ni·ver·zi·tayt
unleaded *bleifrei* blai·frai
unsafe *nicht sicher* nikht zi·kher
until (June) *bis (Juni)* bis (yoo·ni)
unusual *ungewöhnlich* un·ge·vern·likh
up *nach oben* nahkh aw·ben
uphill *aufwärts* owf·verts
upstairs *oben* aw·ben
urgent *dringend* dring·ent
USA *USA* ① pl oo·es·ah
useful *nützlich* nüts·likh

V

vacant *frei* frai
vacation *Ferien* pl fair·i·en
vaccination *Schutzimpfung* ①
  shuts·im·pfung
vagina *Vagina* ① va·gee·na
validate (ticket) *entwerten* ent·ver·ten
valley *Tal* ⑩ tahl
valuable *wertvoll* vert·fol
value (price) *Wert* ⑩ vert
van *Lieferwagen* ⑩ lee·fer·vah·gen

veal *Kalbfleisch* ⓝ *kalp*·flaish

vegetable *Gemüse* ⓝ *ge*·mü·ze

vegetarian *Vegetarier(in)* ⓜ/ⓕ ve·ge·*tah*·ri·er/ve·ge·*tah*·ri·e·rin

vein *Vene* ⓕ *vay*·ne

venereal disease *Geschlechts-krankheit* ⓕ ge·*shlekhts*·krangk·hait

venue *Veranstaltungsort* ⓜ fer·*an*·shtal·tungks·ort

very *sehr* zair

video tape *Videokassette* ⓕ vee·de·o·ka·se·te

view *Aussicht* ⓕ *ows*·zikht

village *Dorf* ⓝ dorf

vine *Rebe* ⓕ *ray*·be

vinegar *Essig* ⓜ *e*·sikh

vineyard *Weinberg* ⓜ *vain*·berk

virus *Virus* ⓜ *vee*·rus

visa *Visum* ⓝ *vee*·zum

visit *besuchen* be·*zoo*·khen

vitamins *Vitamine* ⓝ pl vi·ta·*mee*·ne

vodka *Wodka* ⓕ *vot*·ka

voice *Stimme* ⓕ *shti*·me

volume (amount) *Volumen* ⓝ vo·*loo*·men

volume (book) *Band* ⓜ bant

volume (loudness) *Lautstärke* ⓕ *lowt*·shter·ke

vomit *brechen* *bre*·khen

vote *wählen* *vay*·len

W

wage *Lohn* ⓜ lawn

wait *warten* *var*·ten

waiter *Kellner(in)* ⓜ/ⓕ *kel*·ner/*kel*·ne·rin

waiting room (doctor's) *Wartezimmer* ⓝ *var*·te·tsi·mer

waiting room (train station) *Wartesaal* ⓜ *var*·te·zahl

walk *gehen* *gay*·en

wall (outer) *Mauer* ⓕ *mow*·er

want *wollen* *vo*·len

war *Krieg* ⓜ kreek

wardrobe *Garderobe* ⓕ gar·*draw*·be

warm *warm* varm

warn *warnen* *var*·nen

wash (oneself) *sich waschen* zikh *va*·shen

wash (something) *waschen* *va*·shen

wash cloth (flannel) *Waschlappen* ⓜ *vash*·la·pen

washing machine *Waschmaschine* ⓕ *vash*·ma·shee·ne

washing powder *Waschpulver* ⓝ *vash*·pul·ver

wasp *Wespe* ⓕ *ves*·pe

watch *Uhr* ⓕ oor

watch *beobachten* be·*aw*·bakh·ten

watch (TV) *fernsehen* *fern*·zay·en

water *Wasser* ⓝ *va*·ser

  tap water *Leitungswasser* ⓝ *lai*·tungks·va·ser

water bottle *Wasserflasche* ⓕ *va*·ser·fla·she

waterfall *Wasserfall* ⓜ *va*·ser·fal

watermelon *Wassermelone* ⓕ *va*·ser·me·law·ne

waterproof *wasserdicht* *va*·ser·dikht

waterskiing *Wasserskifahren* ⓝ *va*·ser·shee·fah·ren

wave *Welle* ⓕ *ve*·le

way *Weg* ⓜ vayk

we *wir* veer

weak *schwach* shvakh

wealthy *reich* raikh

weapon *Waffe* ⓕ *va*·fe

wear *tragen* *trah*·gen

weather *Wetter* ⓝ *ve*·ter

wedding *Hochzeit* ⓕ *hokh*·tsait

wedding cake *Hochzeitstorte* ⓕ *hokh*·tsaits·tor·te

wedding present *Hochzeitsgeschenk* ⓝ *hokh*·tsaits·ge·shengk

Wednesday *Mittwoch* ⓜ *mit*·vokh

(this) week *(diese) Woche* ⓕ (*dee*·ze) *vo*·khe

weekend *Wochenende* ⓝ *vo*·khen·en·de

weigh *wiegen* *vee*·gen

weight *Gewicht* ⓝ ge·*vikht*

welcome *willkommen* vil·*ko*·men

welfare *Sozialhilfe* ⓕ zo·*tsyahl*·hil·fe

welfare state *Sozialstaat* ⓜ zo·*tsyahl*·shtaht

well *gut* goot

west *Westen* ⓜ *ves*·ten

wet *nass* nas

what *was* vas
wheel *Rad* ⓝ raht
wheelchair *Rollstuhl* ⓜ rol·shtool
when (adverb) *wann* van
when (conjunction) *wenn* ven
whenever *wann immer* van i·mer
where *wo* vaw
whisky *Whisky* ⓝ vis·ki
white *weiß* vais
who *wer* vair
whole *ganz* gants
why *warum* va·rum
wide *breit* brait
wife *Ehefrau* ⓕ ay·e·frow
wild *wild* vilt
win *gewinnen* ge·vi·nen
winery *Weinkellerei* ⓕ vain·ke·le·rai
wind *Wind* ⓜ vint
window *Fenster* ⓝ fens·ter
windscreen *Windschutzscheibe* ⓕ
   vint·shuts·shai·be
windsurfing *Windsurfen* ⓝ vint·ser·fen
windy *windig* vin·dikh
wine *Wein* ⓜ vain
   red wine *Rotwein* ⓜ rawt·vain
   sparkling wine *Schaumwein* ⓜ
      showm·vain
   white wine *Weißwein* ⓜ vais·vain
wings *Flügel* ⓜ pl flü·gel
winner *Sieger(in)* ⓜ/ⓕ
   zee·ger/zee·ge·rin
winter *Winter* ⓜ vin·ter
wire *Draht* ⓜ draht
wish *wünschen* vün·shen
with *mit* mit
within (an hour) *innerhalb (einer
   Stunde)* i·ner·halp (ai·ner shtun·de)
without *ohne* aw·ne
woman *Frau* ⓕ frow
wonderful *wunderbar* vun·der·bahr
wood *Holz* ⓝ holts
wool *Wolle* ⓕ vo·le
word *Wort* ⓝ vort
work *Arbeit* ⓕ ar·bait
work *arbeiten* ar·bai·ten

work permit *Arbeitserlaubnis* ⓕ
   ar·baits·er·lowp·nis
workout *Training* ⓝ tray·ning
workshop *Werkstatt* ⓕ verk·shtat
world *Welt* ⓕ velt
World Cup *Weltmeisterschaft* ⓕ
   velt·mais·ter·shaft
worms *Würmer* ⓜ pl vür·mer
worried *besorgt* be·zorkt
worse *schlechter* shlekh·ter
worship *einen Gottesdienst besuchen*
   ai·nen go·tes·deenst be·zoo·khen
write *schreiben* shrai·ben
writer *Schriftsteller(in)* ⓜ/ⓕ
   shrift·shte·ler/shrift·shte·le·rin
wrong *falsch* falsh

Y

(this) year *(dieses) Jahr* ⓝ
   (dee·zes) yahr
yellow *gelb* gelp
yes *ja* yah
yesterday *gestern* ges·tern
yet *schon* shawn
not yet *noch nicht* nokh nikht
yoga *Joga* ⓝ yaw·ga
yogurt *Joghurt* ⓜ yaw·gurt
you sg inf *du* doo
you sg&pl pol *Sie* zee
young *jung* yung
your sg inf *dein* dain
your sg&pl pol *Ihr* eer
youth hostel *Jugendherberge* ⓕ
   yoo·gent·her·ber·ge

Z

zero *null* nul
zipper *Reißverschluss* ⓜ rais·fer·shlus
zodiac *Sternzeichen* ⓝ shtern·tsai·khen
zoo *Zoo* ⓜ tsaw
zucchini *Zucchini* ⓕ tsu·kee·ni

Nouns in the dictionary, and adjectives affected by gender, have their gender indicated by ⑦, ⑩ or ⑪. If it's a plural noun, you'll also see pl. Where a word that could be either a noun or a verb has no gender indicated, it's a verb.

A

abbiegen ap·bee·gen *turn*
Abend ⑩ ah·bent *evening*
Abendessen ⑪ ah·bent·e·sen *dinner*
aber ah·ber *but*
Aberglaube ⑩ ah·ber·glow·be *superstition*
abfahren ap·fah·ren *leave (depart)*
Abfahrt ⑦ ap·fahrt *departure*
Abfall ⑩ ap·fal *garbage*
Abfertigungsschalter ⑩ ap·fer·ti·gungks·shal·ter *check-in (desk)*
Abflug ⑩ ap·flook *take off*
Abführmittel ⑪ ap·für·mi·tel *laxatives*
abgelegen ap·ge·lay·gen *remote*
Abgeordnete ⑩&⑦ ap·ge·ord·ne·te *member of parliament*
abgeschlossen ap·ge·shlo·sen *locked*
abhängig ap·heng·ikh *addicted*
Abholzung ⑦ ap·hol·tsung *deforestation*
Abkürzung ⑦ ap·kür·tsung *shortcut*
ablehnen ap·lay·nen *refuse*
Abschleppdienst ⑩ ap·shlep·deenst *breakdown service*
abseits ap·zaits *offside*
Abstrich ⑩ ap·shtrikh *pap smear*
Abtreibung ⑦ ap·trai·bung *abortion*
abwärts ap·verts *downhill*
Abzockerei ⑦ ap·tso·ke·rai *rip-off*
Abzug ⑩ ap·tsook *print (photography)*
Adapter ⑩ a·dap·ter *adaptor*
Adressanhänger ⑩ a·dres·an·heng·er *luggage tag*
Adresse ⑦ a·dre·se *address*
Aerobics pl e·ro·biks *aerobics*
Aerogramm ⑪ air·ro·gram *aerogram*
Afrika ⑪ a·fri·kah *Africa*
Aftershave ⑪ ahf·ter·shayf *aftershave*
ähnlich ayn·likh *similar*
AIDS ⑩ aydz *AIDS*

Aktentasche ⑦ ak·ten·ta·she *briefcase*
Aktivist(in) ⑩/⑦ ak·ti·vist/ak·ti·vis·tin *activist*
Aktuelles ⑪ ak·tu·e·les *current affairs*
Akupunktur ⑦ a·ku·pungk·toor *acupuncture*
Alkohol ⑩ al·ko·hawl *alcohol*
alkoholfreies Getränk ⑪ al·ko·hawl·frai·es ge·trengk *soft drink*
Alkoholiker(in) ⑩/⑦ al·ko·haw·li·ker/ al·ko·haw·li·ke·rin *alcoholic*
alkoholisch al·ko·haw·lish *alcoholic*
alle a·le *all*
Allee ⑦ a·lay *avenue*
allein a·lain *alone*
Allergie ⑦ a·lair·gee *allergy*
alles a·les *everything*
allgemein al·ge·main *general*
alltäglich al·tayk·likh *every day*
alt alt *old • ancient*
Altar ⑩ al·tahr *altar*
Alter ⑪ al·ter *age*
Amateur(in) ⑩/⑦ a·ma·ter(·rin) *amateur*
Ameise ⑦ ah·mai·ze *ant*
Ampel ⑦ am·pel *traffic lights*
sich amüsieren zikh a·mü·zee·ren *enjoy (oneself)*
an an *at • to*
Anarchist(in) ⑩/⑦ a·nar·khist/ a·nar·khis·tin *anarchist*
anbaggern an·ba·gern *chat up*
andere an·de·re *other • different*
anfangen an·fang·en *start*
Anführer ⑩ an·fü·rer *leader*
Angel ⑦ ang·el *fishing rod*
Angestellte ⑩&⑦ an·ge·shtel·te *employee*
Angst (haben) angkst (hah·ben) *(to be) afraid*
anhalten an·hal·ten *stop*

Anhänger ⓜ pl *an*·heng·er *supporters*
ankommen *an*·ko·men *arrive*
Ankunft ⓕ *an*·kunft *arrivals*
ansehen *an*·zay·en *look at*
(an)statt an·*shtat* *instead of*
Anti-Atom- *an*·ti·a·*tawm*· *antinuclear*
Antibiotika ⓝ pl an·ti·bi·*aw*·ti·ka
　antibiotics
Antiquariat ⓝ an·ti·kva·ri·*aht*
　second-hand bookshop
Antiquität ⓕ an·ti·kvi·*tayt antique*
Antiseptikum ⓝ an·ti·*zep*·ti·kum
　antiseptic
Antwort ⓕ *ant*·vort *answer*
antworten *ant*·vor·ten *answer*
Anzahlung ⓕ *an*·tsah·lung *deposit*
Anzeige ⓕ *an*·tsai·ge *advertisement*
Anzeigetafel ⓕ *an*·tsai·ge·tah·fel
　scoreboard
Apfel ⓜ *ap*·fel *apple*
Apfelmost ⓜ *ap*·fel·most *cider*
Apotheke ⓕ a·po·*tay*·ke
　chemist • pharmacy
Aprikose ⓕ a·pri·*kaw*·ze *apricot*
Arbeit ⓕ *ar*·bait *work*
arbeiten *ar*·bai·ten *work*
Arbeiter(in) ⓜ/ⓕ *ar*·bai·ter/*ar*·bai·te·rin
　worker • labourer
Arbeitgeber ⓜ *ar*·bait·gay·ber *employer*
Arbeitserlaubnis ⓕ *ar*·baits·er·lowp·nis
　work permit
arbeitslos *ar*·baits·laws *unemployed*
Arbeitslosengeld ⓝ *ar*·baits·law·zen·gelt
　dole • unemployment benefit
Arbeitslosigkeit ⓕ *ar*·baits·law·zikh·kait
　unemployment
Arbeitsstelle ⓕ *ar*·baits·shte·le *job*
archäologisch ar·khe·o·*law*·gish
　archaeological
Architektur ⓕ ar·khi·tek·*toor*
　architecture
Arm ⓜ arm *arm*
arm arm *poor*
Armut ⓕ *ar*·moot *poverty*
Arzt ⓜ artst *doctor (medical)*
Ärztin ⓕ *erts*·tin *doctor (medical)*
Aschenbecher ⓜ a·shen·be·kher *ashtray*
Asien ⓝ *ah*·zi·en *Asia*
Asthma ⓝ *ast*·ma *asthma*

Asylant(in) ⓜ/ⓕ a·zü·*lant*/a·zü·*lan*·tin
　asylum seeker
Atelier ⓝ a·tel·*yay studio (art)*
atmen *aht*·men *breathe*
Atmosphäre ⓕ at·mos·*fair*·re
　atmosphere
Atomenergie ⓕ a·*tawm*·e·ner·gee
　nuclear energy
Atommüll ⓜ a·*tawm*·mül
　nuclear waste
Aubergine ⓕ aw·ber·*zhee*·ne
　eggplant • aubergine
auch owkh *too • also*
auch nicht owkh nikht *neither*
auf owf *on • at*
auf ... zu owf ... tsoo *towards*
Aufführung ⓕ *owf*·fü·rung *performance*
aufheben owf·*hay*·ben *pick up (object)*
Aufnahme ⓕ *owf*·nah·me *recording*
aufpassen *owf*·pa·sen
　mind (object) • pay attention
Auftritt ⓜ *owf*·trit *gig*
aufwärts *owf*·verts *uphill*
Auge ⓝ *ow*·ge *eye*
Augenblick ⓜ ow·gen·*blik moment*
Augentropfen ⓜ pl ow·gen·*trop*·fen
　eye drops
aus ows *from • out*
aus (Baumwolle) ows (*bawm*·vo·le)
　made of (cotton)
Ausbeutung ⓕ ows·*boy*·tung
　exploitation
Ausgang ⓜ *ows*·gang *exit*
ausgebucht ows·ge·*bookht booked out*
ausgehen *ows*·gay·en
　go out • run out of
mit jemandem ausgehen
　mit *yay*·man·dem ows·*gay*·en
　date someone
ausgeschlossen *ows*·ge·shlo·sen
　excluded
ausgezeichnet ows·ge·*tsaikh*·net
　excellent
Auskunft ⓕ *ows*·kunft *information*
im Ausland im *ows*·lant *abroad*
ausländisch *ows*·len·dish *foreign*
Auspuff ⓜ *ows*·puf *exhaust (car)*
Ausrüstung ⓕ *ows*·rüs·tung *equipment*
Ausschlag ⓜ *ows*·shlahk *rash*

außer *ow-ser apart from • besides*
Aussicht ① *ows-zikht view*
Aussichtspunkt ⓜ *ows-zikhts-pungkt lookout*
Ausstellung ① *ows-shte-lung exhibition*
austeilen *ows-tai-len deal (cards)*
Auster ① *ows-ter oyster*
Australien ⓝ *ows-trah-li-en Australia*
ausverkauft *ows-fer-kowft sold out*
Ausweis ⓜ *ows-vais identification*
Auto ⓝ *ow-to car*
Autobahn ① *ow-to-bahn motorway (tollway)*
Autokennzeichen ⓝ *ow-to-ken-tsai-khen licence plate number*
automatisch *ow-to-mah-tish automatic*
Autor(in) ⓜ/① *ow-tor/ow-taw-rin author*
Autoverleih ⓜ *ow-to-fer-lai car hire*
Avokado ① *a-vo-kah-do avocado*
Axt ① *akst axe*

B

Baby ⓝ *bay-bi baby*
Babynahrung ① *bay-bi-nah-rung baby food*
Babypuder ⓜ *bay-bi-poo-der baby powder*
Babysitter ⓜ *bay-bi-si-ter babysitter*
Bach ⓜ *bakh stream*
Bäckerei ① *be-ke-rai bakery*
Backpflaume ① *bak-pflow-me prune*
Bad ⓝ *baht bath*
Badeanzug ⓜ *bah-de-an-tsook swimsuit*
Badetuch ⓝ *bah-de-tookh bath towel*
Badezimmer ⓝ *bah-de-tsi-mer bathroom*
Bahn ① *bahn track (sports) • railway*
Bahnhof ⓜ *bahn-hawf railway station*
Bahnsteig ⓜ *bahn-shtaik platform*
bald *balt soon*
Balkon ⓜ *bal-kawn balcony*
Ball ⓜ *bal ball*
Ballett ⓝ *ba-let ballet*
Banane ① *ba-nah-ne banana*
Band ① *bent band (music)*
Band ⓜ *bant volume (book)*

Bank ① *bangk bank*
Bankauszug ⓜ *bangk-ows-tsook bankdraft*
Bankkonto ⓝ *bangk-kon-to bank account*
Bär ⓜ *bair bear*
Bargeld ⓝ *bahr-gelt cash*
Batterie ① *ba-te-ree battery*
bauen *bow-en build*
Bauer ⓜ *bow-er farmer*
Bäuerin ① *boy-e-rin farmer*
Bauernhof ⓜ *bow-ern-hawf farm*
Baum ⓜ *bowm tree*
Baumwolle ① *bowm-vo-le cotton*
Bedienungszuschlag ⓜ *be-dee-nungks-tsoo-shlahk service-charge*
bedrohte *be-draw-te endangered*
beenden *be-en-den finish*
Beginn ⓜ *be-gin beginning*
beginnen *be-gi-nen begin*
Begleiter(in) ⓜ/① *be-glai-ter/ be-glai-te-rin companion*
Begräbnis ⓝ *be-grayp-nis funeral*
behindert *be-hin-dert disabled*
bei *bai at*
Beichte ① *baikh-te confession (religious)*
beide *bai-de both*
Bein ⓝ *bain leg (body)*
Beispiel ⓝ *bai-shpeel example*
Bekleidungsgeschäft ⓝ *be-klai-dungks-ge-sheft clothing store*
Belästigung ① *be-les-ti-gung harassment*
Belichtungsmesser ⓜ *be-likh-tungks-me-ser light meter*
beliebt *be-leept popular*
Benzin ⓝ *ben-tseen gas/petrol*
Benzinkanister ⓜ *ben-tseen-ka-nis-ter petrol can*
beobachten *be-aw-bakh-ten watch*
bequem *be-kvaym comfortable*
berauben *be-row-ben rob*
Berg ⓜ *berk mountain*
Berghütte ① *berk-hü-te mountain hut*
Bergsteigen ① *berk-shtai-gen mountaineering*
Bergweg ⓜ *berk-vayk mountain path*

Beruf ⓜ be·*roof*
  occupation • profession
berühmt be·*rümt* famous
berühren be·*rü*·ren touch
beschäftigt be·*shef*·tikht busy (person)
beschützen be·*shü*·tsen protect
sich beschweren zikh be·*shvair*·ren
  complain
besetzt be·*zetst* busy (phone)
Besitzer(in) ⓜ/ⓕ be·*zi*·tser/be·*zi*·tse·rin
  owner
besorgt be·*zorkt* worried
besser be·*ser* better
bestätigen be·*shtay*·ti·gen
  confirm (reservation)
beste *bes*·te best
bestechen be·*shte*·khen bribe
Besteck ⓝ be·*shtek* cutlery
besteigen be·*shtai*·gen
  board (plane, ship)
bestellen be·*shte*·len order
Bestellung ⓕ be·*shte*·lung
  order (restaurant)
bestrafen be·*shtrah*·fen punish
besuchen be·*zoo*·khen visit
Betäubung ⓕ be·*toy*·bung anaesthetic
sich beteiligen zikh be·*tai*·li·gen
  participate
Betrag ⓜ be·*trahk* amount
Betrüger(in) ⓜ/ⓕ be·*trü*·ger/
  be·*trü*·ge·rin cheat
betrunken be·*trung*·ken drunk
Bett ⓝ bet bed
Bettlaken ⓝ *bet*·lah·ken sheet (bed)
Bettler(in) ⓜ/ⓕ *bet*·ler/*bet*·le·rin beggar
Bettwäsche ⓕ *bet*·ve·she linen (bed)
Bettzeug ⓝ *bet*·tsoyk bedding
Beutelmelone ⓕ *boy*·tel·me·law·ne
  cantaloupe
bezahlen be·*tsah*·len pay
Beziehung ⓕ be·*tsee*·ung relationship
BH ⓜ bay·*hah* bra
Bibel ⓕ *bee*·bel bible
Bibliothek ⓕ bi·bli·o·*tayk* library
Biene ⓕ *bee*·ne bee
Bier ⓝ beer beer
Bildschirm ⓜ *bilt*·shirm
  screen (TV, computer)
Billard ⓝ *bil*·yart pool (game)

billig *bi*·likh cheap
Birne ⓕ *bir*·ne pear
bis (Juni) bis (*yoo*·ni) until (June)
bis zu ... bis tsoo ... as far as ...
Biss ⓜ bis bite (animal)
ein bisschen ain *bis*·khen a little
bitte *bi*·te please
um etwas bitten um *et*·vas *bi*·ten
  ask for something
bitter *bi*·ter bitter
Blase ⓕ *blah*·ze blister
Blasenentzündung ⓕ
  blah·zen·en·tsün·dung cystitis
Blatt ⓝ blat leaf
blau blow blue
bleiben *blai*·ben stay (remain)
bleifrei *blai*·frai unleaded
Bleistift ⓜ *blai*·shtift pencil
blind blint blind
Blinddarm ⓜ *blint*·darm appendix
Blindenhund ⓜ *blin*·den·hunt
  guide dog
Blindenschrift ⓕ *blin*·den·shrift Braille
Blitz ⓜ blits lightning • flash
blockiert blo·*keert* blocked
Blume ⓕ *bloo*·me flower
Blumenhändler ⓜ *bloo*·men·hen·dler
  florist
Blumenkohl ⓜ *bloo*·men·kawl
  cauliflower
Blut ⓝ bloot blood
Blutdruck ⓜ *bloot*·druk blood pressure
Blutgruppe ⓕ *bloot*·gru·pe
  blood group
Bluttest ⓜ *bloot*·test blood test
Boden ⓜ *baw*·den floor
Bohne ⓕ *baw*·ne bean
Bonbon ⓝ bong·*bong* candy
Boot ⓝ bawt boat
an Bord an bort aboard
Bordkarte ⓕ *bort*·kar·te boarding pass
Botanischer Garten ⓜ bo·*tah*·ni·sher
  gar·ten botanic garden
Botschaft ⓕ *bawt*·shaft embassy
Botschafter(in) ⓜ/ⓕ *bawt*·shaf·ter/
  bawt·shaf·te·rin ambassador
Boxen ⓝ *bok*·sen boxing
braten *brah*·ten fry

Bratpfanne ① *braht·pfa·ne frying pan*
brauchen *brow·khen need*
braun *brown brown*
brechen *bre·khen vomit*
breit *brait wide*
Bremsen ① pl *brem·zen brakes*
Bremsflüssigkeit ① *brems·flü·sikh·kait brake fluid*
Brennholz ⑪ *bren·holts firewood*
Brennstoff ⑪ *bren·shtof fuel*
Brett ⑪ *bret board (plank)*
Brief ⑪ *breef letter*
Briefkasten ⑪ *breef·kas·ten mailbox*
Briefmarke ① *breef·mar·ke stamp*
Briefumschlag ⑪ *breef·um·shlahk envelope*
brillant *bril·yant brilliant*
Brille ① *bri·le glasses (spectacles)*
bringen *bring·en bring • take (something somewhere)*
Brokkoli ⑪ pl *bro·ko·li broccoli*
Bronchitis ① *bron·khee·tis bronchitis*
Broschüre ① *bro·shü·re brochure*
Brot ⑪ *brawt bread*
Brötchen ⑪ *brert·khen bread roll*
Brücke ① *brü·ke bridge*
Bruder ⑪ *broo·der brother*
Brunnen ⑪ *bru·nen fountain*
Brust ① *brust breast*
Brustkorb ⑪ *brust·korp chest*
Buch ⑪ *bookh book*
buchen *boo·khen book (reserve)*
Buchhalter(in) ⑪/① *bookh·hal·ter/ bookh·hal·te·rin accountant*
Buchhandlung ① *bookh·han·dlung bookshop*
Buddhist(in) ⑪/① *bu·dist/bu·dis·tin Buddhist*
Buffet ⑪ *bü·fay buffet*
bügeln *bü·geln iron (clothes)*
Bühne ① *bü·ne stage (theatre)*
Bundeskanzler(in) ⑪/① *bun·des·kants·ler/bun·des·kants·le·rin prime minister (in Germany & Austria)*
Burg ① *burk castle*
Bürgermeister(in) ⑪/① *bür·ger·mais·ter/bür·ger·mais·te·rin mayor*
Bürgerrechte ⑪ pl *bür·ger·rekh·te civil rights*

Büro ⑪ *bü·raw office*
Büroangestellte ⑪&① *bü·raw·an·ge·shtel·te office worker*
Bus ⑪ *bus bus (city)*
Busbahnhof ⑪ *bus·bahn·hawf bus station*
Bushaltestelle ① *bus·hal·te·shte·le bus stop*
Butter ① *bu·ter butter*

C

Café ⑪ *ka·fay cafe*
Campingplatz ⑪ *kem·ping·plats camping ground*
Cashewnuss ① *kesh·yoo·nus cashew*
CD ① *tsay·day CD*
Celsius ⑪ *tsel·zi·us centigrade*
Chancengleichheit ① *shahng·sen·glaikh·hait equal opportunity*
charmant *shar·mant charming*
Chef(in) ⑪/① *shef/she·fin boss*
chemische Reinigung ① *khay·mi·she rai·ni·gung dry-cleaner*
Chili(sauce) ① *chi·li(·zaw·se) chilli (sauce)*
Christ(in) ⑪/① *krist/kris·tin Christian*
Computerspiel ⑪ *kom·pyoo·ter·shpeel computer game*
Coupon ⑪ *ku·pong coupon*
Couscous ⑪ *kus·kus couscous*
Cousin(e) ⑪/① *ku·zen/ku·zee·ne cousin*
Cracker ⑪ *kre·ker cracker*
Cricket ⑪ *kri·ket cricket*
Curry(pulver) ⑪ *ker·ri(·pul·ver) curry (powder)*

D

Dach ⑪ *dakh roof*
Dachboden ⑪ *dakh·baw·den attic*
Dachs ⑪ *daks badger*
Damenbinden ① pl *dah·men·bin·den sanitary napkins*
Dämmerung ① *de·me·rung dawn • dusk*
danken *dang·ken thank*
Datum ⑪ *dah·tum date (day)*

Decke ① *de*·ke blanket
dein dain *your* sg inf
Demokratie ① de·mo·kra·*tee* democracy
Demonstration ① de·mon·stra·*tsyawn* demonstration
denken *deng*·ken think
Denkmal ① *dengk*·mahl monument
Deo ⑩ *day*·o deodorant
Detail ⑩ de·*tai* detail
Deutsch *doytsh* German
Deutschland ⑩ *doytsh*·lant Germany
Dia ⑩ *dee*·a slide (film)
Diabetis ① di·a·*bay*·tis diabetes
Diät ① di·*ayt* diet
Dichtung ① *dikh*·tung poetry
dick dik thick • fat
Dieb ⑩ deep thief
Dienstag ⑩ *deens*·tahk Tuesday
dieser ⑩ *dee*·zer this (one)
direkt di·*rekt* direct
Diskette ① dis·*ke*·te disk (computer)
Disko(thek) ① dis·ko(·*tayk*) disco
Diskriminierung ① dis·kri·mi·*nee*·rung discrimination
Doktor(in) ⑩/① *dok*·tor/dok·*taw*·rin doctor (title)
Dokumentation ① do·ku·men·ta·*tsyawn* documentary
Dollar ⑩ *do*·lahr dollar
Dolmetscher(in) ⑩/① *dol*·met·sher/ *dol*·met·she·rin interpreter
Dom ⑩ dawm cathedral
Donner ⑩ *do*·ner thunder
Donnerstag ⑩ *do*·ners·tahk Thursday
Dope ⑩ dawp/dohp dope (drugs)
Doppelbett ⑩ *do*·pel·bet double bed
doppelt *do*·pelt double
Doppelzimmer ⑩ *do*·pel·tsi·mer double room
Dorf ⑩ dorf village
dort dort there
Dose ① *daw*·ze can (tin)
Dosenöffner ⑩ *daw*·zen·erf·ner can opener
Dozent(in) ⑩/① do·*tsent*/do·*tsen*·tin lecturer
Drachenfliegen ⑩ *dra*·khen·flee·gen hang-gliding

Draht ⑩ draht wire
draußen *drow*·sen outside
dringend *dring*·ent urgent
dritte *dri*·te third
Droge ① *draw*·ge drug
Drogenabhängigkeit ① *draw*·gen·ap· heng·ikh·kait drug addiction
Drogenhändler ⑩ *draw*·gen·hen·dler drug dealer
Druck ⑩ druk pressure • print (artwork)
Drüsenfieber ⑩ *drü*·zen·fee·ber glandular fever
du doo you sg inf
dumm dum stupid
dunkel *dung*·kel dark
dünn dün thin
durch durkh through
Durchfall ⑩ *durkh*·fal diarrhoea
Durchwahl ① *durkh*·vahl direct-dial
durstig *durs*·tikh thirsty
Dusche ① *doo*·she shower
Dutzend ⑩ *du*·tsent dozen

E

Ebene ① *ay*·be·ne plain
Echse ① *ek*·se lizard
Ecke ① *e*·ke corner
egoistisch e·go·*is*·tish selfish
Ehe ① *ay*·e marriage
Ehefrau ① *ay*·e·frow wife
Ehemann ⑩ *ay*·e·man husband
ehrlich *air*·likh honest
Ei ⑩ ai egg
Eierstockzyste ① *ai*·er·shtok·tsüs·te ovarian cyst
eifersüchtig *ai*·fer·zükh·tikh jealous
in Eile in *ai*·le in a hurry
Eimer ⑩ *ai*·mer bucket
ein(s) ain(s) one
einfach *ain*·fakh simple
einfache Fahrkarte ① *ain*·fa·khe *fahr*·kar·te one-way ticket
einige *ai*·ni·ge some • several
einkaufen gehen *ain*·kow·fen gay·en go shopping
Einkaufszentrum ⑩ *ain*·kowfs·tsen·trum shopping centre
Einkommensteuer ① *ain*·ko·men·shtoy·er income tax

einladen *ain*·lah·den *invite*
einlassen *ain*·la·sen
  admit (allow to enter)
einlösen *ain*·ler·zen *cash (a cheque)*
einmal *ain*·mahl *once*
Einschreiben ⓝ *ain*·shrai·ben
  registered mail
eintreten *ain*·tray·ten *enter*
Eintrittsgeld ⓝ *ain*·trits·gelt
  cover charge
Eintrittskarte ⓕ *ain*·trits·kar·te
  (admission) ticket
Eintrittspreis ⓜ *ain*·trits·prais
  admission price
einzeln aufgeführt *ain*·tseln owf·ge·fürt
  itemised
Einzelzimmer ⓝ *ain*·tsel·tsi·mer
  single room
Eis ⓝ *ais* *ice*
Eiscreme ⓕ *ais*·kraym *ice cream*
Eisdiele ⓕ *ais*·dee·le *ice cream parlour*
Eisenwarengeschäft ⓝ *ai*·zen·vah·ren·
  ge·sheft *hardware store*
Eishockey ⓝ *ais*·ho·ki *ice hockey*
eislaufen *ais*·low·fen *ice skating*
Eispickel ⓜ *ais*·pi·kel *ice axe*
Ekzem ⓝ ek·*tsaym eczema*
Elektrizität ⓕ e·lek·tri·tsi·*tayt electricity*
Elektrogeschäft ⓝ e·*lek*·tro·ge·sheft
  electrical store
Eltern ⓝ pl el·tern *parents*
emotional e·mo·tsyo·*nahl emotional*
empfehlen emp·*fay*·len *recommend*
Empfindlichkeit ⓕ emp·*fint*·likh·kait
  film speed • sensitivity
(am) Ende (am) en·de *(at the) end*
Endstation ⓕ ent·shta·tsyawn *terminal*
Energie ⓕ e·ner·gee *energy*
eng eng *tight*
Englisch ⓝ eng·lish *English*
Enkelkind ⓝ eng·kel·kint *grandchild*
Ente ⓕ en·te *duck*
entscheiden ent·shai·den *decide*
sich entspannen zikh ent·shpa·nen *relax*
entwerfen ent·ver·fen *design*
entwerten ent·ver·ten *validate (ticket)*
Entzündung ⓕ en·*tsün*·dung
  infection • inflammation
Epilepsie ⓕ e·pi·lep·see *epilepsy*

er air *he*
erbrechen er·*bre*·khen *vomit*
Erbse ⓕ erp·se *pea*
Erdbeben ⓝ ert·*bay*·ben *earthquake*
Erdbeere ⓕ ert·*bair*·re *strawberry*
Erde ⓕ er·de *Earth*
Erdnuss ⓕ ert·nus *peanut • ground nut*
Erfahrung ⓕ er·*fah*·rung *experience*
erhalten er·*hal*·ten *receive*
erkältet sein er·*kel*·tet zain *have a cold*
Erlaubnis ⓕ er·*lowp*·nis *permission*
ermüden er·*mü*·den *tire*
ernst ernst *serious*
erstaunlich er·*shtown*·likh *amazing*
erste ers·te *first*
Erwachsene ⓜ&ⓕ er·*vak*·se·ne *adult*
erzählen er·*tsay*·len *tell*
Erziehung ⓕ er·*tsee*·ung *education*
Essen ⓝ e·sen *food*
essen e·sen *eat*
Essig ⓜ e·sikh *vinegar*
etwas et·vas *something • anything*
Euro ⓜ oy·ro *euro*
Europa ⓝ oy·raw·pa *Europe*
Euthanasie ⓕ oy·ta·na·zee *euthanasia*
Express- eks·pres· *express*
Expresspost ⓕ eks·pres·post
  express mail

F

Fabrik ⓕ fa·*breek factory*
fahren fah·ren *travel by vehicle*
Fahrgast ⓜ fahr·gast
  passenger (bus/taxi)
Fahrkarte ⓕ fahr·kar·te *ticket*
Fahrkartenautomat ⓜ fahr·kar·ten·
  ow·to·maht *ticket machine*
Fahrkartenkontrolleur(in) ⓜ/ⓕ fahr·kar·
  ten·kon·tro·ler·(rin) *ticket collector*
Fahrkartenverkauf ⓜ fahr·kar·ten·
  fer·kowf *ticket office*
Fahrplan ⓜ fahr·plahn *timetable*
Fahrrad ⓝ fahr·raht *bicycle*
Fahrradkette ⓕ fahr·raht·ke·te
  bicycle chain
Fahrzeugpapiere ⓝ pl
  fahr·tsoyk·pa·pee·re
  car owner's title (document)
Fallschirmspringen ⓝ
  fal·shirm·shpring·en *parachuting*

F

german–english

229

falsch falsh *false • wrong*
Familie ① fa·mee·li·e *family*
Familienname ⓜ fa·mee·li·en·nah·me *family name*
Familienstand ⓜ fa·mee·li·en·shtant *marital status*
Fan ⓜ fen *fan (sports)*
Farbe ① far·be *colour*
Farben ① pl far·ben *paints*
fast fast *almost*
Fastenzeit ① fas·ten·tsait *Lent*
faul fowl *lazy*
Fax ⓝ faks *fax*
Fechten ⓝ fekh·ten *fencing (sports)*
Feder ① fay·der *spring (coil)*
Fehler ⓜ fay·ler *mistake*
fehlerhaft fay·ler·haft *faulty*
Fehlgeburt ① fayl·ge·burt *miscarriage*
Feier ① fai·er *celebration*
Feige ① fai·ge *fig*
Feinkostgeschäft ⓝ fain·kost·ge·sheft *delicatessen*
Feld ⓝ felt *field*
Feldfrucht ① felt·frukht *crop*
Fels ⓜ fels *rock*
Fenster ⓝ fens·ter *window*
Ferien pl fair·ri·en *holidays/vacation*
Fern- fern· *long-distance*
Fernbedienung ① fern·be·dee·nung *remote control*
Fernbus ⓜ fern·bus *bus (intercity)*
Fernglas ⓝ fern·glahs *binoculars*
fernsehen fern·zay·en *watch TV*
Fernseher ⓜ fern·zay·er *TV set*
Fernsehserie ① fern·zay·zair·ri·e *TV series*
fertig fer·tikh *ready • finished*
Fest ⓝ fest *festival • party*
fest fest *solid*
fettarme Milch ① fet·ar·me milkh *skimmed milk*
feucht foykht *damp*
Feuchtigkeitscreme ① foykh·tikh·kaits·kraym *moisturiser*
Feuer ⓝ foy·er *fire*
Feuerzeug ⓝ foy·er·tsoyk *cigarette lighter*
Fieber ⓝ fee·ber *fever*
Filet ⓝ fi·lay *fillet*

Film ⓜ film *movie (cinema) • film (for camera)*
finden fin·den *find*
Finger ⓜ fing·er *finger*
Firma ① fir·ma *company*
Fisch ⓜ fish *fish*
Fischen ① fi·shen *fishing*
Fitness-Studio ⓝ fit·nes·shtoo·di·o *gym*
flach flakh *flat*
Flagge ① fla·ge *flag*
Flasche ① fla·she *bottle*
Flaschenöffner ⓜ fla·shen·erf·ner *bottle opener*
Fleisch ⓝ flaish *meat*
Fliege ① flee·ge *fly*
fliegen flee·gen *fly*
Flitterwochen pl fli·ter·vo·khen *honeymoon*
Floh ⓜ flaw *flea*
Flohmarkt ⓜ flaw·markt *flea-market*
Flüchtling ⓜ flükht·ling *refugee*
Flug ⓜ flook *flight*
Flügel ⓜ pl flü·gel *wings*
Fluggast ⓜ flook·gast *passenger (plane)*
Flughafen ⓜ flook·hah·fen *airport*
Flughafengebühr ① flook·hah·fen·ge·bür *airport tax*
Fluglinie ① flook·lee·ni·e *airline*
Flugticket ⓝ flook·ti·ket *plane ticket*
Flugzeug ⓝ flook·tsoyk *aeroplane*
Fluss ⓜ flus *river*
folgen fol·gen *follow*
Forderung ① for·de·rung *demand*
Form ① form *shape*
formell for·mel *formal*
Foto ⓝ faw·to *photo*
Fotogeschäft ⓝ faw·to·ge·sheft *camera shop*
Fotograf(in) ⓜ/① fo·to·grahf/ fo·to·grah·fin *photographer*
Fotografie ① fo·to·gra·fee *photograph • photography*
fotografieren fo·to·gra·fee·ren *take a photograph*
Foul ⓝ fowl *foul*
Foyer ⓝ fo·a·yay *foyer*
Frage ① frah·ge *question*
eine Frage stellen ai·ne frah·ge shte·len *ask a question*

Frankreich ⓝ *frangk·raikh France*
Frau ⓕ *frow woman*
frei *frai free (not bound)* • *vacant*
Freibad ⓝ *frai·baht (outdoor) swimming pool*
Freigepäck ⓝ *frai·ge·pek baggage allowance*
Freitag ⓜ *frai·tahk Friday*
fremd *fremt strange*
Fremde ⓜ&ⓕ *frem·de stranger*
Fremdenverkehrsbüro ⓝ *frem·den·fer·kairs·bü·raw tourist office*
Freund ⓜ *froynt male friend* • *boyfriend*
Freundin ⓕ *froyn·din female friend* • *girlfriend*
freundlich *froynt·likh friendly*
Frieden ⓜ *free·den peace*
Friedhof ⓜ *freet·hawf cemetery*
frisch *frish fresh (not stale)*
Frischkäse ⓜ *frish·kay·ze cream cheese*
Friseur(in) ⓜ/ⓕ *fri·zer/fri·zer·rin hairdresser*
Frosch ⓜ *frosh frog*
Frost ⓜ *frost frost*
Frucht ⓕ *frukht fruit*
früh *frü early*
Frühling ⓜ *frü·ling spring (season)*
Frühstück ⓝ *frü·shtük breakfast*
Frühstücksflocke ⓕ *frü·shtüks·flo·ke breakfast cereal*
Frühstücksspeck ⓜ *frü·shtüks·shpek bacon*
fühlen *fü·len feel*
Führer ⓜ *fü·rer (tour) guide* • *guidebook*
Führerschein ⓜ *fü·rer·shain driving licence*
Führung ⓕ *fü·rung guided tour*
füllen *fü·len fill*
Fundbüro ⓝ *funt·bü·raw lost property office*
für *für for*
Fuß ⓜ *foos foot*
Fußball ⓜ *foos·bal football* • *soccer*
Fußgänger(in) ⓜ/ⓕ *foos·geng·er/foos·geng·er·rin pedestrian*
füttern *fü·tern feed*

G

Gabel ⓕ *gah·bel fork*
Gang ⓜ *gang aisle*
Gänge ⓜ pl *geng·e gears*
ganz *gants whole*
Garage ⓕ *ga·rah·zhe garage (car shelter)*
Garderobe ⓕ *gar·draw·be wardrobe* • *cloakroom*
Garnele ⓕ *gar·nay·le prawn*
Garten ⓜ *gar·ten garden*
Gas ⓝ *gahs gas (for cooking)*
Gasflasche ⓕ *gahs·fla·she gas cylinder*
Gaskartusche ⓕ *gahs·kar·tu·she gas cartridge*
Gastfreundschaft ⓕ *gast·froynt·shaft hospitality*
Gebäude ⓝ *ge·boy·de building*
geben *gay·ben give*
Gebet ⓝ *ge·bayt prayer*
Gebirgszug ⓜ *ge·birks·tsook mountain range*
gebraucht *ge·browkht second-hand*
Geburtsdatum ⓝ *ge·burts·dah·tum date of birth*
Geburtsort ⓜ *ge·burts·ort place of birth*
Geburtstag ⓜ *ge·burts·tahk birthday*
Geburtsurkunde ⓕ *ge·burts·oor·kun·de birth certificate*
gefährlich *ge·fair·likh dangerous*
Gefangene ⓜ&ⓕ *ge·fang·e·ne prisoner*
Gefängnis ⓝ *ge·feng·nis prison*
gefiltert *ge·fil·tert filtered*
gefrieren *ge·free·ren freeze*
Gefühle ⓝ pl *ge·fü·le feelings*
gegen *gay·gen against*
gegenüber *gay·gen·ü·ber opposite*
Gegenwart ⓕ *gay·gen·vart present (time)*
Gehacktes ⓝ *ge·hak·tes mince*
Gehalt ⓝ *ge·halt salary*
Geheimnis ⓝ *ge·haim·nis secret*
gehen *gay·en walk*
Gehweg ⓜ *gay·vayk footpath*
Geisteswissenschaften ⓕ pl *gais·tes·vi·sen·shaf·ten humanities*

geizig *gai·*tsikh *stingy*
gelangweilt ge·*lang·*vailt *bored*
gelb gelp *yellow*
Geld ⓝ gelt *money*
Geldautomat ⓜ *gelt·*ow·to·maht
　automatic teller machine (ATM)
Geldbuße ⓕ *gelt·*boo·se
　fine (payment)
Geldschein ⓜ *gelt·*shain *banknote*
Geldwechsel ⓜ *gelt·*vek·sel
　currency exchange
Gelegenheitsarbeit ⓕ
　ge·*lay·*gen·haits·ar·bait *casual work*
Gemüse ⓝ ge·*mü·*ze *vegetable*
Genehmigung ⓕ ge·*nay·*mi·gung
　permit
genug ge·*nook* *enough*
Gepäck ⓝ ge·*pek* *luggage*
Gepäckaufbewahrung ⓕ
　ge·*pek·*owf·be·vah·rung *left luggage*
Gepäckausgabe ⓕ ge·*pek·*ows·gah·be
　luggage claim
gerade ge·*rah·*de *straight (direction)*
Gerechtigkeit ⓕ ge·*rekh·*tikh·kait *justice*
Gericht ⓝ ge·*rikht* *court (legal)*
Geruch ⓜ ge·*rookh* *smell*
Geschäft ⓝ ge·*sheft* *shop • business*
Geschäftsfrau ⓕ ge·*shefts·*frow
　businesswoman
Geschäftsmann ⓜ ge·*shefts·*man
　businessman
Geschäftsreise ⓕ ge·*shefts·*rai·ze
　business trip
Geschenk ⓝ ge·*shengk* *present (gift)*
Geschichte ⓕ ge·*shikh·*te *story*
Geschlechtskrankheit ⓕ
　ge·*shlekhts·*krangk·hait
　venereal disease
geschlossen ge·*shlo·*sen *closed*
geschützte (Tierarten) ⓕ pl ge·*shüts·*te
　(*teer·*ar·ten) *(protected (species)*
Geschwindigkeit ⓕ ge·*shvin·*dikh·kait
　speed
Geschwindigkeitsbegrenzung ⓕ
　ge·*shvin·*dikh·kaits·be·gren·tsung
　speed limit
Gesetz ⓝ ge·*zets* *law*
Gesetzgebung ⓕ ge·*zets·*gay·bung
　legislation
Gesicht ⓝ ge·*zikht* *face*

gestern ges·*tern* *yesterday*
Gesundheit ⓕ ge·*zunt·*hait *health*
Getränk ⓝ ge·*trengk* *drink*
Getränkehandel ⓜ ge·*treng·*ke·han·del
　liquor store
getrennt ge·*trent* *separate (distinct)*
Gewebe ⓝ ge·*vay·*be *fabric*
Gewicht ⓝ ge·*vikht* *weight*
Gewinn ⓜ ge·*vin* *profit*
gewinnen ge·*vi·*nen *win*
Gewürznelke ⓕ ge·*vürts·*nel·ke
　clove (spice)
Gezeiten pl ge·*tsai·*ten *tides*
giftig *gif·*tikh *poisonous*
Giftmüll ⓜ *gift·*mül *toxic waste*
Gin ⓜ dzhin *gin*
Gipfel ⓜ *gip·*fel *peak*
Gitarre ⓕ gi·*ta·*re *guitar*
Glas ⓝ glahs *glass • jar*
glatt glat *slippery*
gleich dort glaikh dort
　right (exactly) there
gleiche *glai·*khe *same*
Gleichheit ⓕ *glaikh·*hait *equality*
Gleis ⓝ glais *platform*
Gleitschirmfliegen ⓝ
　glait·*shirm·*flee·gen *paragliding*
Gletscher ⓜ *glet·*sher *glacier*
Glück ⓝ glük *luck • happiness*
glücklich *glük·*likh *lucky • happy*
Glückwunsch ⓜ *glük·*vunsh
　congratulations
Glühbirne ⓕ *glü·*bir·ne *light bulb*
Gold ⓝ golt *gold*
Golfplatz ⓜ *golf·*plats *golf course*
Gott ⓜ got *god (general)*
Gottesdienst ⓜ go·*tes·*deenst
　church service
Grab ⓝ grahp *grave • tomb*
Grad ⓜ graht *degree*
grafische Kunst ⓕ *grah·*fi·she kunst
　graphic art
Gramm ⓝ gram *gram*
Gras ⓝ grahs *grass • pot (dope)*
gratis *grah·*tis *free (gratis)*
grau grow *grey*
Grenze ⓕ *gren·*tse *border*
Grippe ⓕ *gri·*pe *influenza*
groß graws *big • great • tall*

Größe ⓕ *grer·se* size (general)
Großeltern ⓟ pl *graws·el·tern* grandparents
Großmutter ⓕ *graws·mu·ter* grandmother
Großvater ⓜ *graws·fah·ter* grandfather
grün *grün* green
Grund ⓜ *grunt* reason
Gurke ⓕ *gur·ke* cucumber
Gürtel ⓜ *gür·tel* belt
gut *goot* good • well
gutaussehend *goot·ows·zay·ent* handsome
Gymnastik ⓕ *güm·nas·tik* gymnastics
Gynäkologe ⓜ *gü·ne·ko·law·ge* gynaecologist
Gynäkologin ⓕ *gü·ne·ko·law·gin* gynaecologist

H

Haar ⓝ *hahr* hair
Haarbürste ⓕ *hahr·bürs·te* hairbrush
haben *hah·ben* have
Hafen ⓜ *hah·fen* port • harbour
Hafer(flocken) ⓟ pl *hah·fer·(flo·ken)* oats
Hähnchenschenkel ⓜ *hayn·khen·sheng·kel* chicken drumstick
Halal- *ha·lal·* halal
Hälfte ⓕ *helf·te* half
Hallenbad ⓝ *ha·len·baht* (indoor) swimming pool
hallo *ha·lo/ha·law* hello
halluzinieren *ha·lu·tsi·nee·ren* hallucinate
Hals ⓜ *hals* throat
Halskette ⓕ *hals·ke·te* necklace
Halsschmerzen pl *hals·shmer·tsen* sore throat
Halt ⓜ *halt* stop
Hammer ⓜ *ha·mer* hammer
Hamster ⓜ *hams·ter* hamster
Hand ⓕ *hant* hand
Handel ⓜ *han·del* trade
handgemacht *hant·ge·makht* handmade
Handschuh ⓜ *hant·shoo* glove
Handtasche ⓕ *hant·ta·she* handbag
Handtuch ⓝ *han·tookh* towel

Handwerk ⓝ *hant·verk* crafts
Handy ⓝ *hen·di* mobile phone
Hang ⓜ *hang* slope
Hängematte ⓕ *heng·e·ma·te* hammock
hart *hart* hard (not soft)
Haschee ⓝ *ha·shay* hash
Haupt- *howpt·* main
Hauptplatz ⓜ *howpt·plats* main square
Haus ⓝ *hows* house
Hausarbeit ⓕ *hows·ar·bait* housework
nach Hause *nahkh how·ze* (go) home
Hausfrau ⓕ *hows·frow* homemaker
Hausmann ⓜ *hows·man* homemaker
Haut ⓕ *howt* skin
heilig *hai·likh* holy
Heiligabend ⓜ *hai·likh·ah·bent* Christmas Eve
Heilige ⓜ&ⓕ *hai·li·ge* saint
Heim ⓝ *haim* home
Heimweh haben *haim·vay hah·ben* to be homesick
heiraten *hai·rah·ten* marry
heiß *hais* hot
Heizgerät ⓝ *haits·ge·rayt* heater
helfen *hel·fen* help
hell *hel* light (weight)
Helm ⓜ *helm* helmet
Hemd ⓝ *hemt* shirt
Herausgeber(in) ⓜ/ⓕ *he·rows·gay·ber/he·rows·gay·be·rin* editor
Herbst ⓜ *herpst* autumn • fall
Herd ⓜ *hert* stove
Hering ⓜ *hay·ring* herring
Heringe pl *hay·ring·e* tent pegs
Heroin ⓝ *he·ro·een* heroin
Herz ⓝ *herts* heart
Herzleiden ⓝ *herts·lai·den* heart condition
Herzschrittmacher ⓜ *herts·shrit·ma·kher* pacemaker (heart)
Heuschnupfen ⓜ *hoy·shnup·fen* hay fever
heute *hoy·te* today
heute Abend *hoy·te ah·bent* tonight
hier *heer* here
Hilfe ⓕ *hil·fe* help
Himbeere ⓕ *him·bair·re* raspberry
Himmel ⓜ *hi·mel* sky
Hindu ⓜ&ⓕ *hin·du* Hindu

hinten *hin·ten at the back*
hinter *hin·ter behind*
hinüber *hi·nü·ber across (to)*
historisch *his·taw·rish historical*
Hitze ① *hi·tse heat*
HIV-positiv *hah·ee·fow·paw·zi·teef HIV positive*
hoch *hawkh high (up)*
Hochebene ① *hawkh·ay·be·ne plateau*
Hochzeit ① *hokh·tsait wedding*
Hochzeitsgeschenk ⑩ *hokh·tsaits·ge·shengk wedding present*
Hochzeitstorte ① *hokh·tsaits·tor·te wedding cake*
Hockey ⑩ *ho·ki hockey*
Höhe ① *her·e altitude*
Höhle ① *her·le cave*
Holz ⑩ *holts wood*
homöopathisches Mittel ⑩ *haw·mer·o·pah·ti·shes mi·tel homeopathic medicine*
homosexuell *haw·mo·zek·su·el homosexual*
Honig ⑩ *haw·nikh honey*
hören *her·ren hear • listen*
Hörgerät ⑩ *her·ge·rayt hearing aid*
Horoskop ⑩ *ho·ros·kawp horoscope*
Hose ① *haw·ze trousers/pants*
Hotel ⑩ *ho·tel hotel*
hübsch *hüpsh pretty*
Hüfttasche ① *hüft·ta·she bumbag*
Hügel ⑩ *hü·gel hill*
Huhn ⑩ *hoon chicken*
Hühnerbrust ① *hü·ner·brust chicken breast*
Hülsenfrucht ① *hül·zen·frukht legume*
Hund ⑩ *hunt dog*
hundert *hun·dert hundred*
hungrig *hung·rikh hungry*
husten *hoos·ten cough*
Hustensaft ⑩ *hoos·ten·zaft cough medicine*
Hut ⑩ *hoot hat*
Hütte ① *hü·te hut*
Hüttenkäse ⑩ *hü·ten·kay·ze cottage cheese*

I

ich *ikh I*
Idee ① *i·day idea*
Idiot ⑩ *i·di·awt idiot*

ihr *eer her • their*
Ihr *eer your (polite)*
illegal *i·le·gahl illegal*
immer *i·mer always • forever*
Immigration ① *i·mi·gra·tsyawn immigration*
in *in in • at*
inbegriffen *in·be·gri·fen included*
Indien ⑩ *in·di·en India*
Industrie ① *in·dus·tree industry*
Informationstechnologie ① *in·for·ma·tsyawns·tekh·no·lo·gee IT*
Ingenieuer(in) ⑩/① *in·zhe·nyer(·rin) engineer*
Ingenieurwesen ⑩ *in·zhe·nyer·vay·zen engineering*
Ingwer ⑩ *ing·ver ginger*
Injektion ① *in·yek·tsyawn injection (medical)*
injizieren *in·yi·tsee·ren inject*
innen *i·nen inside*
Innenstadt ① *i·nen·shtat city centre*
innerhalb (einer Stunde) *i·ner·halp (ai·ner shtun·de) within (an hour)*
Insekt ⑩ *in·zekt insect*
Insektenschutzmittel ⑩ *in·zek·ten·shuts·mi·tel insect repellant*
Insel ① *in·zel island*
Installateur(in) ⑩/① *in·sta·la·ter/ in·sta·la·ter·rin plumber*
interessant *in·tre·sant interesting*
international *in·ter·na·tsyo·nahl international*
Internet ⑩ *in·ter·net Internet*
Interview ⑩ *in·ter·vyoo interview*
Intrauterinpessar ⑩ *in·tra·u·te·reen·pe·sahr IUD*
irgendein *ir·gent·ain any*
irgendetwas *ir·gent·et·vas anything*
irgendwo *ir·gent·vaw anywhere*
Irland ⑩ *ir·lant Ireland*

J

ja *yah yes*
Jacke ① *ya·ke jacket*
Jagd ① *yahkt hunting*
Jahr ⑩ *yahr year*
Jahreszeit ① *yah·res·tsait season*

Japan ⑩ *yah*·pahn Japan
Jeans pl dzheens jeans
jeder *yay*·der everyone
jeder ⑩ *yay*·der each • every
jemand *yay*·mant someone
Jetlag ⑩ *dzhet*·leg jet lag
jetzt yetst now
Jockey ⑩ *dzho*·ki jockey
Joga ⑩ *yaw*·ga yoga
Joggen ⑩ *dzho*·gen jogging
Joghurt ⑩ *yaw*·gurt yogurt
Journalist(in) ⑩/⑪ zhur·na·*list*/
  zhur·na·*lis*·tin journalist
Juckreiz ⑩ *yuk*·raits itch
jüdisch *yü*·dish Jewish
Jugendherberge ⑪ *yoo*·gent·her·ber·ge
  youth hostel
jung yung young
Junge ⑩ *yung*·e boy
Jura ⑩ *yoo*·ra law (subject)

K

Kabel ⑩ *kah*·bel cable
Kaffee ⑩ *ka*·fay coffee
Kakao ⑩ ka·*kow* cocoa
Kakerlake ⑪ *kah*·ker·lah·ke cockroach
Kalbfleisch ⑩ *kalp*·flaish veal
Kalender ⑩ ka·*len*·der calendar
kalt kalt cold
Kamera ⑪ *ka*·me·ra camera
Kamm ⑩ kam comb
Kampf ⑩ kampf fight
Kampfsport ⑩ *kampf*·shport
  martial arts
Kanada ⑩ *ka*·na·dah Canada
Kanarienvogel ⑩ ka·*nah*·ri·en·faw·gel
  canary
Kaninchen ⑩ ka·*neen*·khen rabbit
Kantine ⑪ kan·*tee*·ne canteen
Kapelle ⑪ ka·*pe*·le
  chapel • band (music)
Kapitalismus ⑩ ka·pi·ta·*lis*·mus
  capitalism
kaputt ka·*put* broken
Karte ⑪ *kar*·te map • ticket
Karten pl *kar*·ten cards
Kartoffel ⑪ kar·*to*·fel potato
Karton ⑩ kar·*tong* box • carton
Karwoche ⑪ *kahr*·vo·khe Holy Week

Käse ⑩ *kay*·ze cheese
Kasino ⑩ ka·*zee*·no casino
Kasse ⑪ *ka*·se cash register • checkout •
  ticket counter
Kassette ⑪ ka·*se*·te cassette
Kassierer(in) ⑩/⑪ ka·*see*·rer/
  ka·*see*·re·rin cashier
Katholik(in) ⑩/⑪ ka·to·*leek*/
  ka·to·*lee*·kin Catholic
Kätzchen ⑩ *kets*·khen kitten
Katze ⑪ *ka*·tse cat
kaufen *kow*·fen buy
Kaugummi ⑩ *kow*·gu·mi chewing gum
Kaviar ⑩ *kah*·vi·ahr caviar
Keilriemen ⑩ *kail*·ree·men fanbelt
keine *kai*·ne none
Keks ⑩ kayks biscuit • cookie
Keller ⑩ *ke*·ler cellar
Kellner(in) ⑩/⑪ *kel*·ner/*kel*·ne·rin
  waiter
kennen *ke*·nen know (a person)
Keramik ⑪ ke·*rah*·mik ceramic
Kerze ⑪ *ker*·tse candle
Kessel ⑩ *ke*·sel kettle
Ketchup ⑩ *ket*·chap ketchup
Kette ⑪ *ke*·te chain
Kichererbse ⑪ *ki*·kher·erp·se chickpea
Kiefer ⑩ *kee*·fer jaw
Kilogramm ⑩ *kee*·lo·gram kilogram
Kilometer ⑩ ki·lo·*may*·ter kilometre
Kind ⑩ kint child
Kinder pl *kin*·der children
Kinderbetreuung ⑪ *kin*·der·be·troy·ung
  childminding
Kindergarten ⑩ *kin*·der·gar·ten
  kindergarten
Kinderkrippe ⑪ *kin*·der·kri·pe creche
Kindersitz ⑩ *kin*·der·zits child seat
Kino ⑩ *kee*·no cinema
Kiosk ⑩ *kee*·osk convenience store
Kirche ⑪ *kir*·khe church
Kissen ⑩ *ki*·sen pillow
Kissenbezug ⑩ *ki*·sen·be·tsook
  pillowcase
Kiwifrucht ⑪ *kee*·vi·frukht kiwifruit
Klasse ⑪ *kla*·se class
klassisch *kla*·sish classical
Klavier ⑩ kla·*veer* piano
Kleid ⑩ klait dress

Kleidung ⓕ *klai*-dung *clothing*
klein klain *little* • *small* • *short (height)*
Kleingeld ⓝ *klain*-gelt *loose change*
klettern *kle*-tern *climb*
Klettern ⓝ *kle*-tern *rock climbing*
Klima ⓝ *klee*-ma *climate*
Klimaanlage ⓕ *klee*-ma-an-lah-ge
   air-conditioning
klingeln *kling*-eln *ring (of phone)*
Klippe ⓕ *kli*-pe *cliff*
Kloster ⓝ *klaws*-ter
   convent • *monastery*
Knappheit ⓕ *knap*-hait *shortage*
Kneipe ⓕ *knai*-pe *pub*
Knie ⓝ *knee* *knee*
Knoblauch ⓜ *knawp*-lowkh *garlic*
Knöchel ⓜ *kner*-khel *ankle*
Knochen ⓜ *kno*-khen *bone*
Knopf ⓜ knopf *button*
Knoten ⓜ *knaw*-ten *lump (health)*
Koch ⓜ kokh *chef* • *cook*
kochen *ko*-khen *cook*
Kocher ⓜ *ko*-kher *camping stove*
Köchin ⓕ *ker*-khin *chef* • *cook*
Köder ⓜ *ker*-der *bait*
Koffer ⓜ *ko*-fer *suitcase*
Kofferraum ⓜ *ko*-fer-rowm *boot* • *trunk*
Kohl ⓜ kawl *cabbage*
Kokain ⓝ ko-ka-*een* *cocaine*
Kollege ⓜ ko-*lay*-ge *colleague*
Kollegin ⓕ ko-*lay*-gin *colleague*
kommen *ko*-men *come*
Kommunion ⓕ ko-mun-*yawn*
   communion
Komödie ⓕ ko-*mer*-di-e *comedy*
Kompass ⓜ *kom*-pas *compass*
Konditorei ⓕ kon-dee-to-*rai* *cake shop*
Kondom ⓝ kon-*dawm* *condom*
König ⓜ *ker*-nikh *king*
Königin ⓕ *ker*-ni-gin *queen*
können *ker*-nen
   be able to • *have permission to*
konservativ kon-zer-va-*teef* *conservative*
Konsulat ⓝ kon-zu-*laht* *consulate*
Kontaktlinsen ⓕ pl kon-*takt*-lin-zen
   contact lenses
Kontostand ⓜ *kon*-to-shtant
   balance (account)
Kontrollstelle ⓕ kon-*trol*-shte-le
   checkpoint

Konzert ⓝ kon-*tsert* *concert*
Konzerthalle ⓕ kon-*tsert*-ha-le
   concert hall
Kopf ⓜ kopf *head*
Kopfsalat ⓜ *kopf*-za-laht *lettuce*
Kopfschmerzen pl *kopf*-shmer-tsen
   headache
Kopfschmerztablette ⓕ
   kopf-shmerts-ta-ble-te *aspirin*
Korb ⓜ korp *basket*
Körper ⓜ *ker*-per *body*
korrupt ko-*rupt* *corrupt*
koscher *kaw*-sher *kosher*
kosten *kos*-ten *cost*
köstlich *kerst*-likh *delicious*
Kraft ⓕ kraft *power*
Krampf ⓜ krampf *cramp*
krank krangk *sick*
Krankenhaus ⓝ *krang*-ken-hows
   hospital
Krankenpfleger ⓜ *krang*-ken-pflay-ger
   nurse
Krankenschwester ⓕ
   krang-ken-shves-ter *nurse*
Krankenwagen ⓜ *krang*-ken-vah-gen
   ambulance
Krankheit ⓕ *krangk*-hait *disease*
Kräuter pl *kroy*-ter *herbs*
Krebs ⓜ krayps *cancer*
Kreditkarte ⓕ kre-*deet*-kar-te
   credit card
Kreisverkehr ⓜ *krais*-fer-kair
   roundabout
Kreuz ⓝ kroyts *cross (religious)*
Krieg ⓜ kreek *war*
Kritik ⓕ kri-*teek* *review (arts)*
Küche ⓕ *kü*-khe *kitchen*
Kuchen ⓜ *koo*-khen *cake*
Kuckucksuhr ⓕ *ku*-kuks-oor
   cuckoo clock
Kugelschreiber ⓜ *koo*-gel-shrai-ber
   pen (ballpoint)
Kuh ⓕ koo *cow*
Kühler ⓜ *kü*-ler *radiator*
Kühlschrank ⓜ *kül*-shrangk *refrigerator*
sich kümmern um zikh *kü*-mern um
   look after
Kunde ⓜ *kun*-de *client*
kündigen *kün*-di-gen *resign*
Kundin ⓕ *kun*-din *client*

Kunst ① *kunst art*
Kunstgalerie ① *kunst·ga·le·ree art gallery*
Kunstgewerbe ⑩ *kunst·ge·ver·be arts & crafts*
Kunsthandwerk ⑩ *kunst·hant·verk handicrafts*
Künstler(in) ⑩/① *künst·ler/künst·le·rin artist*
Kunstsammlung ① *kunst·zam·lung art collection*
Kunstwerk ⑩ *kunst·verk work of art*
Kupplung ① *kup·lung clutch (car)*
Kürbis ⑩ *kür·bis pumpkin*
kurz *kurts short*
kurzärmelig *kurts·er·me·likh short-sleeved*
Kuss ⑩ *kus kiss*
küssen *kü·sen kiss*
Küste ① *küs·te coast*

L

lächeln *le·kheln smile*
lachen *la·khen laugh*
Lachs ⑩ *laks salmon*
Lage ① *lah·ge situation*
Lager ⑩ *lah·ger lager*
Lamm ⑩ *lam lamb*
Land ⑩ *lant country • countryside*
Landschaft ① *lant·shaft scenery*
Landwirtschaft ① *lant·virt·shaft agriculture*
lang *lang long*
langärmelig *lang·er·me·likh long-sleeved*
langsam *lang·zahm slow • slowly*
langweilig *lang·vai·likh boring*
Laptop ⑩ *lep·top laptop*
Lastwagen ⑩ *last·vah·gen truck*
Lauch ⑩ *lowkh leek*
laufen *low·fen run*
Läuse ⑩ pl *loy·ze lice*
laut *lowt loud • noisy*
Lautstärke ① *lowt·shter·ke volume (loudness)*
Lawine ① *la·vee·ne avalanche*
leben *lay·ben to live*
Leben ⑩ *lay·ben life*

Lebenslauf ⑩ *lay·bens·lowf resume • CV*
Lebensmittelhändler ⑩ *lay·bens·mi·tel·hen·dler greengrocer*
Lebensmittelladen ⑩ *lay·bens·mi·tel·lah·den grocery store*
Lebensmittelvergiftung ① *lay·bens·mi·tel·fer·gif·tung food poisoning*
Leber ① *lay·ber liver*
Leder ⑩ *lay·der leather*
ledig *lay·dikh single (of person)*
leer *lair empty*
legen *lay·gen put (horizontal)*
Lehrer(in) ⑩/① *lair·rer/lair·re·rin teacher • instructor*
leicht *laikht easy*
Leichtathletik ① *laikht·at·lay·tik athletics*
leihen *lai·en borrow*
Leinen ⑩ *lai·nen linen (fabric)*
Leitungswasser ⑩ *lai·tungks·va·ser tap water*
Lenker ⑩ *leng·ker handlebar*
lernen *ler·nen learn*
Lesbierin ① *les·bi·e·rin lesbian*
lesen *lay·zen read*
letzte *lets·te last*
Licht ⑩ *likht light*
lieben *lee·ben love*
liebevoll *lee·be·fol caring*
Liebhaber(in) ⑩/① *leep·hah·ber/ leep·hah·be·rin lover*
Lied ⑩ *leet song*
liefern *lee·fern deliver*
Lieferwagen ⑩ *lee·fer·vah·gen van*
liegen *lee·gen lie (not stand)*
Lift ⑩ *lift lift • elevator*
lila *lee·la purple*
Limonade ① *li·mo·nah·de lemonade*
Limone ① *li·maw·ne lime*
Linie ① *lee·ni·e line*
links *lingks left (direction)*
linksgerichtet *lingks·ge·rikh·tet left-wing*
Linse ① *lin·ze lentil*
Lippen ⑩ pl *li·pen lips*
Lippenbalsam ⑩ *li·pen·bal·zahm lip balm*
Lippenstift ⑩ *li·pen·shtift lipstick*

Liter ⓜ *lee*-ter *litre*
Löffel ⓜ *ler*-fel *spoon*
Lohn ⓜ lawn *wage*
Lohnsatz ⓜ *lawn*-zats *rate of pay*
Lokal ⓝ lo-*kahl* *bar*
Luft ⓕ luft *air*
Luftkrankheit ⓕ *luft*-krangk-hait *airsickness*
Luftpost ⓕ *luft*-post *airmail*
Luftpumpe ⓕ *luft*-pum-pe *pump*
Luftverschmutzung ⓕ *luft*-fer-shmu-tsung *air pollution*
Lügner(in) ⓜ/ⓕ *lüg*-ner/*lüg*-ne-rin *liar*
Lungen ⓕ pl *lung*-en *lungs*
lustig *lus*-tikh *funny*
luxuriös luk-su-ri-*ers* *luxury*

M

machen *ma*-khen *make*
Mädchen ⓝ *mayt*-khen *girl*
Magen ⓜ *mah*-gen *stomach*
Magen-Darm-Katarrh ⓜ *mah*-gen-*darm*-ka-tar *gastroenteritis*
Magenschmerzen ⓜ pl *mah*-gen-shmer-tsen *stomachache*
Magenverstimmung ⓕ *mah*-gen-fer-shti-mung *indigestion*
Majonnaise ⓕ ma-yo-*nay*-ze *mayonnaise*
Makler(in) ⓜ/ⓕ *mahk*-ler/*mahk*-le-rin *real estate agent*
Maler(in) ⓜ/ⓕ *mah*-ler/*mah*-le-rin *painter*
Malerei ⓕ mah-le-*rai* *painting (the art)*
Mama ⓕ *ma*-ma *mum • mom*
Mammogramm ⓝ ma-mo-*gram* *mammogram*
manchmal *mankh*-mahl *sometimes*
Mandarine ⓕ man-da-*ree*-ne *mandarin*
Mandel ⓕ *man*-del *almond*
Mann ⓜ man *man*
Mannschaft ⓕ *man*-shaft *team*
Mantel ⓜ *man*-tel *overcoat • cloak*
Margarine ⓕ mar-ga-*ree*-ne *margarine*
Marihuana ⓝ ma-ri-hu-*ah*-na *marijuana*
Markt ⓜ markt *market*
Marktplatz ⓜ *markt*-plats *market square*
Marmelade ⓕ mar-me-*lah*-de *jam*

Maschine ⓕ ma-*shee*-ne *machine*
Masern pl *mah*-zern *measles*
Massage ⓕ ma-*sah*-zhe *massage*
Masseur(in) ⓜ/ⓕ ma-*ser*(-rin) *masseur/masseuse*
Material ⓝ ma-te-ri-*ahl* *material*
Matratze ⓕ ma-*tra*-tse *mattress*
Matte ⓕ *ma*-te *mat*
Mauer ⓕ *mow*-er *wall (outer)*
Maurer(in) ⓜ/ⓕ *mow*-rer/*mow*-re-rin *bricklayer*
Maus ⓕ mows *mouse*
Mechaniker(in) ⓜ/ⓕ me-*khah*-ni-ker/ me-*khah*-ni-ke-rin *mechanic*
Medien pl *may*-di-en *media*
Meditation ⓕ me-di-ta-*tsyawn* *meditation*
Medizin ⓕ me-di-*tseen* *medicine*
Meer ⓝ mair *sea*
Meeresküste ⓕ *mair*-res-küs-te *seaside*
Meerrettich ⓜ *mair*-re-tikh *horseradish*
Mehl ⓝ mayl *flour*
mehr mair *more*
nicht mehr nikht mair *not any more*
mein main *mine • my*
Meinung ⓕ *mai*-nung *opinion*
Meisterschaften ⓕ pl *mais*-ter-shaf-ten *championships*
Melodie ⓕ me-lo-*dee* *tune*
Melone ⓕ me-*law*-ne *melon*
Mensch ⓜ mensh *person*
Menschen ⓜ pl *men*-shen *people*
Menschenrechte ⓝ pl *men*-shen-rekh-te *human rights*
menschlich *mensh*-likh *human*
Menstruation ⓕ mens-tru-a-*tsyawn* *menstruation*
Menstruationsbeschwerden ⓕ pl mens-tru-a-*tsyawn*-be-shver-den *period pain*
Messe ⓕ *me*-se *mass (Catholic) • trade fair*
Messer ⓝ *me*-ser *knife*
Metall ⓝ me-*tal* *metal*
Meter ⓜ *may*-ter *metre*
Metzgerei ⓕ mets-ge-*rai* *butcher's shop*
mieten *mee*-ten *rent • hire*
Mietvertrag ⓜ *meet*-fer-trahk *lease*
Migräne ⓕ mi-*gray*-ne *migraine*

Mikrowelle ① *mee·kro·ve·le microwave*
Milch ① *milkh milk*
Milchprodukte ⓝ pl *milkh·pro·duk·te dairy products*
Militär ⓝ *mi·li·tair military*
Millimeter ⓜ *mi·li·may·ter millimetre*
Million ① *mi·lyawn million*
Mineralwasser ⓝ *mi·ne·rahl·va·ser mineral water*
Minute ① *mi·noo·te minute*
mischen *mi·shen mix*
mit *mit with*
Mitglied ⓝ *mit·gleet member*
Mittag ⓜ *mi·tahk noon*
Mittagessen ⓝ *mi·tahk·e·sen lunch*
Mitteilung ① *mi·tai·lung message*
Mitternacht ① *mi·ter·nakht midnight*
Mittwoch ⓜ *mit·vokh Wednesday*
Möbel ⓝ pl *mer·bel furniture*
Modem ⓝ *maw·dem modem*
mögen *mer·gen to like*
möglich *merk·likh possible*
Mohrrübe ① *mawr·rü·be carrot*
Monat ⓜ *maw·nat month*
Montag ⓜ *mawn·tahk Monday*
Morgen ⓜ *mor·gen morning (6am – 10am)*
morgen *mor·gen tomorrow*
morgen früh *mor·gen frü tomorrow morning*
Moschee ① *mo·shay mosque*
Moskitospirale ① *mos·kee·to·shpi·rah·le mosquito coil*
Moslem ⓜ *mos·lem Muslim*
Moslime ① *mos·lee·me Muslim*
Motor ⓜ *maw·tor/mo·tawr engine*
Motorboot ⓝ *maw·tor·bawt motorboat*
Motorrad ⓝ *maw·tor·raht motorcycle*
Möwe ① *mer·ve seagull*
müde *mü·de tired*
Müll ⓜ *mül rubbish*
Mülleimer ⓜ *mül·ai·mer rubbish bin*
Mund ⓜ *munt mouth*
Mundfäule ① *munt·foy·le thrush (medical condition)*
Münzen ① pl *mün·tsen coins*
Muschel ① *mu·shel mussel*
Museum ⓝ *mu·zay·um museum*
Musik ① *mu·zeek music*

Musiker(in) ⓜ/① *moo·zi·ker/ moo·zi·ke·rin musician*
Muskel ⓜ *mus·kel muscle*
Muskelzerrung ① *mus·kel·tser·rung sprain*
Müsli ⓝ *müs·li muesli*
mutig *moo·tikh brave*
Mutter ① *mu·ter mother*

N

nach *nahkh after • towards*
Nachkomme ⓜ *nahkh·ko·me descendant*
Nachmittag ⓜ *nahkh·mi·tahk afternoon*
Nachname ⓜ *nahkh·nah·me surname*
Nachrichten pl *nahkh·rikh·ten news*
nächste *naykhs·te next • nearest*
Nacht ① *nakht night*
Nadel ① *nah·del sewing needle • syringe*
Nagelknipser ⓜ pl *nah·gel·knip·ser nail clippers*
nahe *nah·e close (nearby)*
in der Nähe *in dair nay·e nearby*
nähen *nay·en sew*
Name ⓜ *nah·me name*
Nase ① *nah·ze nose*
nass *nas wet*
Natur ① *na·toor nature*
Naturheilkunde ① *na·toor·hail·kun·de naturopathy*
Naturreservat ⓝ *na·toor·re·zer·vaht nature reserve*
neben *nay·ben next to*
neblig *nay·blikh foggy*
Neffe ⓜ *ne·fe nephew*
nehmen *nay·men take*
nein *nain no*
nett *net nice • kind*
Netz ⓝ *nets net*
neu *noy new*
Neujahrstag ⓜ *noy·yahrs·tahk New Year's Day*
Neuseeland ⓝ *noy·zay·lant New Zealand*
nicht *nikht not*
Nichte ① *nikh·te niece*
Nichtraucher- *nikht·row·kher· non-smoking*

nichts nikhts *nothing*
nie nee *never*
Niederlande pl nee·der·lan·de *Netherlands*
niedrig nee·drikh *low*
noch nicht nokh nikht *not yet*
Nonne ① no·ne *nun*
Norden ⓜ nor·den *north*
normal nor·mahl *ordinary*
normale Post ① nor·mah·le post *surface mail*
Notfall ⓜ nawt·fal *emergency*
Notizbuch ⓝ no·teets·bookh *notebook*
notwendig nawt·ven·dikh *necessary*
Nudeln pl noo·deln *noodles • pasta*
null nul *zero*
Nummer ① nu·mer *number*
nur noor *only*
Nuss ① nus *nut*
nützlich nüts·likh *useful*

O

obdachlos op·dakh·laws *homeless*
oben aw·ben *upstairs*
Objektiv ⓝ op·yek·teef *lens (camera)*
Obsternte ① awpst·ern·te *fruit picking*
oder aw·der *or*
Ofen ⓜ aw·fen *oven*
offen o·fen *open*
offensichtlich o·fen·zikht·likh *obvious*
öffentlich er·fent·likh *public*
öffnen erf·nen *open*
Öffnungszeiten ① pl erf·nungks·tsai·ten *opening hours*
oft oft *often*
ohne aw·ne *without*
Ohr ⓝ awr *ear*
Ohrenstöpsel ⓜ aw·ren·shterp·sel *earplugs*
Ohrringe ⓜ pl awr·ring·e *earrings*
Öl ⓝ erl *oil*
Olive ① o·lee·ve *olive*
Olivenöl ⓝ o·lee·ven·erl *olive oil*
Olympische Spiele ⓝ pl o·lüm·pi·she shpee·le *Olympic Games*
Oma ① aw·ma *grandmother*
Onkel ⓜ ong·kel *uncle*
Opa ⓜ aw·pa *grandfather*

Oper ① aw·per *opera*
Operation ① o·pe·ra·tsyawn *operation*
Opernhaus ⓝ aw·pern·hows *opera house*
Optiker(in) ⓜ/① op·ti·ker/op·ti·ke·rin *optician*
orange o·rahngzh *orange (colour)*
Orange ① o·rahng·zhe *orange*
Orangenmarmelade ① o·rahng·zhen·m ar·me·lah·de *marmalade*
Orangensaft ⓜ o·rahng·zhen·zaft *orange juice*
Orchester ⓝ or·kes·ter *orchestra*
organisieren or·ga·ni·zee·ren *organise*
Orgasmus ⓜ or·gas·mus *orgasm*
Orgel ① or·gel *organ (church)*
Original- o·ri·gi·nahl· *original (not copied)*
örtlich ert·likh *local*
Osten ⓜ os·ten *east*
der Nahe Osten ⓜ dair nah·e os·ten *Middle East*
Ostern ⓝ aws·tern *Easter*
Österreich ① ers·ter·raikh *Austria*
Ozean ⓜ aw·tse·ahn *ocean*
Ozonschicht ① o·tsawn·shikht *ozone layer*

P

Paar ⓝ pahr *pair (couple)*
ein paar ain pahr *a few*
Packung ① pa·kung *packet (general)*
Paket ⓝ pa·kayt *package • parcel*
Pampelmuse ① pam·pel·moo·ze *grapefruit*
eine Panne haben ai·ne pa·ne hah·ben *break down*
Papa ⓜ pa·pa *dad*
Papagei ⓜ pa·pa·gai *parrot*
Papier ⓝ pa·peer *paper*
Papiertaschentücher ⓝ pl pa·peer·ta·shen·tü·kher *tissues*
Paprika ① pap·ri·kah *paprika • capsicum • bell pepper*
Parfüm ⓝ par·füm *perfume*
Park ⓜ park *park*
Parkplatz ⓜ park·plats *carpark*
Parlament ⓝ par·la·ment *parliament*

Partei ① par·*tai* party (politics)

Pass ⓜ pas pass • passport

Passnummer ① *pas*·nu·mer
  passport number

Pause ① *pow*·ze intermission

eine Pause machen ai·ne *pow*·ze
  ma·khen rest

Pedal ⓝ pe·*dahl* pedal

Penis ⓜ *pay*·nis penis

Pension ① pahng·*zyawn*
  boarding house • bed & breakfast

pensioniert pahng·zyo·*neert* retired

Person ① per·*zawn* person

Personalausweis ⓜ
  per·zo·*nahl*·ows·vais
  identification card

persönlich per·*zern*·likh personal

Petersilie ① pay·ter·*zee*·li·e parsley

Petition ① pe·ti·*tsyawn* petition

Pfad ⓜ pfaht path • trail

Pfanne ① *pfa*·ne pan

Pfeffer ⓜ *pfe*·fer pepper

Pfefferminzbonbons ⓜ pl
  pfe·fer·*mints*·bong·bongs mints

Pfeife ① *pfai*·fe pipe

Pferd ⓝ pfert horse

Pfirsich ⓜ *pfir*·zikh peach

Pflanze ① *pflan*·tse plant

Pflaster ⓝ *pflas*·ter Band-aids

Pflaume ① *pflow*·me plum

pflücken *pflü*·ken pick (flowers)

Pfund ⓝ pfunt pound (weight)

Phantasie ① fan·ta·*zee* imagination

Physik ① fü·*zeek* physics

Picknick ⓝ *pik*·nik picnic

Pilgerfahrt ① *pil*·ger·fahrt pilgrimage

Pille ① *pi*·le pill

die Pille ① dee *pi*·le the Pill

Pilz ⓜ pilts mushroom

Pinzette ① pin·*tse*·te tweezers

PKW-Zulassung ①
  pay·kah·vay·*tsoo*·la·sung
  car registration

Plakat ⓝ pla·*kaht* poster

Planet ⓜ pla·*nayt* planet

Plastik ⓝ *plas*·tik plastic

Platz ⓜ plats
  place • seat (train, cinema) • square
  (town) • court (tennis)

Platz ⓜ **am Gang** plats am gang
  aisle seat

Poker ⓝ *paw*·ker poker (game)

Politik ① po·li·*teek* politics • policy

Politiker(in) ⓜ/① po·*lee*·ti·ker/
  po·*lee*·ti·ke·rin politician

Polizei ① po·li·*tsai* police

Polizeirevier ⓝ po·li·*tsai*·re·veer
  police station

Pollen ⓜ *po*·len pollen

Pony ⓝ *po*·ni pony

Porto ⓝ *por*·to postage

Post ① post mail

Postamt ⓝ *post*·amt post office

Postkarte ① *post*·kar·te postcard

postlagernd *post*·lah·gernt
  poste restante

Postleitzahl ① *post*·lai·tsahl postcode

praktisch *prak*·tish practical

prämenstruelle Störung ①
  pray·mens·tru·e·le *shter*·rung
  premenstrual tension

Präsident(in) ⓜ/① pre·zi·*dent*/
  pre·zi·*den*·tin president

Preis ⓜ prais price

Premierminister(in) ⓜ/①
  prem·*yay*·mi·nis·ter/
  prem·*yay*·mi·nis·te·rin prime minister

Priester ⓜ *prees*·ter priest

privat pri·*vaht* private

Privatklinik ① pri·*vaht*·klee·nik
  private hospital

pro praw per

produzieren pro·du·*tsee*·ren produce

Programm ⓝ pro·*gram* program

Projektor ⓜ pro·*yek*·tor projector

Prosa ① *praw*·za fiction

Prostituierte ① pros·ti·tu·*eer*·te
  prostitute

Protest ⓜ pro·*test* protest

protestieren pro·tes·*tee*·ren protest

Prozent ⓝ pro·*tsent* percent

prüfen *prü*·fen check

Psychologie ① psü·kho·lo·*gee*
  psychology

Pullover ⓜ pu·*law*·ver jumper • sweater

Pumpe ① *pum*·pe pump

Punkt ⓜ pungkt point

Puppe ① *pu*·pe doll

Q

Qualifikationen ① pl
kva·li·fi·ka·tsyaw·nen *qualifications*
Qualität ① kva·li·tayt *quality*
Quarantäne ① ka·ran·tay·ne
quarantine
Querschnittsgelähmte ⓜ&①
kvair·shnits·ge·laym·te *paraplegic*
Quittung ① kvi·tung *receipt*

R

Rabatt ⓜ ra·bat *discount*
Rad ⓝ raht *wheel*
radfahren raht·fah·ren *cycle*
Radfahrer(in) ⓜ/① raht·fah·rer/
raht·fah·re·rin *cyclist*
Radio ⓝ rah·di·o *radio*
Radsport ⓜ raht·shport *cycling*
Radweg ⓜ raht·vayk *bike path*
Rahmen ⓜ rah·men *frame*
Rallye ① re·li *rally*
Rasiercreme ① ra·zeer·kraym
shaving cream
rasieren ra·zee·ren *shave*
Rasierer ⓜ ra·zee·rer *razor*
Rasierklingen pl ra·zeer·kling·en
razor blades
Rassismus ⓜ ra·sis·mus *racism*
Rat ⓜ raht *advice*
raten rah·ten *advise • guess*
Ratte ① ra·te *rat*
Raub ⓜ rowp *robbery*
rauchen row·khen *smoke*
Raum ⓜ rowm *space*
realistisch re·a·lis·tish *realistic*
Rebe ① ray·be *vine*
Rechnung ① rekh·nung *bill • check*
rechts rekhts *right (direction)*
rechtsgerichtet rekhts·ge·rikh·tet
right-wing
Rechtsanwalt ⓜ rekhts·an·valt *lawyer*
Rechtsanwältin ① rekhts·an·vel·tin
lawyer
recyceln ri·sai·keln *recycle*
Regal ⓝ re·gahl *shelf*
Regeln ① pl ray·geln *rules*
Regen ⓜ ray·gen *rain*

Regenmantel ⓜ ray·gen·man·tel
raincoat
Regenschirm ⓜ ray·gen·shirm *umbrella*
Regierung ① re·gee·rung *government*
Region ① re·gyawn *region*
Regisseur(in) ⓜ/① re·zhi·ser/
re·zhi·ser·rin *director*
reich raikh *wealthy*
Reifen ⓜ rai·fen *tyre*
Reifenpanne ① rai·fen·pa·ne *puncture*
rein rain *pure*
Reinigung ① rai·ni·gung *cleaning*
Reis ⓜ rais *rice*
Reise ① rai·ze *journey • trip*
Reisebüro ⓝ rai·ze·bü·raw
travel agency
Reiseführer ⓜ rai·ze·fü·rer *guidebook*
Reisekrankheit ① rai·ze·krangk·hait
travel sickness
reisen rai·zen *travel*
Reisende ⓜ/① rai·zen·de
passenger (train)
Reisepass ⓜ rai·ze·pas *passport*
Reiseroute ① rai·ze·roo·te *itinerary*
Reisescheck ⓜ rai·ze·shek
travellers cheque
Reiseziel ⓝ rai·ze·tseel *destination*
Reißverschluss ⓜ rais·fer·shlus *zipper*
Reiten ⓝ rai·ten *horse riding*
reiten rai·ten *ride (horse)*
Reitweg ⓜ rait·vayk *bridle path*
Religion ① re·li·gyawn *religion*
religiös re·li·gyers *religious*
Reliquie ① re·lee·kvi·e *relic (religious)*
Rennbahn ① ren·bahn *racetrack*
rennen re·nen *run*
Rennen ⓝ re·nen *race (sport)*
Rennrad ⓝ ren·raht *racing bike*
Rentner(in) ⓜ/① rent·ner/rent·ne·rin
pensioner
reparieren re·pa·ree·ren *repair*
Republik ① re·pu·bleek *republic*
Reservereifen ⓜ re·zer·ve·rai·fen
spare tyre
reservieren re·zer·vee·ren *reserve*
Reservierung ① re·zer·vee·rung
reservation
Restaurant ⓝ res·to·rahng *restaurant*
retten re·ten *save (someone)*

Rettich ⓜ re·tikh *radish*
R-Gespräch ⓝ air·ge·shpraykh
  collect call • reverse-charge call
Rhythmus ⓜ rüt·mus *rhythm*
Richter(in) ⓜ/ⓕ rikh·ter/rikh·te·rin
  judge
richtig rikh·tikh *right (correct)*
riesig ree·zikh *huge*
Rindfleisch ⓝ rint·flaish *beef*
Ring ⓜ ring *ring (on finger)*
Risiko ⓝ ree·zi·ko *risk*
Ritt ⓜ rit *ride*
Rock ⓜ rok *skirt*
Rockgruppe ⓕ rok·gru·pe *rock group*
Rockmusik ⓕ rok·mu·zeek
  rock (music)
Rodeln ⓝ raw·deln *tobogganing*
Roggenbrot ⓝ ro·gen·brawt *rye bread*
roh raw *raw*
Rollschuhfahren ⓝ rol·shoo·fah·ren
  in-line skating
Rollstuhl ⓜ rol·shtool *wheelchair*
Rolltreppe ⓕ rol·tre·pe *escalator*
romantisch ro·man·tish *romantic*
rosa raw·za *pink*
Rosenkohl ⓜ raw·zen·kawl
  Brussels sprouts
Rosine ⓕ ro·zee·ne *raisin*
rot rawt *red*
Rotwein ⓜ rawt·vain *red wine*
Route ⓕ roo·te *route*
Rücken ⓜ rü·ken *back (body)*
Rückfahrkarte ⓕ rük·fahr·kar·te
  return (ticket)
Rucksack ⓜ ruk·zak
  backpack • knapsack
Rückzahlung ⓕ rük·tsah·lung *refund*
Rudern ⓝ roo·dern *rowing*
Rugby ⓝ rag·bi *rugby*
ruhig roo·ikh *quiet*
Ruinen ⓕ pl ru·ee·nen *ruins*
Rum ⓜ rum *rum*
rund runt *round*

S

Sabbat ⓜ za·bat *Sabbath*
Safe ⓜ sayf *safe*
Safe Sex ⓜ sayf seks *safe sex*

Saft ⓜ zaft *juice*
sagen zah·gen *say*
Sahne ⓕ zah·ne *cream*
Salami ⓕ za·lah·mi *salami*
Salat ⓜ za·laht *salad*
Salz ⓝ zalts *salt*
Samstag ⓜ zams·tahk *Saturday*
Sand ⓜ zant *sand*
Sandalen ⓕ pl zan·dah·len *sandals*
Sänger(in) ⓜ/ⓕ zeng·er/zeng·e·rin
  singer
Sardine ⓕ zar·dee·ne *sardine*
Sattel ⓜ za·tel *saddle*
sauber zow·ber *clean*
Sauce ⓕ zaw·se *sauce*
Sauerstoff ⓜ zow·er·shtof *oxygen*
Sauerteigbrot ⓝ zow·er·taik·brawt
  sourdough bread
Sauna ⓕ zow·na *sauna*
Schach ⓝ shakh *chess*
Schaf ⓝ shahf *sheep*
Schaffner(in) ⓜ/ⓕ shaf·ner/shaf·ne·rin
  conductor
Schal ⓜ shahl *scarf*
Schatten ⓜ sha·ten *shade • shadow*
einen Schaufensterbummel machen
  ai·nen show·fens·ter·bu·mel ma·khen
  go window-shopping
Schaumwein ⓜ showm·vain
  sparkling wine
Schauspiel ⓝ show·shpeel
  play (theatre) • drama
Schauspieler(in) ⓜ/ⓕ show·shpee·ler/
  show·shpee·le·rin *actor*
Scheck ⓜ shek *cheque (bank)*
einen Scheck einlösen ai·nen shek
  ain·ler·zen *cash a cheque*
Scheckkarte ⓕ shek·kar·te *cheque card*
Scheinwerfer ⓜ pl shain·ver·fer
  headlights
Schere ⓕ shair·re *scissors*
schieben shee·ben *push*
Schiedsrichter(in) ⓜ/ⓕ sheets·rikh·ter/
  sheets·rikh·te·rin *referee*
schießen shee·sen *shoot (gun)*
Schiff ⓝ shif *ship*
Schild ⓝ shilt *sign*
Schinken ⓜ shing·ken *ham*
schlafen shlah·fen *sleep*

schläfrig *shlayf*·rikh *sleepy*

Schlafsack ⓜ *shlahf*·zak *sleeping bag*

Schlaftabletten ⓕ pl *shlahf*·ta·ble·ten *sleeping pills*

Schlafwagen ⓜ *shlahf*·vah·gen *sleeping car*

Schlafzimmer ⓜ *shlahf*·tsi·mer *bedroom*

Schläger ⓜ *shlay*·ger *racquet*

Schlamm ⓜ *shlam* *mud*

Schlange ⓕ *shlang*·e *queue • snake*

Schlauch ⓜ *shlowkh* *tube (tyre)*

schlecht *shlekht* *bad • off (of food)*

schlechter *shlekh*·ter *worse*

schließen *shlee*·sen *close (shut)*

Schließfächer ⓜ pl *shlees*·fe·kher *luggage lockers*

Schloss ⓜ *shlos* *lock • palace*

Schlucht ⓕ *shlukht* *gorge*

Schlüssel ⓜ *shlü*·sel *key*

schmackhaft *shmak*·haft *tasty*

Schmalz ⓜ *shmalts* *lard*

Schmand ⓜ *shmant* *sour cream*

Schmerz ⓜ *shmerts* *pain*

schmerzhaft *shmerts*·haft *sore • painful*

Schmerzmittel ⓝ *shmerts*·mi·tel *painkillers*

Schmetterling ⓜ *shme*·ter·ling *butterfly*

Schmiermittel ⓝ *shmeer*·mi·tel *lubricant*

Schminke ⓕ *shming*·ke *make-up*

Schmuck ⓜ *shmuk* *jewellery*

schmutzig *shmu*·tsikh *dirty*

Schnecke ⓕ *shne*·ke *snail*

Schnee ⓜ *shnay* *snow*

Schneefeld ⓝ *shnay*·felt *snowfield*

schneiden *shnai*·den *cut*

Schneider(in) ⓜ/ⓕ *shnai*·der/ *shnai*·de·rin *tailor*

schnell *shnel* *quick*

Schnorcheln ⓝ *shnor*·kheln *snorkelling*

Schnuller ⓜ *shnu*·ler *dummy • pacifier*

Schnur ⓕ *shnoor* *string*

Schokolade ⓕ *sho*·ko·*lah*·de *chocolate*

schon *shawn* *yet • already*

schön *shern* *beautiful*

Schönheitssalon ⓜ *shern*·haits·za·long *beauty salon*

Schottland ⓝ *shot*·lant *Scotland*

Schramme ⓕ *shra*·me *bruise*

Schrank ⓜ *shrangk* *cupboard*

Schraubenzieher ⓜ *shrow*·ben·tsee·er *screwdriver*

schrecklich *shrek*·likh *terrible*

Schreibarbeit ⓕ *shraip*·ar·bait *paperwork*

schreiben *shrai*·ben *write*

Schreibwarenhandlung ⓕ *shraip*·vah·ren·han·dlung *stationer*

schreien *shrai*·en *shout*

Schrein ⓜ *shrain* *shrine*

Schreiner(in) ⓜ/ⓕ *shrai*·ner/*shrai*·ne·rin *carpenter*

Schriftsteller(in) ⓜ/ⓕ *shrift*·shte·ler/ *shrift*·shte·le·rin *writer*

schüchtern *shükh*·tern *shy*

Schuhe ⓜ pl *shoo*·e *shoes*

Schuld ⓕ *shult* *(someone's) fault*

schulden *shul*·den *owe*

schuldig *shul*·dikh *guilty*

Schule ⓕ *shoo*·le *school*

Schulter ⓕ *shul*·ter *shoulder*

Schüssel ⓕ *shü*·sel *bowl*

Schutzimpfung ⓕ *shuts*·im·pfung *vaccination*

schwach *shvakh* *weak*

schwanger *shvang*·er *pregnant*

Schwangerschaftserbrechen ⓝ *shvang*·er·shafts·er·bre·khen *morning sickness*

Schwangerschaftstest ⓜ *shvang*·er·shafts·test *pregnancy test kit*

Schwanz ⓜ *shvants* *tail*

schwarz *shvarts* *black*

schwarzer Pfeffer ⓜ *shvar*·tser *pfe*·fer *black pepper*

schwarzweiß *shvarts*·vais *B&W (film)*

Schwein ⓝ *shvain* *pig*

Schweinefleisch ⓝ *shvai*·ne·flaish *pork*

Schweiz ⓕ *shvaits* *Switzerland*

schwer *shvair* *difficult (task) • heavy*

Schwester ⓕ *shves*·ter *sister*

Schwiegermutter ⓕ *shvee*·ger·mu·ter *mother-in-law*

Schwiegersohn ⓜ *shvee*·ger·zawn *son-in-law*

Schwiegertochter ⓕ *shvee*·ger·tokh·ter *daughter-in-law*

Schwiegervater ⓜ *shvee*·ger·fah·ter *father-in-law*

schwierig shvee·rikh difficult
Schwimmbad @ shvim·baht swimming pool
schwimmen shvi·men swim
Schwimmweste ① shvim·ves·te lifejacket
schwindelig shvin·de·likh dizzy
schwul shvool gay
schwül shvül muggy
Secondhandgeschäft @ se·kend·hend·ge·sheft second-hand shop
See @ zay lake
seekrank zay·krangk seasick
Segeln @ zay·geln sailing
segnen zayg·nen bless
sehen zay·en see • look
sehr zair very
Seide ① zai·de silk
Seife ① zai·fe soap
Seifenoper ① zai·fen·aw·per soap opera
Seil @ zail rope
Seilbahn ① zail·bahn cable car
sein zain his
sein zain be
seit (Mai) zait (mai) since (May)
Seite ① zai·te side • page
Sekretär(in) @/① ze·kre·tair/ ze·kre·tair·rin secretary
Sekundarschule ① ze·kun·dahr·shoo·le high school
Sekunde ① ze·kun·de second
Selbstbedienung ① zelpst·be·dee·nung self-service
selbstständig zelpst·shten·dikh self-employed
selten zel·ten rare
senden zen·den send
Senf @ zenf mustard
Serie ① zair·ri·e series
Serviette ① zer·vye·te napkin
Sessellift @ ze·se·lift chairlift (skiing)
Sex @ seks sex
Sexismus @ sek·sis·mus sexism
sexy sek·si sexy
Shampoo @ sham·poo shampoo
Shorts pl shorts shorts • boxer shorts
Show ① shoh show
sicher zi·kher safe
Sicherheit ① zi·kher·hait safety

Sicherheitsgurt @ zi·kher·haits·gurt seatbelt
Sicherung ① zi·khe·rung fuse
sie zee she • they
Sie zee you sg&pl pol
Sieger(in) @/① zee·ger/zee·ge·rin winner
silbern zil·bern silver
Silvester @ zil·ves·ter New Year's Eve
Singapur @ zing·a·poor Singapore
singen zing·en sing
Single @ singl single (of person)
sinnlich zin·likh sensual
Sitz @ zits seat (car)
sitzen zi·tsen sit
Skateboarden @ skayt·bor·den skateboarding
Skibrille ① shee·bri·le goggles (skiing)
skifahren shee·fah·ren ski
Skulptur ① skulp·toor sculpture
Slipeinlage ① slip·ain·lah·ge panty liner
Snack @ snek snack
Snowboarden @ snoh·bor·den snowboarding
Socken pl zo·ken socks
sofort zo·fort immediately
Sohn @ zawn son
Sojamilch ① zaw·ya·milkh soy milk
Sojasauce ① zaw·ya·zaw·se soy sauce
Sommer @ zo·mer summer
Sonne ① zo·ne sun
Sonnenaufgang @ zo·nen·owf·gang sunrise
Sonnenbrand @ zo·nen·brant sunburn
Sonnenbrille ① zo·nen·bri·le sunglasses
Sonnencreme ① zo·nen·kraym sunblock
Sonnenuntergang @ zo·nen·un·ter·gang sunset
sonnig zo·nikh sunny
Sonntag @ zon·tahk Sunday
Soße ① zaw·se sauce
Souvenir @ zu·ve·neer souvenir
Souvenirladen @ zu·ve·neer·lah·den souvenir shop
Sozialhilfe ① zo·tsyahl·hil·fe welfare
sozialistisch zo·tsya·lis·tish socialist

Sozialstaat ⓜ zo·*tsyahl*·shtaht *welfare state*

Spanien ⓝ *shpah*·ni·en *Spain*

sparen *shpah*·ren *save (money)*

Spargel ⓜ *shpar*·gel *asparagus*

Spaß ⓜ shpahs *fun*

Spaß haben shpahs *hah*·ben *have fun*

spät shpayt *late*

Spaten ⓜ *shpah*·ten *spade*

Speichen ⓝ pl *shpai*·khen *spokes*

Speisekarte ① *shpai*·ze·kar·te *menu*

Speisewagen ⓜ *shpai*·ze·vah·gen *dining car*

Spezialist(in) ⓜ/① shpe·tsya·*list*/shpe·tsya·*lis*·tin *specialist*

speziell shpe·*tsyel* *special*

Spiegel ⓜ *shpee*·gel *mirror*

Spiel ⓝ shpeel *match (sport)*

spielen *shpee*·len *play (game)* • *play (instrument)*

Spielzeug ⓝ *shpeel*·tsoyk *toy*

Spinat ⓜ shpi·*naht* *spinach*

Spinne ① *shpi*·ne *spider*

Spitze ① *shpi*·tse *lace*

Spitzhacke ① *shpits*·ha·ke *pickaxe*

Spitzname ⓜ *shpits*·nah·me *nickname*

Sport ⓜ shport *sport*

Sportler(in) ⓜ/① *shport*·ler/*shport*·le·rin *sportsperson*

Sprache ① *shprah*·khe *language*

Sprachführer ⓜ *shprahkh*·fü·rer *phrasebook*

sprechen *shpre*·khen *speak*

springen *shpring*·en *jump*

Spritze ① *shpri*·tse *syringe*

Spülung ① *shpü*·lung *conditioner*

Staat ⓜ shtaht *state*

Staatsangehörigkeit ① *shtahts*·an·ge·her·rikh·kait *nationality*

Staatsbürgerschaft ① *shtahts*·bür·ger·shaft *citizenship*

Stadion ⓝ *shtah*·di·on *stadium*

Stadium ⓝ *shtah*·di·um *stage*

Stadt ① shtat *city* • *town*

Standby-Ticket ⓝ stend·*bai*·ti·ket *stand-by ticket*

stark shtark *strong*

Start ⓜ shtart *start (sport)*

statt shtat *instead of*

Statue ① *shtah*·tu·e *statue*

Steak ⓝ stayk *steak (beef)*

Stechmücke ① *shtekh*·mü·ke *mosquito*

Stecker ⓜ *shte*·ker *plug (electricity)*

stehlen *shtay*·len *steal*

Stehplatz ⓜ *shtay*·plats *standing room*

steil shtail *steep*

Stein ⓜ shtain *stone*

stellen *shte*·len *put (vertical)*

sterben *shter*·ben *die*

Stereoanlage ① *shtair*·re·o·an·lah·ge *stereo*

Sterne ⓜ pl *shter*·ne *stars*

Sternzeichen ⓝ *shtern*·tsai·khen *star sign* • *zodiac*

Steuer ① *shtoy*·er *tax*

Stich ⓜ shtikh *bite (insect)*

Stickerei ① shti·ke·*rai* *embroidery*

Stiefel ⓜ *shtee*·fel *boot (footwear)*

Stil ⓜ shteel *style*

stilles Wasser ⓝ *shti*·les va·ser *still water*

Stimme ① *shti*·me *voice*

Stock ⓜ shtok *floor (storey)*

stoned stohnd *stoned (drugged)*

stoppen *shto*·pen *stop*

Stöpsel ⓜ *shterp*·sel *plug (bath)*

stornieren shtor·*nee*·ren *cancel*

Strand ⓜ shtrant *beach*

Straße ① *shtrah*·se *street* • *road*

Straßenbahn ① *shtrah*·sen·bahn *tram*

Straßenkarte ① *shtrah*·sen·kar·te *road map*

Straßenkinder ⓝ pl *shtrah*·sen·kin·der *street kids*

Straßenmusiker(in) ⓜ/① *shtrah*·sen·moo·zi·ker/*shtrah*·sen·moo·zi·ke·rin *busker*

Streichhölzer ⓝ pl *shtraikh*·herl·tser *matches*

streiken *shtrai*·ken *(to be) on strike*

Streit ⓜ shtrait *quarrel*

streiten *shtrai*·ten *argue*

Strom ⓜ shtrawm *current (electricity)*

Stromschnellen ① pl *shtrawm*·shne·len *rapids*

Strümpfe ⓜ pl *shtrümp*·fe *stockings*

Strumpfhose ① *shtrumpf*·haw·ze *pantyhose*

Stück ⓝ shtük *piece*

Student(in) ⓜ/① shtu·*dent*/shtu·*den*·tin *student*

Studentenausweis ⓜ shtu·*den*·ten·ows·vais *student card*

studieren shtu·*dee*·ren *study*

Studio ⓝ *shtoo*·di·o *studio*

Stufe ① *shtoo*·fe *step (stairs)*

Stuhl ⓜ shtool *chair*

stumm shtum *mute*

stur shtoor *stubborn*

Sturm ⓜ shturm *storm*

suchen nach *zoo*·khen nahkh *look for*

Süchtige ⓜ/① *zükh*·ti·ge *addict*

Süden ⓜ *zü*·den *south*

Supermarkt ⓜ *zoo*·per·markt *supermarket*

Suppe ① *zu*·pe *soup*

Surfbrett ⓝ *serf*·bret *surfboard*

surfen *ser*·fen *surf*

süß züs *sweet/candy*

Süßigkeiten ⓝ pl *zü*·sikh·kai·ten *lollies*

Synagoge ① *zü*·na·gaw·ge *synagogue*

synthetisch *zün*·tay·tish *synthetic*

T

Tabak ⓜ *ta*·bak *tobacco*

Tabakladen ⓜ *ta*·bak·lah·den *tobacconist*

Tag ⓜ tahk *day*

Tagebuch ⓝ *tah*·ge·bookh *diary (journal)*

täglich *tayk*·likh *daily*

Tal ⓝ tahl *valley*

Tampons ⓜ pl *tam*·pons *tampons*

Tankstelle ① *tangk*·shte·le *service station*

Tante ① *tan*·te *aunt*

tanzen *tan*·tsen *dance*

Tasche ① *ta*·she *bag • pocket*

Taschenbuch ⓝ *ta*·shen·bookh *paperback*

Taschenlampe ① *ta*·shen·lam·pe *torch • flashlight*

Taschenmesser ⓝ *ta*·shen·me·ser *penknife*

Taschenrechner ⓜ *ta*·shen·rekh·ner *calculator*

Tasse ① *ta*·se *cup*

Tastatur ① tas·ta·*toor* *keyboard*

taub towp *deaf*

Tauchen ⓝ *tow*·khen *diving*

Taufe ① *tow*·fe *baptism • christening*

tausend *tow*·zent *thousand*

Taxi ⓝ *tak*·si *taxi*

Taxistand ⓜ *tak*·si·shtant *taxi stand*

Technik ① *tekh*·nik *technique*

Tee ⓜ tay *tea*

Teelöffel ⓜ *tay*·ler·fel *teaspoon*

Teil ⓝ tail *part*

teilen *tai*·len *share*

Teilzeit ① *tail*·tsait *part-time*

Telefon ⓝ te·le·*fawn* *telephone*

Telefonauskunft ① te·le·*fawn*·ows·kunft *directory enquiries*

Telefonbuch ⓝ le·le·*fawn*·bookh *phone book*

telefonieren te·le·fo·*nee*·ren *phone*

Telefonkarte ① te·le·*fawn*·kar·te *phone card*

Telefonzelle ① te·le·*fawn*·tse·le *phone box*

Telefonzentrale ① te·le·*fawn*·tsen·trah·le *telephone centre*

Telegramm ⓝ te·le·*gram* *telegram*

Teleskop ⓝ te·les·*kawp* *telescope*

Teller ⓜ *te*·ler *plate*

Tempel ⓜ *tem*·pel *temple*

Temperatur ① tem·pe·ra·*toor* *temperature (weather)*

Tennis ⓝ *te*·nis *tennis*

Tennisplatz ⓜ *te*·nis·plats *tennis court*

Teppich ⓜ *te*·pikh *rug*

Termin ⓜ ter·*meen* *appointment*

Terminkalender ⓜ ter·*meen*·ka·len·der *diary (for appointments)*

Terrasse ① te·ra·se *patio*

Test ⓜ test *test*

teuer *toy*·er *expensive*

Theater ⓝ te·*ah*·ter *theatre*

Theaterkasse ① te·*ah*·ter·ka·se *ticket office (theatre)*

Theke ① *tay*·ke *counter (at bar)*

Thermosflasche ① *ter*·mos·fla·she *thermos*

Thunfisch ⓜ *toon*-fish *tuna*
tief teef *deep*
Tier ⓝ teer *animal*
Tisch ⓜ tish *table*
Tischdecke ⓕ *tish*-de-ke *tablecloth*
Tischtennis ⓝ *tish*-te-nis *table tennis*
Toast ⓜ tawst *toast*
Toaster ⓜ *taws*-ter *toaster*
Tochter ⓕ *tokh*-ter *daughter*
Tofu ⓜ *taw*-fu *tofu*
Toilette ⓕ to-a-*le*-te *toilet*
Toilettenpapier ⓝ to-a-*le*-ten-pa-peer *toilet paper*
toll tol *terrific*
Tomate ⓕ to-*mah*-te *tomato*
Tomatensauce ⓕ to-*mah*-ten-zaw-se *tomato sauce*
Topf ⓜ topf *pot (ceramics)*
Töpferwaren ⓕ pl *terp*-fer-vah-ren *pottery*
Tor ⓝ tawr *gate • goal*
Torhüterin ⓕ *tawr*-hü-te-rin *goalkeeper*
Torwart ⓜ *tawr*-vart *goalkeeper*
ein Tor schießen ain *tawr* shee-sen *score a goal*
tot tawt *dead*
töten *ter*-ten *kill*
Tour ⓕ toor *tour*
Tourist(in) ⓜ/ⓕ tu-*rist*/tu-*ris*-tin *tourist*
Touristenklasse ⓕ tu-*ris*-ten-kla-se *economy class*
tragen *trah*-gen *carry • wear*
Training ⓝ *tray*-ning *workout*
trampen *trem*-pen *hitchhike*
Transitraum ⓜ tran-*zeet*-rowm *transit lounge*
Transport ⓜ trans-*port* *transport*
trauen *trow*-en *trust*
träumen *troy*-men *dream*
traurig *trow*-rikh *sad*
treffen *tre*-fen *meet*
Treppe ⓕ *tre*-pe *stairway*
treten *tray*-ten *kick*
trinken *tring*-ken *drink*
Trinkgeld ⓝ *tringk*-gelt *tip (gratuity)*
trocken *tro*-ken *dry*
Trockenobst ⓝ *tro*-ken-awpst *dried fruit*
trocknen *trok*-nen *dry (clothes)*
Truthahn ⓜ *troot*-hahn *turkey*

T-Shirt ⓝ *tee*-shert *T-shirt*
tun toon *do*
Tür ⓕ tür *door*
Turm ⓜ turm *tower*
Türsteher ⓜ *tür*-shtay-er *bouncer (club heavy)*
Tüte ⓕ *tü*-te *carton (milk)*
Typ ⓜ tüp *type*
typisch *tü*-pish *typical*

U

U-Bahn ⓕ *oo*-bahn *subway (underground)*
U-Bahnhof ⓜ *oo*-bahn-hawf *metro station*
Übelkeit ⓕ *ü*-bel-kait *nausea*
über *ü*-ber *about • above • over*
Überbrückungskabel ⓝ *ü*-ber-brü-kungks-kah-bel *jumper leads*
Überdosis ⓕ *ü*-ber-daw-zis *overdose*
überfüllt ü-ber-*fült* *crowded*
Übergepäck ⓝ *ü*-ber-ge-pek *excess baggage*
übermorgen *ü*-ber-mor-gen *day after tomorrow*
übernachten ü-ber-*nakh*-ten *stay (at a hotel)*
Überraschung ⓕ ü-ber-*ra*-shung *surprise*
Überschwemmung ⓕ ü-ber-*shve*-mung *flooding*
übersetzen ü-ber-*ze*-tsen *translate*
Uhr ⓕ oor *clock • watch*
Ultraschall ⓜ *ul*-tra-shal *ultrasound*
umarmen um-*ar*-men *hug*
Umfrage ⓕ *um*-frah-ge *polls*
Umkleideraum ⓜ *um*-klai-de-rowm *changing room*
Umsatzsteuer ⓕ *um*-zats-shtoy-er *sales tax*
umsteigen *um*-shtai-gen *change (trains)*
Umtausch ⓜ *um*-towsh *exchange*
Umwelt ⓕ *um*-velt *environment*
Umweltverschmutzung ⓕ *um*-velt-fer-shmu-tsung *pollution*
unbequem *un*-be-kvaym *uncomfortable*
und unt *and*

unfair un·fair *unfair*
Unfall ⓜ un·fal *accident*
ungefähr un·ge·fair *approximately*
ungewöhnlich un·ge·vern·likh *unusual*
Ungleichheit ① un·glaikh·hait *inequality*
Uniform ① u·ni·form *uniform*
Universität ① u·ni·ver·zi·tayt *university*
Universum ⓝ u·ni·vair·zum *universe*
unmöglich un·merk·likh *impossible*
unschuldig un·shul·dikh *innocent*
unser un·zer *our*
unten un·ten *down • at the bottom*
unter un·ter *among • below • under*
Unterhemd ⓝ un·ter·hemt *singlet*
Unterkunft ① un·ter·kunft *accommodation*
Unterschrift ① un·ter·shrift *signature*
Untertitel ⓝ pl un·ter·tee·tel *subtitles*
Unterwäsche ① un·ter·ve·she *underwear*
Urlaub ⓜ oor·lowp *holiday*

V

Vagina ① va·gee·na *vagina*
Vater ⓜ fah·ter *father*
Vegetarier(in) ⓜ/① ve·ge·tah·ri·er/ ve·ge·tah·ri·e·rin *vegetarian*
Vene ① vay·ne *vein*
Ventilator ven·ti·lah·tor *fan (machine)*
Verabredung ① fer·ap·ray·dung *date (appointment)*
Veranstaltungskalender ⓜ fer·an·shtal·tungks·ka·len·der *entertainment guide*
Veranstaltungsort ⓜ fer·an·shtal·tungks·ort *venue*
Verband ⓜ fer·bant *bandage*
Verbandskasten ⓜ fer·bants·kas·ten *first-aid kit*
Verbindung ① fer·bin·dung *connection*
verbrennen fer·bre·nen *burn*
verdienen fer·dee·nen *earn*
Vergangenheit ① fer·gang·en·hait *past*
Vergaser ⓜ fer·gah·zer *carburettor*
vergessen fer·ge·sen *forget*
vergewaltigen fer·ge·val·ti·gen *rape*

Verhaftung ① fer·haf·tung *arrest*
verhindern fer·hin·dern *prevent*
Verhütungsmittel ⓝ fer·hü·tungks·mi·tel *contraceptives*
verkaufen fer·kow·fen *sell*
Verkehr ⓜ fer·kair *traffic*
Verlängerung ① fer·leng·e·rung *extension (visa)*
verlegen fer·lay·gen *embarrassed*
verletzen fer·le·tsen *hurt*
Verletzung ① fer·le·tsung *injury*
verlieren fer·lee·ren *lose*
Verlobte ⓜ&① fer·lawp·te *fiance • fiancee*
Verlobung ① fer·law·bung *engagement (marriage)*
verloren fer·law·ren *lost*
Vermieter(in) ⓜ/① fer·mee·ter/ fer·mee·te·rin *landlord/landlady*
vermissen fer·mi·sen *miss (feel absence of)*
Vermittlung ① fer·mit·lung *operator*
vernünftig fer·nünf·tikh *sensible*
verpassen fer·pa·sen *miss (the bus)*
Verpflegung ① fer·pflay·gung *provisions*
verrückt fer·rükt *crazy*
Versicherung ① fer·zi·khe·rung *insurance*
Verspätung ① fer·shpay·tung *delay*
versprechen fer·shpre·khen *promise*
verstehen fer·shtay·en *understand*
Verstopfung ① fer·shtopf·ung *constipation*
versuchen fer·zoo·khen *try (attempt)*
Vertrag ⓜ fer·trahk *contract*
Verwaltung ① fer·val·tung *administration*
Verwandte ⓜ&① fer·van·te *relation (family)*
verzeihen fer·tsai·en *forgive*
Videokassette ① vee·de·o·ka·se·te *video tape*
viel feel *a lot (of) • plenty*
viele fee·le *many*
vielleicht fi·laikht *maybe*
Viertel ⓝ feer·tel *quarter*
vierzehn Tage ⓜ pl feer·tsayn tah·ge *fortnight*

Virus ⓜ vee·rus
virus (health) • *virus (computer)*
Visum ⓝ vee·zum *visa*
Vitamine ⓟ pl vi·ta·mee·ne *vitamins*
Vogel ⓜ faw·gel *bird*
Volksentscheid ⓜ folks·ent·shait
referendum
voll fol *full*
Vollkornbrot ⓝ fol·korn·brawt
wholemeal bread
Vollkornreis ⓜ fol·korn·rais *brown rice*
Vollzeit ⓕ fol·tsait *full-time*
Volumen ⓝ vo·loo·men *volume*
von fon *from*
vor fawr *in front of* • *before*
vor kurzem fawr kur·tsem *recently*
vor uns fawr uns *ahead*
vorbereiten fawr·be·rai·ten *prepare*
vorgestern fawr·ges·tern
day before yesterday
Vorhängeschloss ⓝ fawr·heng·e·shlos
padlock
Vormittag ⓜ fawr·mi·tahk
morning (10am–12pm)
Vorname ⓜ fawr·nah·me
Christian/given name
Vorort ⓜ fawr·ort *suburb*
Vorrat ⓜ fawr·raht *stock*
vorsichtig fawr·zikh·tikh *careful*
Vorwahl ⓕ fawr·vahl *area code*
vorziehen fawr·tsee·en *prefer*

W

wachsen vak·sen *grow*
sich waschen zikh va·shen
wash (oneself)
Waffe ⓕ va·fe *weapon*
Wagen ⓜ vah·gen *carriage (train)*
wählen vay·len *choose* • *vote*
Wahlen ⓟ pl vah·len *elections*
Wählton ⓜ vayl·tawn *dial tone*
wahr vahr *true*
während vair·rent *during*
Währung ⓕ vair·rung *currency*
Wald ⓜ valt *forest*
wandern van·dern *hike*
Wanderstiefel ⓜ pl van·der·shtee·fel
hiking boots

Wanderweg ⓜ van·der·vayk
hiking route
wann van *when*
wann immer van i·mer *whenever*
Warenhaus ⓝ vah·ren·hows
department store
warm varm *warm*
warnen var·nen *warn*
warten var·ten *wait*
Wartesaal ⓜ var·te·zahl
waiting room (train station)
Wartezimmer ⓝ var·te·tsi·mer
waiting room (doctor's)
warum va·rum *why*
was vas *what*
Wäscheleine ⓕ ve·she·lai·ne
clothesline
waschen va·shen *wash (something)*
Wäscherei ⓕ ve·she·rai *laundrette*
Waschküche ⓕ vash·kü·khe
laundry (room)
Waschlappen ⓜ vash·la·pen
wash cloth (flannel)
Waschmaschine ⓕ vash·ma·shee·ne
washing machine
Waschpulver ⓝ vash·pul·ver
washing powder
Wasser ⓝ va·ser *water*
wasserdicht va·ser·dikht *waterproof*
Wasserfall ⓜ va·ser·fal *waterfall*
Wasserflasche ⓕ va·ser·fla·she
water bottle
Wasserhahn ⓜ va·ser·hahn *faucet* • *tap*
Wassermelone ⓕ va·ser·me·law·ne
watermelon
Wasserskifahren ⓝ va·ser·shee·fah·ren
waterskiing
Watte-Pads pl va·te·pedz *cotton balls*
Wechselgeld ⓝ vek·sel·gelt
change (coins)
Wechselkurs ⓜ vek·sel·kurs
exchange rate
wechseln vek·seln *exchange (money)*
Wecker ⓜ ve·ker *alarm clock*
Weg ⓜ vayk *track (path)* • *way*
wegen vay·gen *because of*
Wegweiser ⓜ vayk·vai·zer *signpost*
sich weh tun zikh vay toon
hurt (yourself)

Wehrdienst ⓜ *vair*·deenst
military service

Weihnachten ⓝ *vai*·nakh·ten *Christmas*

Weihnachtsbaum ⓜ *vai*·nakhts·bowm
Christmas tree

Weihnachtsfeiertag ⓜ
vai·nakhts·fai·er·tahk *Christmas Day*

weil vail *because*

Wein ⓜ vain *wine*

Weinberg ⓜ *vain*·berk *vineyard*

Weinbrand ⓜ *vain*·brant *brandy*

Weintrauben ① pl vain·trow·ben *grapes*

weiß vais *white*

Weißbrot ⓝ *vais*·brawt *white bread*

weißer Pfeffer ⓜ *vai*·ser pfe·fer
white pepper

weißer Reis ⓜ *vai*·ser rais *white rice*

Weißwein ⓜ *vais*·vain *white wine*

weit vait *far*

Welle ① *ve*·le *wave*

Welt ① velt *world*

Weltmeisterschaft ① velt·mais·ter·shaft
World Cup

wenig vay·nikh *(a) little*

wenige vay·ni·ge *few*

weniger vay·ni·ger *less*

wenn ven *when* • *if*

wer vair *who*

Werkstatt ① verk·shtat
garage (car repair)

Werkzeug ⓝ verk·tsoyk *tools*

Wert ⓜ vert *value (price)*

wertvoll vert·fol *valuable*

Wespe ① *ves*·pe *wasp*

Westen ⓜ *ves*·ten *west*

Wette ① *ve*·te *bet*

Wetter ⓝ *ve*·ter *weather*

Whisky ⓜ *vis*·ki *whisky*

wichtig vikh·tikh *important*

wie vee *how*

wie viel vee feel *how much*

wieder vee·der *again*

wiederverwertbar vee·der·fer·vert·bahr
recyclable

wiegen vee·gen *weigh*

wild vilt *wild*

willkommen vil·ko·men *welcome*

Wind ⓜ vint *wind*

Windel ① *vin*·del *nappy (diaper)*

Windeldermatitis ①
vin·del·der·ma·tee·tis *nappy rash*

windig *vin*·dikh *windy*

Windschutzscheibe ① *vint*·shuts·shai·be
windscreen

Windsurfen ⓝ *vint*·ser·fen *windsurfing*

Winter ⓜ *vin*·ter *winter*

winzig *vin*·tsikh *tiny*

wir veer *we*

wissen *vi*·sen *know (something)*

Wissenschaft ① *vi*·sen·shaft *science*

Wissenschaftler(in) ⓜ/① *vi*·sen·shaft·ler/
vi·sen·shaft·le·rin *scientist*

Witz ⓜ vits *joke*

wo vaw *where*

Wochenende ⓝ *vo*·khen·en·de
weekend

Wodka ⓜ *vot*·ka *vodka*

Wohlfahrt ① vawl·fahrt *social welfare*

wohnen *vaw*·nen *reside*

Wohnung ① *vaw*·nung
apartment (flat)

Wohnwagen ⓜ *vawn*·vah·gen *caravan*

Wolke ① *vol*·ke *cloud*

wolkig *vol*·kikh *cloudy*

Wolle ① *vo*·le *wool*

wollen *vo*·len *want*

Wort ⓝ vort *word*

Wörterbuch ⓝ *ver*·ter·bookh *dictionary*

wunderbar vun·der·bahr *wonderful*

wünschen *vün*·shen *wish*

Würfel ⓜ *vür*·fel *dice*

Würmer ⓜ pl vür·mer *worms*

Wurst ① vurst *sausage*

würzig *vür*·tsikh *spicy*

Wüste ① *vüs*·te *desert*

wütend *vü*·tent *angry*

Z

Zahl ① tsahl *number*

zählen tsay·len *count*

Zahlung ① *tsah*·lung *payment*

Zahn ⓜ tsahn *tooth*

Zahnarzt ⓜ *tsahn*·artst *dentist*

Zahnärztin ① *tsahn*·erts·tin *dentist*

Zahnbürste ① *tsahn*·bürs·te *toothbrush*

Zähne ⓝ pl tsay·ne *teeth*

Zahnfleisch ⓝ *tsahn*·flaish *gum (mouth)*

Zahnpasta ① *tsahn*·pas·ta *toothpaste*

Zahnschmerzen pl *tsahn*-shmer-tsen
toothache

Zahnseide ① *tsahn*-zai-de *dental floss*

Zahnstocher ⓜ *tsahn*-shto-kher
toothpick

Zauberer(in) ⓜ/① *tsow*-be-rer/
tsow-be-re-rin *magician*

Zaun ⓜ tsown *fence*

Zehe ① *tsay*-e *toe • clove (of garlic)*

zehn tsayn *ten*

zeigen *tsai*-gen *show • point*

Zeit ① tsait *time*

Zeitschrift ① tsait-shrift *magazine*

Zeitung ① *tsai*-tung *newspaper*

Zeitungshändler ⓜ *tsai*-tungks-hen-dler
newsagency

Zeitungskiosk ⓜ *tsai*-tungks-kee-osk
newsstand

Zeitunterschied ⓜ *tsait*-un-ter-sheet
time difference

Zelt ⓝ tselt *tent*

zelten *tsel*-ten *camp*

Zeltplatz ⓜ *tselt*-plats *campsite*

Zentimeter ⓜ tsen-ti-*may*-ter *centimetre*

Zentralheizung ① tsen-*trahl*-hai-tsung
central heating

Zentrum ⓝ *tsen*-trum *centre*

zerbrechen tser-*bre*-khen *break*

zerbrechlich tser-*brekh*-likh *fragile*

Zertifikat ⓝ tser-ti-fi-*kaht* *certificate*

Zeugnis ⓝ *tsoyk*-nis *reference (work)*

Ziege ① *tsee*-ge *goat*

ziehen *tsee*-en *pull*

Ziel ⓝ tseel *target • finish (sport)*

Zigarette ① tsi-ga-*re*-te *cigarette*

Zigarre ① tsi-*gar*-re *cigar*

Zimmer ⓝ *tsi*-mer *room*

Zimmernummer ① *tsi*-mer-nu-mer
room number

Zirkus ⓜ *tsir*-kus *circus*

Zitrone ① tsi-*traw*-ne *lemon*

Zoll ⓜ tsol *customs*

Zoo ⓜ tsaw *zoo*

zu tsoo *too • at*

zu Hause tsoo *how*-ze *(at) home*

Zucchini ① tsu-*kee*-ni
zucchini • courgette

Zucker ⓜ *tsu*-ker *sugar*

Zuckererbse ① *tsu*-ker-erp-se *snow pea*

Zufall ⓜ *tsoo*-fal *chance*

Zug ⓜ tsook *train*

zugeben *tsoo*-gay-ben
admit (accept as true)

Zukunft ① *tsoo*-kunft *future*

Zulassung ① *tsoo*-la-sung
car registration

zum Beispiel tsum *bai*-shpeel
for example

Zündung ① *tsün*-dung *ignition*

zurück tsu-*rük* *back (return)*

zurückkommen tsu-*rük*-ko-men *return*

zusammen tsu-*za*-men *together*

Zusammenstoß ⓜ tsu-*za*-men-staws
crash

zustimmen *tsoo*-shti-men *agree*

Zutat ① *tsoo*-taht *ingredient*

zweimal *tsvai*-mahl *twice*

zweite *tsvai*-te *second*

Zwerchfell ⓝ *tsverkh*-fel *diaphragm*

Zwiebel ① *tsvee*-bel *onion*

Zwillinge ⓜ pl *tsvi*-ling-e *twins*

zwischen *tsvi*-shen *between*

M

N

O

P

The topics covered in this book are listed below in German. If you're having trouble understanding German, show this page to the person you're talking to so they can look up the relevant section.

What kind of traveller are you?

A You're eating chicken for dinner *again* because it's the only word you know.

B When no one understands what you say, you step closer and shout louder.

C When the barman doesn't understand your order, you point frantically at the beer.

D You're surrounded by locals, swapping jokes, email addresses and experiences; other travellers want to borrow your phrasebook or audio guide.

If you answered A, B or C, you NEED Lonely Planet's language products...

- **Lonely Planet Phrasebooks** – every phrase you need in every language you want
- **Lonely Planet Language & Culture** – laugh and learn as you explore the richness of English idiom as it's spoken around the world
- **Lonely Planet Fast Talk** – enjoy hassle-free sightseeing, shopping and dining using our essential phrases for short trips and weekends away
- **Lonely Planet Small Talk** – pack light with our quick-hit language guide featuring 10 languages per book
- **Lonely Planet Phrasebook & Audio CD** – read, listen and talk like a local with our complete phrasebook plus a bonus CD of 400 key phrases
- **Lonely Planet Phrasebooks for iPhone and iPod touch** – download more than 600 phrases with corresponding audio, available on the App Store

...and this is why

- **Talk to everyone everywhere**
  Over 120 languages, more than any other publisher
- **The right words at the right time**
  Quick-reference colour sections, two-way dictionary, easy pronunciation, every possible subject – and audio to support it

Lonely Planet Offices

Australia
90 Maribyrnong St, Footscray,
Victoria 3011
☎ 03 8379 8000
fax 03 8379 8111
✉ talk2us@lonelyplanet.com

USA
150 Linden St, Oakland,
CA 94607
☎ 510 250 6400
Toll free 800 275 8555
fax 510 893 8572

UK
2nd fl, 186 City Rd,
London EC1V 2NT
☎ 020 7106 2100
fax 020 7106 2101

lonelyplanet.com